WordPress Developm Start Guide

Build beautiful and dynamic websites for your domain
from scratch

Rakhitha Nimesh Ratnayake

BIRMINGHAM - MUMBAI

WordPress Development Quick Start Guide

Commissioning Editor: Kunal Chaudhari
Acquisition Editor: Reshma Raman
Content Development Editor: Roshan Kumar
Technical Editor: Shweta Jadhav
Copy Editor: Safis Editing
Project Coordinator: Hardik Bhinde
Proofreader: Safis Editing
Indexer: Pratik Shirodkar
Graphics: Alishon Mendonsa
Production Coordinator: Deepika Naik

First published: October 2018

Production reference: 1291018

Published by Packt Publishing Ltd.
Livery Place
35 Livery Street
Birmingham
B3 2PB, UK.

ISBN 978-1-78934-287-1

www.packtpub.com

`mapt.io`

Mapt is an online digital library that gives you full access to over 5,000 books and videos, as well as industry leading tools to help you plan your personal development and advance your career. For more information, please visit our website.

Why subscribe?

- Spend less time learning and more time coding with practical eBooks and Videos from over 4,000 industry professionals

- Improve your learning with Skill Plans built especially for you

- Get a free eBook or video every month

- Mapt is fully searchable

- Copy and paste, print, and bookmark content

Packt.com

Did you know that Packt offers eBook versions of every book published, with PDF and ePub files available? You can upgrade to the eBook version at `www.packt.com` and as a print book customer, you are entitled to a discount on the eBook copy. Get in touch with us at `customercare@packtpub.com` for more details.

At `www.packt.com`, you can also read a collection of free technical articles, sign up for a range of free newsletters, and receive exclusive discounts and offers on Packt books and eBooks.

Contributors

About the author

Rakhitha Nimesh Ratnayake is a freelance web developer, writer, and open source enthusiast. He has over 9 years of experience in developing WordPress applications and plugins. He develops premium WordPress plugins for individual clients and the CodeCanyon marketplace. User Profiles Made Easy and WP Private Content Pro are the most popular plugins developed by him. Rakhitha is the creator of WPExpertDeveloper, where he shares his latest WordPress plugins. *Building Impressive Presentations with impress.js* was his first book, which was published by Packt Publishing. He is also the author of the first three editions of *WordPress Web Application Development*. In his spare time, he likes to read books and spend time with his family.

I would like to thank my loving wife, Dulari; my daughter, Hesara; my parents; and my wife's parents for the help and encouragement provided throughout this book. I would also like to thank Packt Publishing, especially Senior Acquisition Editor, Reshma Raman, for inviting me to write this book; Content Development Editor, Roshan Kumar, and the reviewer for providing honest feedback to improve this book. Finally, I would like to thank you for reading my book and being one of the most important people who helped me make this book a success.

About the reviewer

Olivier Pons is a high skilled developer who's been building websites for many years. He's a teacher in France: at the University of Sciences of Aix-en-Provence, CESI and three other ones, where he teaches Python, Django, advanced JavaScript, nginx and Apache and Linux. In 2011, he left a full time job as a Php expert to concentrate on his own company, HQF Development. He currently runs a number of web sites, and you will easily find his web development blog if you google for "Olivier Pons". He's currently making a Unity mcq mobile application, which works together with a Django website. He works as teacher, high skilled developer and helps big companies and CTOs in making the best choice for their Web projects.

> *I would like to thank my family and friends for their never-ending support. I am also thankful to Packt Publishing and its amazing collection of videos, without whom none of this would be possible. I'd also like to thank Rakhitha Nimesh Ratnayake, author of the book, for putting together a very helpful guide about Wordpress Development; as well as Hardik Bhinde for giving me the opportunity to review this amazing book.*

Packt is searching for authors like you

If you're interested in becoming an author for Packt, please visit `authors.packtpub.com` and apply today. We have worked with thousands of developers and tech professionals, just like you, to help them share their insight with the global tech community. You can make a general application, apply for a specific hot topic that we are recruiting an author for, or submit your own idea.

Table of Contents

Preface

WordPress is the most widely used CMS in the world. As a developer, WordPress is the ideal way to share your knowledge with a large community as well as build a profitable business. Getting started with WordPress development has been a challenge for novice developers, compared to building everything from scratch in other frameworks. It's very easy to build WordPress sites by connecting bits and pieces without actually knowing what's happening under the hood. Many developers tend to follow this path and face maintenance and security nightmares in the long run. This book is structured to explain the components used in WordPress development, when and where to use them, and why you should be using each component in specific scenarios.

You will begin this book by learning the basic development setup and coding standards of WordPress. Mastering the built-in database is one of the keys to becoming a expert in WordPress development. In this section, you will learn about the database structure, and examine the data usage of the built-in features and their limitations in order to plan the data needs of your application. Then you will move onto an important topic: the theme and plugin development process. In this section, you will learn how themes and plugins fit into an application while understanding basic to advanced techniques for extending themes and plugins.

With the basics covered, we explore the use of the wide range of APIs provided by WordPress and see how we can leverage them to rapidly build solutions. Next, we move onto another essential section, where we explore the techniques for capturing, processing, and displaying user data while integrating third-party components into the site's design. Finally, you will learn how to test and deploy the application with secure and maintainable code, while providing the best performance for end users.

By the end of this book, you will have the ability to choose the right components for any development task and build flexible solutions that work with existing plugins and themes.

Who this book is for

This book is intended for web developers and site owners who are planning to build custom websites with WordPress. Also, web developers could use this book as a starting point for getting into plugin and theme development.

What this book covers

Chapter 1, *Introduction to WordPress Development*, covers the basic installation and configuration process of WordPress. Setting up the development environment, an introduction to WordPress coding standards, and understanding the WordPress file/folder structure are the highlights of this chapter.

Chapter 2, *Managing Database Structure, Storage, and Retrieval*, introduces you to the existing WordPress database table structure and its role in custom development. Executing basic queries, managing custom tables, and tracking the database usage of various features are the highlights of this chapter.

Chapter 3, *Designing Flexible Frontends with Theme Development*, explores the role and features of a theme in custom development. In-depth coverage of template hierarchy, custom template design, and custom development techniques in themes are the highlights of this chapter.

Chapter 4, *Building Custom Modules with Plugin Development*, explores the role of plugins and introduces the basics of developing a simple plugin. Understanding plugin life cycle events, identifying advantages of building plugins, and developing a plugin covering life cycle events are the highlights of this chapter.

Chapter 5, *Extending Plugins with Add-ons, Filters, and Actions*, focuses on extending existing plugins and core features with the use of add-ons and WordPress hooks. Customizing third-party plugins, integrating multiple plugins, and identifying the extendable features of existing plugins are the highlights of this chapter.

Chapter 6, *Practical Usage of WordPress APIs*, explores WordPress APIs and their functionality in custom development. Mastering the use of shortcodes, building custom routes with the Rewrite API, and allowing remote connections with REST APIs are the highlights of this chapter.

Chapter 7, *Managing Custom Post Types and Processing Forms*, explains the primary data capturing and managing process with custom post types and custom forms. Building object-oriented plugins for handling property management site with custom post types and building custom forms in the frontend are the highlights of this chapter.

Chapter 8, *Discovering Key Modules in Development*, dives into the process of improving user experience with interactive designs and customized backend features. Integrating UI components, working with page builders, and simplifying backend admin features are the highlights of this chapter.

Chapter 9, *Enhancing Security, Performance, and Maintenance,* covers the non-functional aspects of development for building quality and reliable sites. Identifying the process of testing, steps for securing sites, migrating sites using plugins, and exploring the primary tasks of maintenance are the highlights of this chapter.

To get the most out of this book

Basic knowledge of PHP, JavaScript, HTML and CSS is required. You also need a computer, a browser, and an Internet connection with the following working environment:

- An Apache web server
- PHP version 5.4 or higher
- WordPress version 4.9.8
- MySQL version 5.6+ OR MariaDB 10.0+

Download the example code files

You can download the example code files for this book from your account at www.packt.com. If you purchased this book elsewhere, you can visit www.packt.com/support and register to have the files emailed directly to you.

You can download the code files by following these steps:

1. Log in or register at www.packt.com.
2. Select the **SUPPORT** tab.
3. Click on **Code Downloads & Errata**.
4. Enter the name of the book in the **Search** box and follow the onscreen instructions.

Once the file is downloaded, please make sure that you unzip or extract the folder using the latest version of:

- WinRAR/7-Zip for Windows
- Zipeg/iZip/UnRarX for Mac
- 7-Zip/PeaZip for Linux

The code bundle for the book is also hosted on GitHub at `https://github.com/PacktPublishing/WordPressDevelopmentQuickStartGuide`. In case there's an update to the code, it will be updated on the existing GitHub repository.

We also have other code bundles from our rich catalog of books and videos available at `https://github.com/PacktPublishing/`. Check them out!

Download the color images

We also provide a PDF file that has color images of the screenshots/diagrams used in this book. You can download it here: `http://www.packtpub.com/sites/default/files/downloads/9781789342871_ColorImages.pdf`.

Code in action

Visit the following link to check out videos of the code being run:

`http://bit.ly/2AzlbTj`

Conventions used

There are a number of text conventions used throughout this book.

`CodeInText`: Indicates code words in text, database table names, folder names, filenames, file extensions, pathnames, dummy URLs, user input, and Twitter handles. Here is an example: "We need to use the `self::$instance` object as we are within the `static` function."

A block of code is set as follows:

```
add_action( 'plugins_loaded', 'wqcpt_plugin_init' );
function wqcpt_plugin_init(){
  global $wqcpt;
  $wqcpt = WPQuick_CPT::instance();
}
```

When we wish to draw your attention to a particular part of a code block, the relevant lines or items are set in bold:

```
add_action( 'plugins_loaded', 'wqcpt_plugin_init' );
function wqcpt_plugin_init(){
  global $wqcpt;
  $wqcpt = WPQuick_CPT::instance();
}
```

Bold: Indicates a new term, an important word, or words that you see onscreen. For example, words in menus or dialog boxes appear in the text like this. Here is an example: "Select **System info** from the **Administration** panel."

Warnings or important notes appear like this.

Tips and tricks appear like this.

Get in touch

Feedback from our readers is always welcome.

General feedback: If you have questions about any aspect of this book, mention the book title in the subject of your message and email us at customercare@packtpub.com.

Errata: Although we have taken every care to ensure the accuracy of our content, mistakes do happen. If you have found a mistake in this book, we would be grateful if you would report this to us. Please visit www.packt.com/submit-errata, selecting your book, clicking on the Errata Submission Form link, and entering the details.

Piracy: If you come across any illegal copies of our works in any form on the Internet, we would be grateful if you would provide us with the location address or website name. Please contact us at copyright@packt.com with a link to the material.

If you are interested in becoming an author: If there is a topic that you have expertise in and you are interested in either writing or contributing to a book, please visit authors.packtpub.com.

Reviews

Please leave a review. Once you have read and used this book, why not leave a review on the site that you purchased it from? Potential readers can then see and use your unbiased opinion to make purchase decisions, we at Packt can understand what you think about our products, and our authors can see your feedback on their book. Thank you!

For more information about Packt, please visit packt.com.

Introduction to WordPress Development 1

WordPress is the most widely-used CMS in the world, and the demand for developers is on the rise. Beginner WordPress developers are often restricted to using existing plugins and making minor modifications with the theme functions file. As a developer, you need a thorough understanding of WordPress core modules and components, along with a proper development setup to tackle complex application requirements.

This chapter focuses on introducing you to the prerequisites of WordPress development while clearing up some of the misconceptions about development. Unlike other frameworks, WordPress doesn't have an MVC architecture or similar. So, developers have the freedom to find their own techniques. We will begin by having a high-level overview of how developers can use the existing features in development, as well as the techniques for integrating our code with WordPress components. Then, we will move on to installing WordPress and discussing the use of configuration files with default and advanced configurations. Development tools and coding standards are the keys for producing quality code, and hence we will discuss the use of WordPress-specific coding standards as well as the use of popular open source development tools.

In this chapter, we will cover the following topics:

- Installing and configuring a development environment for WordPress
- How to use a WordPress configuration file
- A high-level overview of the WordPress file/directory structure and their use in development
- A brief introduction to WordPress coding standards and its usage
- Using popular tools for debugging code

By the end of this chapter, you will have the necessary knowledge to understand the key development areas of WordPress and preparing the development environment for a smooth workflow.

Introduction to WordPress development

This book is intended for beginner WordPress developers and site owners who want to build custom websites with WordPress. We dive into developing solutions with WordPress, it's important to understand what exactly development is, and the areas involved. There are many people who call themselves WordPress developers and yet haven't done anything beyond changing some theme designs and using the theme functions file. WordPress development can range from simple theme design changes to building a complex web application.

Here are the components involved in WordPress development:

- **Theme functions file**: The first technique you encounter when getting started with development. Usually, we can add small code snippets using filters and actions to change the functionality of theme or plugins. Since this file is updated on theme updates, it's not recommended to add your own custom code. However, there are exceptions when using your own theme or a theme without version updates. This is a good starting point to add some code and learn how WordPress can be customized with actions and filters.

- **Child themes**: This is the next step in development, before diving into complex implementations using plugins. The child theme is a theme that we create based on an existing theme. We can either override all files in the child theme or only add the necessary files to override. If you are starting WordPress development and want to add some quick code snippets, creating a child theme and using the functions file is the ideal solution. In development, the child theme should be used for minor implementations such as design changes or displaying more/less data on frontend screens. Since we only use the `functions.php` file for code changes, this technique is not recommended for implementing advanced features. However, modern themes are packed with features and hence there may be exceptions for doing advanced implementations in child themes.

- **Plugins**: As a developer, developing plugins is the most important aspect of building custom websites. Plugins allow you to build independent and extendable solutions. Usually, it's a good practice to add any customization into a separate plugin or a site-specific common plugin based on its scope. You can create plugins to customize existing WordPress backend and frontend features, theme functionality, as well as developing completely new features beyond WordPress's built-in modules.

- **Addons**: Even though we call these addons, they are a plugin that extends the features of another plugin. In WordPress development, we are not going to build everything from scratch as there is a huge free plugin repository and thousands of premium plugins for doing all kinds of things. Most of these existing plugins are not going to align perfectly to our requirements. Therefore, we need a way to customize the features of such plugins without losing the changes on plugin updates. Addons extend the features of plugins by using actions, filters, and APIs provided by the plugin.

These are the main components and files for developing your own solutions in WordPress. Now, we need to shift focus to major areas involved in development and how they fit into WordPress. Let's review the use of existing features in development as well as custom build features.

Posts, pages, and custom post type management

Since its inception, WordPress was used as a basic CMS with the primary focus on blogging. After so many years, posts and pages are still the main aspect of WordPress, with the addition of custom post types. The primary feature of many sites is the management of posts. So, you need to master each and every aspect of post creation, editing, displaying, and managing additional data. With the arrival of custom post types, developers can match many of the user data capturing application requirements. Since the basic features such as creating, editing, displaying, and listing are inbuilt with custom post types, developers can focus on extending these features at a rapid pace.

Many large-scale applications such as event management systems, online shops, realestate sites, and job management sites are modeled using custom post types, and hence it's a primary feature in WordPress development.

User management

This is another built-in module with comprehensive functionality for user data, access levels, and permissions. You may find the need for registered members in many modern applications and sites. So, you can use the features of existing user modules to handle basic user data and permissions, while developing advanced features such as frontend login, registration, and profile management with the extension of core features.

Similar to custom post types, you will find many applications with one of the primary features as user management. Forums, online student management systems, and CRMs are some of the examples of high-level user management applications with WordPress.

Form data management

The process of capturing, processing, and displaying user data is the primary feature of many websites. We already discussed the use of custom post types for simplifying the data modeling process. However, inbuilt custom post type features are only available in the backend. Form management is essential for capturing the user data to the custom post types from the frontend. There are certain limitations that force us to use form management from scratch without using custom post types on some occasions. Such limitations include the use of existing database tables, hooks, and built-in templates in custom post types.

We can add forms using theme templates, shortcodes, or existing hooks. Modern JavaScript libraries will be used to process them while using custom database tables to enhance flexibility. So, this is another essential skill in WordPress development.

Building custom layouts and extending theme layouts

Each WordPress site or application is built around a theme and set of plugins. In general, most people prefer to use a high-quality existing theme, while some of them require a complete theme built for them from scratch. Regardless of these preferences, you need to be skilled in theme development, in order to cater to modern trends. Widget-based dynamic screens, responsive layouts, and dynamic content displays based on user preferences are some of the modern trends used in themes. The most common form of development is the customization of existing theme layouts and building new post/page templates.

Modern applications may also require you to add complex features into the theme instead of separating them into plugins. So, you need to have hands-on experience in theme files as well as common theme hooks for building advanced user interfaces.

These are some of the frequently involved areas in WordPress development, and hence you need to be familiar in order to deliver rapid solutions. Apart from these areas, you can extend most WordPress features using existing hooks, as well as build custom features such as APIs, integration of third-party UI components, and so on.

Setting up the development environment

In order to get started with WordPress development, you will need a working development environment that supports WordPress. So, we need to focus on the essential steps for building a development environment, such as the following:

- Installing a development stack that supports PHP, Apache, and MySQL or Maria DB
- Installing and configuring WordPress
- Setting up web browsers and code editors

Let's take a quick look at each of these options for building the ideal development environment for WordPress.

Installing the development stack

The most basic requirements for running WordPress include PHP, Apache server, and a MySQL database. So, we need to either install these components from scratch or use existing tools such as WAMP, XAMPP, or MAMP. Since this book is about a quick start to WordPress development, we are going to use existing tools without wasting time on manual installation. You can choose the tool depending on your operating system. For this book, we are going to use the WAMP server on the Windows platform.

The WAMP server offers a built-in installation process, and all you need is to provide the requested inputs while going through several well-defined installation screens. Since this is already discussed in several online resources, we are not going to explain the installation process here. You can refer to `http://www.wampserver.com/en/` for instructions on setting up WAMP.

Installing and configuring WordPress

Once the development stack is installed, we can move to the WordPress installation process. WordPress offers one of the simplest automated processes for installing a software framework. The complete installation process takes no more than 5-6 steps and a few minutes. Since it's already documented comprehensively in the WordPress codex, we are not going to waste time explaining it from scratch. You can refer to `https://codex.wordpress.org/Installing_WordPress#Detailed_Instructions` for the complete installation process.

Even though installation is a simple process, configuration might vary based on your requirements as well as different environments. Therefore, we are going to discuss the configuration in detail in the upcoming sections.

Setting up web browsers and code editors

As a developer, you should already have at least two browsers installed on your system. WordPress is frequently updated with modern versions of libraries and trends, such as responsive design. So, you need to make sure that the available browsers are updated to the latest versions. Also, you may have to install all popular browsers such as Chrome, Firefox, Opera, Safari, and Internet Explorer to adhere to browser compatibility.

A code editor is another important aspect of development, where developers need to choose one that favors their personal interests. Some popular code editors include Sublime Text, Brackets, Textmate, and Notepad++. When choosing a code editor, you need to look for essential features, such as the following:

- Supported programming languages
- Syntax highlighting and code readability
- Autocompletion
- Simplified indentation and formatting
- Version management
- File/folder search and replacement

Many of these editors are fully featured solutions and hence all these features are available by default. In such cases, you can make the decision based on your personal preferences. At this point, our development environment is ready with the most common tools for getting started.

Preparing development tools

Even though we can start the development right away, it's important to have the necessary tools that make our tasks easier as developers, while saving precious time. You can find hundreds of developer tools created to test and debug the code and help you pinpoint the issues in your implementations. Here, we are going to look at some of the most essential tools to support your development.

Client-side monitoring with browser development tools

There was a time when we had to install different extensions to use development tools in different browsers. Now, development tools have become the norm in the latest versions of all modern browsers. These tools provide a wide range of facilities to debug your code. The following screenshot previews the developer tools section of the Chrome browser:

The preceding screenshot previews the **Console** tab, where you will see errors, notices, and information related to user requests. This tab simplifies the process of tracking and fixing errors in your client-side coding. We can also use other tabs such as **Sources**, **Network**, **Performance**, **Security** to track AJAX requests, file loading precedence, memory, and bandwidth usage, along with possible security risks.

> *"AJAX is a short term for Asynchronous JavaScript and XML. AJAX is a set of web development techniques using many web technologies on the client side to create asynchronous web applications. With Ajax, web applications can send and retrieve data from a server asynchronously (in the background) without interfering with the display and behavior of the existing page."*

> – *Wikipedia*

Other browsers provide built-in development tools with similar features. The Firefox browser consists of **Inspector,Console, Debugger, Style Editor, Performance, Memory, Network,** and **Storage** tabs. Internet Explorer consists of **DOM Explorer, Console, Debugger, Network, UI Responsiveness, Profiler,** and **Memory** tabs. The main feature set is consistent across all browsers. As a developer, you should use browser tools at least for simple tasks, such as monitoring errors, inspecting HTML tags, tracking AJAX requests, and testing CSS styles.

Server-side monitoring with WordPress plugins

The WordPress plugin repository provides quite a few plugins to help developers track errors, performance issues, styles used in requests, executed hooks, loaded scripts, and various kind of other useful features. It's up to you to choose the number of plugins to use, and which plugins to use. In this section, we are going to look at some of the most popular plugins for debugging and testing.

Query Monitor

This is the most widely used plugin among the recently updated plugins in the debug category. The primary functionality of this plugin is to monitor the database queries in user requests and help you optimize them. We use many plugins to build a WordPress site, and hence each user request may execute a large number of queries. In most scenarios, a considerable amount of queries are not relevant to the user request and executed due to low quality coding from plugin developers. This plugin allows you to track queries by plugin, making it easier to identify the plugins responsible for executing a large number of queries, as well as unnecessary ones.

The following screenshot previews the use of **Query Monitor** to track the queries executed by the WordPress core and individual plugins:

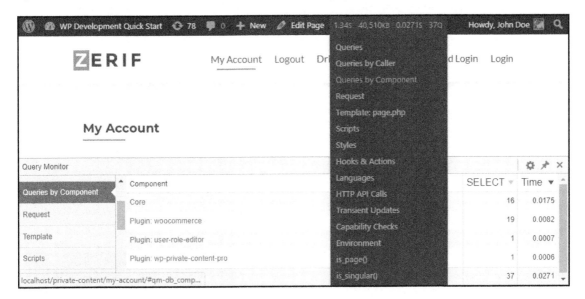

Apart from monitoring queries, you can also use this plugin to check hooks, scripts, and styles loaded in the current user request. Query Monitor is a must-use plugin for WordPress. You can find more details about Query Monitor plugin at `https://wordpress.org/plugins/query-monitor/`.

Debug This

This is one of the more recently created plugins to support developers. Unlike **Query Monitor**, this plugin doesn't have a primary feature. Instead, it offers a wide range of features for tracking all types of features in WordPress. You can track shortcodes, post types, PHP class/function usage, media attachments, and many other things, along with the features we already discussed in Query Monitor.

The following screenshot previews the use of **Debug This** with the list of available features:

As you may notice, this is an extremely useful tool for developers. The only drawback is the output of information as plain arrays, making it difficult to read. Even though it lacks the proper organization of information using user-friendly screens, you can resolve complex issues without using your own `var_dump` inside the code. You can find more details about the Debug This plugin at `https://wordpress.org/plugins/debug-this/`.

Apart from these two plugins, there are more useful plugins to help developers write quality code and save time with error handling and optimization. The following is a list of such plugins to be used in development:

- **What The File** (`https://wordpress.org/plugins/what-the-file/`): This plugin allows you to quickly track the templates and template parts used in the current user request. It also supports BuddyPress-based themes.
- **Debug Bar** (`https://wordpress.org/plugins/debug-bar/`): This plugin is similar to the **Debug This** plugin. However, it provides fewer features and a better user interface.

We looked at most popular testing and debugging plugins in the WordPress plugin repository. There are premium plugins and online services for further improving the development process. You can test these plugins and see which ones fit into your development environment.

Working with the configuration file

WordPress uses a configuration file called `wp-config.php`, located inside the root directory of your WordPress installation. In the preceding section, we went through the installation process, and this file was generated automatically based on the specified information. In order to use the advanced features of WordPress, as well as making manual modifications based on system changes, we will explain this file thoroughly. Let's take a quick look at the initial contents of this file using the following code:

```
define('DB_NAME', 'wpquick');
define('DB_USER', 'wpadmin');
define('DB_PASSWORD', ' GBm+Hq1T1Clyq ');
define('DB_HOST', 'localhost');
define('DB_CHARSET', 'utf8mb4');
define('DB_COLLATE', '');

define('AUTH_KEY',          '}ezywl=_z-&_r-
Ter]^)GafZQ!;T}sG{`RI?y.!BDgKKtW6WLqk>FnH<p1@ZsHZ`');
define('SECURE_AUTH_KEY',   'm1+,]G-])dt)%T:9ziw;|,]s&k^
^Z0Vp.7DaSC0U)GT>*GY:jW@');
define('LOGGED_IN_KEY',     '&W_%WB%jjS0+_oBN:-cz5]qK<Jv*1{oM
vji[~}k(uN*`g>wczC}<6?8t!BX{Z;G');
define('NONCE_KEY',
'vL9gM*pJPP3BC>I29+8*f[[)%kI$>)^clg%T;`9ONs17RXAkzm]oX18Y~1c.;n%6');
define('AUTH_SALT',         'y>:&&$GBm+Hq1T1Clyq=Vp{Mk>f;nRofa/f!i}ex(m&-
rs&dkT!ja0ilwJD~Lk4qQ');
define('SECURE_AUTH_SALT', 'PQMwuucwM`=0z7AwEJO@##
}kQ]+o,bl2CZ()!d|*_FEl)>iI');
define('LOGGED_IN_SALT',    'XD1T]5pBg4jTg=e#XA2u{CTrdP!SU|aD o&Rq4/}:
!Gu_2;)u-nW}0(/EEu4Ysb');
define('NONCE_SALT',
'CCX2?iAcCJ{Se5!ViEUO(/E0~/`ez_TZ=oAFrZ?DMru/RzLz(iPv(LwV%L0#a5px');

$table_prefix  = 'wp_';
define('WP_DEBUG', false);

if ( !defined('ABSPATH') )
   define('ABSPATH', dirname(__FILE__) . '/');
require_once(ABSPATH . 'wp-settings.php');
```

The first section of the file handles database configurations for your site. As you can see, database details are already added based on the inputs you provided in the installation process. You need to modify this section manually when you move the site from a local environment to a live environment, or when you make changes in database details such as username and password. Once database details are modified and saved, it will immediately impact the loading of your site.

The next section defines the WordPress security keys. These keys are automatically generated on WordPress installation. In scenarios where you don't have the security keys, you can go to `https://api.wordpress.org/secret-key/1.1/salt/` and generate a new set of keys. This section consists of four keys and four salts for your website. These keys are used to secure the cookies for your users. You don't have to know the meaning of each key or remember the keys. WordPress will use these keys to generate hash values of cookie names as well as cookie values, making it difficult to hack your authentication details. No matter how many security precautions we take, there is a chance of your site getting hacked due to the open source nature of WordPress and use of third-party plugins. In such situations, you can regenerate and add these keys to the config file. This will invalidate all existing cookies and hence all users will have to log in again.

The next two lines define the table prefix and the debug mode. The prefix is configured by the input you provide in the installation process. It's recommended to change the prefix to anything other than `wp`, to improve security. By default, the debug mode is set to `FALSE` and hence you won't see any PHP errors on your site. In a development environment, you should change this value to `TRUE`, in order to identify the errors in code. Once development is completed, you should change it back to `FALSE` before uploading the file to a live server. The final few lines define the file path, and load the settings file.

This is the most basic version of the `wp-config.php` file, and it's adequate for handling basic WordPress sites.

An overview of advanced configurations

As a developer, you will have to build from simple WordPress blogs to fully functional web applications. So, advanced configurations become important for security, advanced features, and the performance of applications. Let's take a quick look at how you can modify the configuration file using other configuration options.

Securing plugins and upload directories

Due to the open source nature of WordPress, everyone knows where plugins and files are stored in your site. Therefore, the process of hacking or spamming your site becomes easier for potential attackers. As a solution, we can move plugin and upload directories to a different path using the config file, to increase the difficulty of finding paths to attack.

Let's add more configurations to change the default location of these directories:

```
define( 'WP_PLUGIN_DIR', $_SERVER['DOCUMENT_ROOT'] .
'/example.com/modules/' );
define( 'WP_PLUGIN_URL', 'http://localhost/ example.com /modules/');
define( 'UPLOADS', 'modules/media' );
```

The first two lines move the plugin directory from `wp-content/plugins` to the `modules` directory in your root directory. Since the path has changed to the root directory, it will be difficult for attackers to identify the path. These configurations only change the directory. If you already have plugins in the `wp-content/plugins` directory, you will have to move them manually to a new directory. The next line changes the media upload path from `wp-content/uploads` to the `modules/media` directory inside the main installation.

The process of moving the theme directory is not straightforward as the path is configured relative to the `wp-content` directory. Therefore, you will have to change the main path of the `wp-content` directory in situations where you want to change the theme directory. You may use these configurations manually, or use existing plugins to help secure your site.

Configuring advanced debugging settings

Earlier, we enabled debugging in the development environment by setting `WP_Debug` to `TRUE`. There are more settings to control the debugging process and provide more information on issues in our code. Let's walk through some of the advanced options for developers.

Script debugging

In general, conflicts in JavaScript files are a common problem due to the use of different script versions in different plugins and themes. Identifying these errors is a cumbersome process when using minified versions and concatenated script files. Let's take a look at some of the rules used for resolving these issues:

```
define( 'SCRIPT_DEBUG', true );
define( 'CONCATENATE_SCRIPTS', false );
```

The first line enables script debugging by loading the uncompressed file instead of the minified version. The second line prevents concatenation of multiple scripts, allowing you to track the line of the error. You should use these configuration rules when you are experiencing script issues in WordPress core files.

Logging errors and customizing php.ini rules

We can either display the coding errors in the browser or log them to a separate log file. It's at the preference of the developer, but I think logging the errors is the ideal solution for future reference. Also, sometimes we need to change the PHP configurations to make our code work. Many hosting servers will not allow you to directly edit the php.ini file, and hence we can use the wp-config.php file to override the default settings of the php.ini file.

> Some hosting providers don't provide access to change the php.ini file, and you will have to request modification through server support.

Consider the following configuration rules for error logging with php.ini modifications:

```
@ini_set( 'log_errors', 'On' );
@ini_set( 'display_errors', 'Off' );
@ini_set( 'error_log', '/home/example.com/logs/php_error.log' );
```

First, we enable error logging in PHP and disable displaying errors in the browser by using the display_errors setting. Then, we define the path of the file where errors will be logged. You need to create this directory first and provide the necessary write permissions before this rule takes effect.

In this section, we had a brief overview of some of the most basic and advanced configurations in WordPress development. There are many other settings to help developers, as well as control features. You can take a look at the available configurations and their use in the WordPress codex at https://codex.wordpress.org/Editing_wp-config.php. Now, we have the complete setup to begin development tasks on top of WordPress.

Understanding the role of the WordPress file and directory structure

Beginning WordPress development is not a complex task. It's about making minor theme changes, installing and customizing existing plugins, and using the available hooks. As you move on, complex requirements come your way with the expectation of future-proof solutions. Trying to build such solutions without considering future WordPress, plugin, and theme versions can lead to a nightmare. Getting used to existing WordPress files/directories and knowing their role is vital in developing maintainable solutions. In this section, we are going to look at the existing files and directories of a default WordPress installation.

The following is a screenshot of typical files and directories inside your WordPress installation:

Let's look at some of the most important files and directories inside WordPress:

- `wp-admin`: This is where WordPress stores files related to admin-side functionality. The files in this directory are based around the `admin.php` file. Primary functionalities of these files include checking admin permission, connecting to the database, and loading the admin dashboard features. This directory is upgraded with WordPress version updates and hence the content of these files is replaced.

- `wp-content`: This is where WordPress stores user-uploaded files such as plugins, themes, and media files. We can add additional files/directories here without being affected by WordPress version updates. So, the content in this directory will not be replaced.
- `wp-includes`: This is the largest directory in WordPress with over 800 files to power the features of the admin dashboard as well as frontend functionality. The primary file in this directory is `functions.php`, considered as the main WordPress API. This directory is upgraded with WordPress version updates and hence the content of these files is replaced.
- `.htaccess`: This file is where you describe configuration rules for your Apache server. By default, it will contain minimal rules. You can manually add configuration rules based on your requirements. There are plugins that automatically add the necessary configuration rules to this file. This file is used for the configuration of WordPress permalinks. Changing the permalink structure from the WordPress settings section is the simplest way to track rule changes in this file.
- `index.php`: This file is responsible for initializing WordPress based on user requests, and serving the response.
- `wp-config.php`: This file is used for all the configurations for your site including databases, secret keys, plugins, and theme directory paths. So, it's very important to keep this file as secure as possible. This file is not replaced on WordPress version upgrades and hence you can use your own configurations.

Here, we looked at the most important files and directories involved in development. You can also check the comments of other core files to understand their functionality.

How to choose files and directories for development

The process of WordPress development is slightly more challenging compared to other PHP frameworks. With any other framework, we choose a specific framework version and develop the features for that specific version. It's entirely optional to upgrade our solution's future versions of the framework. However, it's the opposite with WordPress. We can't stick with a specific WordPress version for a long time, especially due to security concerns. Most of you will want to upgrade the version as soon as WordPress releases a new version. Therefore, it's important to develop solutions that don't break with version upgrades. Basically, we should be able to upgrade WordPress without touching any of our code.

So, the first thing you need to understand is where you can place your code files and how you can use the core WordPress files/directories in development. We discussed the main files and directories inside the WordPress directory in the previous section. Let's narrow it down to the files and folders used for custom development. Basically, we have to choose files and folders that are not replaced by WordPress updates. Among the files and folders we discussed, `wp-content`, `wp-config.php`, and `htaccess` are not affected by upgrades. So, our development should focus on these files and folders.

As we mentioned, `wp-content` is the directory where all the user-uploaded files are stored. So, we need to add our code files inside this directory. Let's explore the contents of this directory to understand where and what kinds of files can be created.

The following is a screenshot of files and folders inside your `wp-content` folder:

The preceding screenshot contains both default directories and custom directories created based on custom requirements. Let's have a brief overview of the role of each folder:

- `plugins`: This is where WordPress stores all the plugins required to run your site. You will get Akismet Anti-Spam and Hello Dolly plugins on initial installation. Afterwards, you can use this directory to add your own plugins as well as install existing plugins from other developers. This directory can be considered as the heart of WordPress development.

- `themes`: This is where WordPress stores all your themes that power the design and initial functionality of your site. Initial installation contains a few default themes such as **Twenty Seventeen, Twenty Sixteen**, and so on. Afterwards, you can use this directory to add your own themes as well as install existing themes from other developers. Unlike plugins, you can only use one theme from this directory at any given time.

- `uploads`: This is where all the user-uploaded files for posts, pages, and plugins will be stored. This directory is not created until you upload the first file. Usually, all the media files for posts and pages will be stored with a sub-directory structure of year/month format. You can create unlimited sub-directories to handle files for plugins and themes.

- `languages`: This directory is not available on initial installation and is created when you change the language in WordPress. So, it's not important for the development tasks.

- `mu-plugins`: This directory stores must-use plugins for your site and is not available on initial installation. A must-use plugin is a plugin that's mandatory to run the site and hence it's not possible to deactivate. These plugins are automatically enabled on all sites of your WordPress installation. Even though these plugins are useful in some scenarios, it's not ideal to use them due to some of the limitations in executing certain hooks. So, we are not considering them for the development tasks of this book.

- `upgrade`: This directory is not available by default and is used for storing temporary files for WordPress version upgrades. So, it's important for our development tasks.

- `cache and logs`: These are some of the custom directories created by plugins or themes to handle certain features. I have used them in this screenshot to explain the use of custom folders. You can create such custom folders to handle files related to themes or plugins.

After having a quick overview of files and directories, we can come to the conclusion that our primary focus should be on the `plugins`, `themes`, and `uploads` directories inside the `wp-content` directory. Using code and media files in these directories ensures our solutions are not wiped out by version upgrades.

A brief overview of WordPress coding standards

In programming, writing working code is not the only responsibility of the developers. They are responsible for writing quality code that is extendable for future enhancements, as well as making sure the code is easily understandable for other developers. This is where coding standards become an important aspect of development. Coding standards are a set of rules and conventions specific to a programming language, and all developers are expected to follow them to make the code consistent.

I assume that you are familiar with PHP coding standards and ready to develop WordPress with that experience. However, WordPress itself has a set of coding standards and some of these rules are slightly different to PHP standards. The coding standards are currently divided into four sections, called PHP, HTML, CSS, and JavaScript. As a developer, you need to be familiar with WordPress coding standards, especially when you are developing themes and plugins for the WordPress repository.

Let's take a look at some of the main PHP coding standards used in WordPress:

- **Single quotes and double quotes**: PHP processes single quotes quicker than double quotes since the parser doesn't have to detect and execute any variables. That's why it's better to use single quotes for strings that don't have any evaluations.
- **Indentation**: You should use tabs instead of spaces for indenting the code.
- **Opening and closing brackets**: You should always use opening and closing brackets even when it's not necessary for single line evaluations.
- **Using spaces**: WordPress recommends putting spaces after commas, and on both sides of logical, comparison, string, and assignment operators.
- **Naming conventions**: You should always use lowercase letters and underscores for naming variables, functions, actions, filters, and so on. The `camelCase` method is not recommended in WordPress coding standards.
- **Dynamic hooks**: Hooks are unique to WordPress and hence the guidelines suggest using interpolation by wrapping the variable in curly brackets, instead of using concatenation.

These are some of the common coding standards for WordPress, and you can find the complete set of standards, including CSS, JavaScript, and HTML, at `https://codex.wordpress.org/WordPress_Coding_Standards`. Those developers who are familiar with pure PHP coding will notice the slight changes in WordPress standards, such as using lots of spaces and not using camel case for functions. So, it's a challenge even for experienced developers to come out of your comfort zone and write code the WordPress way.

The preceding section illustrated the main PHP coding standards. Most of you should have a general idea of these standards, as you have already worked with PHP. However, there are WordPress-specific coding styles/conventions due to hook-based architecture. Many of you may not be aware of these conventions, which are essential for building themes and plugins that don't conflict with others.

Let's have a quick overview of some of these conventions, which will be discussed in detail throughout the book:

- **Loading scripts and styles**: Usually, we can load scripts and styles anywhere in an HTML page by using `<script>` and `<link>` tags. WordPress uses built-in PHP functions to load scripts and styles. Therefore, it's recommended that you load these files only within an action called `wp_enqueue_scripts`. Loading these files outside this action could result in conflicts with WordPress core features as well as other `plugins` or `themes`.

- **Loading third-party libraries**: Libraries such as **jQuery**, **Underscore**, **and Backbone.js** are used frequently in modern web development. Usually, developers have the option to include these libraries within their code files or load them from a CDN for faster performance. This technique is not feasible in WordPress as many plugins from different developers are involved. Therefore, we need to load one common version of the library to avoid conflicts in code. So, we have to use the library version that comes built-in with WordPress.

- **Using proper events for execution**: In pure PHP programming, we can execute code anywhere and anytime based on our preferences. WordPress uses an event-driven architecture with hooks, and hence code is executed through events in a predefined manner. Unless we use the correct events, our code is going to conflict with code from other. For example, we need to access `$_POST` variables within or after an `init` hook. Trying to access this data before the necessary event could lead to errors in your code.

We had a brief introduction to the coding standards and conventions needed to get started with WordPress development. Often, you will find it sufficient for development projects for specific clients. However, you will sometimes need further knowledge, especially on event-based conventions for plugin and theme development. We will cover the necessary coding conventions throughout the upcoming chapters.

Summary

The goal of this chapter was to get the environment ready and understand the prerequisites for complex development tasks. We explored the techniques for integrating our code into WordPress, as well as identifying the most used modules in development.

We had a brief overview of the installation and configuration of the development environment, while identifying the necessary tools for simplifying our tasks. Finally, we went through the WordPress file and directory structure to understand how our solutions can be provided in a future-proof manner.

In Chapter 2, *Managing Database Structure, Storage, and Retrieval*, we will be exploring the existing WordPress database structure and its use, while discussing the practical uses of custom database tables.

Managing Database Structure, Storage, and Retrieval

2

The database is the primary location for storing application data. WordPress provides a built-in database with pre-defined tables, compared to traditional web applications, where the database is designed from scratch. Getting used to the pros and cons of the existing database table is the key to developing quality themes and plugins.

In this chapter, we will learn the power and limitations of the existing database tables in Wordpress. You will get an overview of existing database tables and their role, while understanding how data is managed in common functions such as post creation, user creation, media uploads, and so on. You will also learn the uses of custom tables in development, and using the query functions to retrieve data.

In this chapter, we will cover the following topics:

- Understanding the role of default database tables
- Tracking and understanding database usage of primary features
- Creating and managing custom tables
- Implementing CRUD operations
- A brief overview of the multisite database structure

By the end of this chapter, you will have the necessary knowledge to maximize the use of existing database tables in development, while using custom tables for advanced use cases.

Introduction to the WordPress database

The process of planning and designing a database is one of the most critical phases of any project. A well-planned database design eases the process for future growth while increasing performance in data storage and retrieval. Usually, it's the responsibility of the development team to identify the entities and relationships between these entities. WordPress, on the other hand, is a CMS and hence offers an existing database to handle core features. So, the process of planning a database is not part of the responsibility as a developer in most scenarios. Instead, developers have a tougher task of understanding the core tables and managing the data needs with its limitations. Of course, you can create and use your own database tables for any requirement. But, doing so eliminates the whole purpose of developing on top of WordPress.

The WordPress database currently supports MySQL and MariaDB, with MariaDB being the most preferred choice. However, most of the existing WordPress sites still use MySQL. On successful installation, WordPress will create eleven database tables to cater for the core functionality. Since its inception, backward compatibility was one of the top priorities of the WordPress team. Therefore, you may not see major changes in these eleven tables in the near future.

Understanding the role of built-in database tables

The WordPress database structure is designed to store a minimum amount of data required for core features. Therefore, developers need to have a thorough understanding of the existing tables in order to use them effectively to build flexible websites. Let's take a look at the entity relationship diagram of the latest WordPress versions:

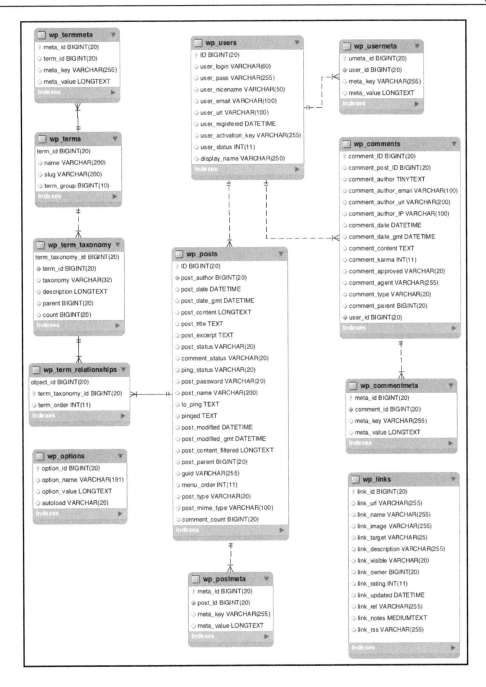

As may notice, all the existing tables don't have more than one or two relationships with other tables, and hence understanding and working with the database becomes a simpler task. Now, we are going to look at each database table with important columns, its role, and how it works with other tables. You need to refer to the preceding diagram to visualize the points in our discussion.

Posts-related database tables

Three database tables are directly involved with posts and six tables handle posts-related data. Many of the existing WordPress sites are either basic sites with a few pages, or blogs with hundreds of posts. So, the data of the majority of the sites are managed by these six database tables. Let's take a look at the two tables directly related to posts.

wp_posts

This is the primary data storage location of many WordPress sites and applications. This table consists of the main data for posts, pages, and custom post types. This table consists of twenty-three columns. Let's identify some of the most important columns in this table:

post_author	This is where you find the ID of the user who created the post or page. This column is used to form the relationship with the wp_users table.
post_content	The complete content of the post/page is stored in this column. So, the data in this column can range from a few words to thousands of words and images.
post_title	The title of the post/page is stored in this column. It's used to identify the page in the backend as well as highlight the title in the frontend.
post_excerpt	The data in this column is optional and used for keeping a summary of the post/page. Usually, this is used in post lists (archive) pages to show a glimpse of what the post is about, and encourage users to read the entire post.
post_status	WordPress-specific post statuses are stored in this column. These statuses defines a step in the life cycle of a post. Default statuses include publish, pending, private, future, inherit, trash, draft, and auto-draft. Most of these statuses are self-explanatory. However, you may need explanations on the inherit and auto-draft statuses. WordPress provides the ability to store revisions of posts in the database. When we update a post, the previous post data in the database automatically becomes a revision with the status marked as **inherit**. Also, WordPress automatically saves posts at certain time intervals, and those revisions are marked as **auto-draft**.

post_password	This stores the password of password-protected posts or pages.
post_parent	This column stores the ID of the parent post. WordPress supports child posts for attachments, pages, and post revisions.
guid	The complete URL of the post/page is stored in this column.
post_type	This stores the type post with a unique key. Default post types includes post, page, revision, attachment, and nav_menu_item. Apart from these types, you can create any new type using custom post types.

Usually, this table is intended for built-in types such as posts, pages, menus, and attachments. With the introduction of custom post types, this table is used widely for storing data such as products, forum topics, properties, and anything that you can think of.

wp_postmeta

This is the secondary storage for posts where optional data related to posts and pages are stored. This table consists of four columns. Let's identify some of the most important columns in this table:

post_id	This is where you find the ID of the post for these additional data. This column is used to form the relationship with the wp_posts table.
meta_key	All the additional post data is saved as key-value pairs. This column defines the identification for post data. A unique key should be used for this column with alpha numeric characters, underscores, and dashes. By default, WordPress stores **edit lock** info for posts and pages. As you add data to posts or create menus, you will see more keys stored with underscore prefixes. This is different to what we have used as developers, where we store such data in a different table with these keys as columns.
meta_value	This column contains the posts-related data for the specified meta keys. Usually, these values are stored as plain text or serialized values.

Usually, this table is used to store administration-level values and custom fields added from the post edit screen. In large sites with custom post types, this table becomes crucial. In such sites, we can store data such as product options in an online store, property details in real-estate sites, and job details in a job management site.

Terms-related tables

We can find four tables in this section, targeted for handling post-specific categorization. We use the term *taxonomoy* in WordPress for these categorizations. By default, we have two taxonomies called categories and tags. These tables are capable of handling these two taxonomy types as well as your own taxonomy types. Let's take a look at each of these four tables in detail.

wp_terms

This is used to store the choices for taxonomies. You should be aware of categories and tags in WordPress posts. We call those types taxonomies. The choice inside a taxonomy is called a term. **Category** is a taxonomy and choices we create such as Health, Sports, and Travel are considered terms. This table consists of four columns. Let's identify some of the most important columns in this table:

name	Stores the title of the term that displays on the frontend of the site
slug	Stores the unique identifier for the term

Initial WordPress installation generates two taxonomies, called category and post tag. However, no terms are created by default and only contains **Uncategorized** as a term. We can use this table to create post tags or category choices. Also, we can use this in custom scenarios for creating terms such as WordPress, PHP, and jQuery for job skills in a job management site.

wp_termmeta

This is the secondary location for storing data for terms. This table consists of four columns and works similar to other metadata tables using key-value pairs.

By default, this table is not used frequently. You may use this table to store additional details of your own terms. Assume you have terms for articles such as sports, health, travel. You want to display the archive pages of each of these categories using a different design. In such a scenario, you can store the CSS, images, templates in a term metatable and use this info to load the design.

wp_term_relationships

This used to form the relationship between posts and terms. This table consists of three columns and only IDs are used as data. Let's identify some of the most important columns in this table:

object_id	Stores the ID of the post or custom post type that connects with the taxonomy
term_taxonomy_id	Stores the ID of the taxonomy

This is purely an associative table, which connects two tables using IDs. As a developer, you just need to assign the relationship, and this table doesn't have different uses based on the type of the site.

wp_term_taxonomy

This table stores the type of categorizations called taxonomies. This table consists of six columns. Let's identify some of the most important columns in this table:

term_id	This is the ID of the term and is used to form the connection with the wp_terms table.
taxonomy	This is the unique slug for the taxonomy. Default taxonomies are category and post_tag.
parent	Stores the parent term when using sub-terms in your site.
count	Stores the number of posts and custom post types that belong to this taxonomy.

This table contains default taxonomies for category and `post_tag`, to be used in normal WordPress posts. We can create custom taxonomies such as job skills in a job management site, product types in an online store, property features in a real-estate site, and so on.

User-related tables

User data is managed using two tables in the existing database. By default, we have very basic details about users stored in these tables. Modern sites bring the concept of personalized content, and hence user management is becoming more and more important. So, you see extensive use of these tables in many websites. Let's take a look at each of these two tables in detail.

wp_users

This is the primary storage location for users, consisting of ten columns. Let's identify some of the most important columns in this table:

user_login	Used as the username for the site. You can allow users to change it using your own implementations. However, this value needs to be unique.
user_pass	Stores the encrypted password for the user.
user_email	Used as the email of the user. Since WordPress allows users to login with email, this value needs to be unique for each user.
user_registered	Stores the registration date and is often used to sort the list of users or assign the membership period on membership-based sites.

The data in this table doesn't change based on the type of site you are developing, and hence you only need to have knowledge on inserting, updating, and deleting users in this table.

wp_usermeta

Used as the secondary location for user data. By default, it keeps track of names, descriptions, capabilities, and so on. This table consists of four columns. Let's identify some of the most important columns in this table:

user_id	This is where you find the ID of the user that this data belongs to. This column is used to form the relationship with the wp_users table.
meta_key	All the additional user data is saved as key-value pairs. This column defines the identification for user data. A unique key should be used for this column with alpha numeric characters, underscores, and dashes. This is different to what we have used as developers, where we store such data in a different table with these keys as columns.
meta_value	This column contains the user-related data for the specified metakeys. Usually, these values are stored as plain text or serialized values.

Apart from default options, we can use this table to store simple custom user data such as date of birth, country, city, and advanced user data such as interests, and profile pictures.

Options and comments tables

This section consists of three tables used for configurations and comments. Let's take a look at these tables in detail.

wp_options

This stores all the built-in and custom settings for WordPress. This is another table similar to wp_postmeta and wp_usermeta, where key-value pairs are used for keeping data. Default options in this table include the site URL, site description, date format, and so on.

Developers can use this table to store settings for their themes or plugins. Usually, plugin or theme settings are stored as a single row in this table as a serialized value. However, you can store as many options based on your preference.

wp_comments

This stores comments for posts, pages, and custom post types. This table consists of fifteen columns. Let's identify some of the most important in the following table:

comment_post_ID	Stores the post, page, or custom post type ID where the comment belongs.
comment_author	Keeps the name of the user who created this comment.
comment_content	Used to keep the comment added by the user. This column can contain plain text values as well as HTML depending on the allowed options in the site.
comment_approved	In most sites, a comment needs to be approved before it appears for public. This column stores Boolean status on whether a comment is approved or pending approval.
comment_type	Stores the type of comment. Default comment types includes comment, pingbacks, and trackbacks. We can also use custom comment types.
user_id	ID of the user who created the comment. This column is used to form the connection with the wp_users table.

Usually, this table is used for basic comments of posts, pages, and custom post types. However, we can think beyond the convention by using comments in innovative ways. We can use comments for features such as answers of a question-based site such as stackoverflow, user messages in a forum topic, or reviews in an online product marketplace.

wp_commentmeta

This is used as the secondary location for storing additional comment data. This table consists of four columns and works similar to other metadata tables in WordPress.

There are no default usages of this table. We can use this table to store additional data such as ratings in a product review site, verified status in a question-answer site, and so on.

In this section, we looked at all eleven default database tables in WordPress and their role in development. You have to understand each and every column of these tables with the possible values, as most of the WordPress development is done on top of the core features.

Understanding the importance of database usage

In today's world, many of the developers doesn't have in-depth knowledge of WordPress core features and yet, capable of turning your requirement into a working solution. However, these solutions are often based on assumptions, rather than knowing the exact process and data usage under the hood.

Tracking database usage and knowing the exact data needs of any given process is crucial for building flexible and extendable solutions that integrate perfectly with other parts of the site. Let's identify some of the use cases where you need perfect knowledge of data usage in WordPress features:

Building existing features on the frontend

WordPress offers a powerful backend with many features for administration-level users. Post creation and user management are some of the top features in backend. Comparatively, existing WordPress frontend features are less powerful and mainly focus on displaying data. So, it's a common requirement to transfer these backend features to the frontend, allowing users with lesser permissions to create content from the frontend without giving access to the backend.

In such scenarios, we need to know the exact data used in the backend process, so that we can emulate it on the frontend process. Often, developers don't have necessary knowledge of all data stored in such a process. So, the frontend aspect of this feature works perfectly, but breaks the backend due to lack of data.

Let's consider a simple scenario where you want to let users upload files using a form on your site, and store the files in a WordPress media library. At first glance, you will see that media files are stored in the `wp_posts` table and contains the necessary data. So, you will save the data to the `wp_posts` table. However, you may not notice that additional metadata for files are stored in the `wp_postmeta` table. Therefore, your frontend implementation may break the core features or other plugins that rely on this data.

Customizing existing plugins

Use of other existing plugins is almost certain in WordPress site development. Often, these plugins don't fit directly for our needs, and hence the customization becomes an obvious choice. Understanding the use of data becomes even more crucial since some of these custom plugins lack documentation and code quality compared to core features. Customizing a plugin without knowing its data usage can lead to major conflicts compared to core features.

In such scenarios, we need a thorough examination of documentation to manually track database usage and when possible get the support of the developer to build custom solutions. Let me pick up and example from one of our own plugins. We have a user profile management plugin where we store additional user details in the `wp_usermeta` table. Since searching hundreds of rows per user in the `wp_usermeta` table is a cumbersome task, we also store all additional data in a single row as a search cache. We have seen many developers customizing the plugin to update user data, without knowing the need for a search cache value. Even though user data is updated, users don't appear in search results due to the missing search cache value. Such scenarios are common in plugin customizations and it's a must identify and avoid them using data tracking methods.

We have looked at the most common situations where tracking and knowing the data usage becomes critical. You may find other less common situations where consistency of the data becomes essential.

How to track database usage in WordPress

We identified the importance of tracking and knowing the data needs of core features as well as custom features. The next question is how we can track and understand data to avoid potential conflicts. So, we need a method that logs/shows all queries run within a user request. There are numerous ways to track database queries, including premium enterprise tools and the command line. As you are beginning WordPress development, we are going to look at some of the simpler and useful methods that expand your knowledge.

Using MySQL/MariaDB log files

This is one of the simpler and must-know methods as a developer. Both MySQL and MariaDB allow us to create a log file where we can track all the steps in connecting, initializing, and executing queries in a database. First, we need to add some configurations to the MySQL/MariaDB `ini` file. Since we are using WAMP for the development tasks of this book, you can click on the WAMP icon, go to the MySQL section, and open the `my.ini` file. You can use the same process for MAMP or any other tools that offer MySQL/MariaDB configuration.

 In Linux servers, the MySQL/MariaDB configuration file is often `/etc/mysql/my.cnf`; if you don't find it try to locate it using `sudo updatedb ; locate my.cnf`.

Next, you can add the following lines to the end of the file to configure the log file output:

```
[mysqld]
log-output = FILE
general-log = 1
general_log_file=C:/wamp/logs/general-query.log
```

 In linux servers, you can use `/var/log/mysql/mysql-debug.log` instead of `C:/wamp/logs/general-query.log` for the log file path. After modifying, restart MySQL/MariaDB server like this: `/etc/init.d/mysql restart`.

Once the rules are added, you should save and restart the WAMP server. Now, you can refresh your WordPress site to test a user request.

 Keep in mind that many of the hosting providers don't allow access to MySQL/MariaDB logs.

Then, open the log file in given location and you will see many queries executed within that request. So, you can use this method to track database changes by clearing the file, executing the request, and viewing the updated log file. The limitation of this method is that it shows all queries including numerous SELECT queries. Since we only want to track INSERT, UPDATE, and DELETE queries, it's not the perfect method.

Comparing database backups

This is one of the easier methods to compare the changes, instead of reviewing executed queries, and identify them. In this method, we take a database backup using phpMyAdmin, execute the user request, and take another database backup. Then, we can use a file compare tool like **MELD** (http://meldmerge.org/) to check how the database is changed within the request. The limitation of this process is that you need to manually take database backups, and comparing may become time-consuming for larger databases.

Creating a manual query logger

This is the ideal method where we create our own query logger and specify which queries we need to track. Let's look at the implementation of this method using the following code:

```
function wpc_filter_query( $query ) {
   if (strpos($query, 'INSERT') !== false || strpos($query, 'UPDATE') !==
false || strpos($query, 'DELETE') !== false)
     error_log('#### $query', 0);

   return $query;
};
add_filter( 'query', 'wpc_filter_query', 10, 1 );
```

The preceding code uses WordPress **query** filter to filter all the queries that are executed in user request. A complete `sql` query is parsed as a parameter and we filter INSERT, UPDATE, and DELETE queries. Then, we can log the queries to a preferred file. Here, we are adding the queries to PHP error log for illustration purposes. You can check the expected queries using the log file at `wamp/logs/php_error.log`. You can include this code in the `functions.php` file of the theme, until we get into plugin development.

You can choose one of the preferred methods or an external database tool to track database usage for any user request, and understand the must-use data of different processes.

Tracking database usage of common WordPress features

At this point, you should be able to configure and track database usage for both backend and frontend user requests. In this section, we will be looking at the usage of database in the most common WordPress features, and understand the need for storing the specified data.

Post creation

Being the most frequently used feature in WordPress sites, you need thorough understanding of the database usage. First, you need to go to **Posts | Add New** section and clear the existing query logs. Then, you can add the data and publish a post to track the database usage. The **Post creation** screen offers wide range of features and hence database usage may vary based on the amount of options you use. Let's track the queries by using the most common options in post creation:

```
INSERT INTO `wp_posts` (`post_author`, `post_date`...........) VALUES (1,
'2018-07-13 08:43:22'.....)
UPDATE `wp_posts` SET `post_author` = 1, `post_date` = '2018-07-13
08:43:30' ..... WHERE `ID` = 48
INSERT INTO `wp_postmeta` (`post_id`, `meta_key`, `meta_value`) VALUES (48,
'test field', '1')
INSERT INTO `wp_term_relationships` (`object_id`, `term_taxonomy_id`)
VALUES (48, 23)
UPDATE `wp_term_taxonomy` SET `count` = 3 WHERE `term_taxonomy_id` = 23
INSERT INTO `wp_term_relationships` (`object_id`, `term_taxonomy_id`)
VALUES (48, 24)
UPDATE `wp_term_taxonomy` SET `count` = 4 WHERE `term_taxonomy_id` = 24
```

The log file will contain a large amount of queries. Many of them are generated due to the WordPress autosaving process and temporary data storage for transients, cache, and admin-level options. We have omitted such queries and included the essential ones for understanding post creation.

In this scenario, we have assigned existing categories, tags and custom fields, along with the main post content. As you can see, the process starts with a INSERT query to the `wp_posts` table, where all primary post-specific data is stored. This query is executed as soon as you load the post creation screen. Then, WordPress updates the already created post when you hit the **Publish** button. The next query adds the custom field data to the `wp_postmeta` table. If you have multiple custom fields, you will see multiple such queries, one for each field.

Next, two queries relate the post with the category and update the post count for that specific category. The remaining two queries use the same process for tags instead of category. Here, we have seen the use of four database tables in post creation. Instead of using existing categories and tags, we can create new ones to analyze the use of all six post related tables in post creation. I recommend you further track the database usage by changing post statuses, adding a featured image, changing post formats, and changing post visibility.

Page creation

This is similar to post creation process where we use **Pages** | **Add New** section to load the page creation screen. We have less options in page creation compared to post creation process. Therefore, we should notice a decrease in the number of queries executed in this process. Let's take a look at the executed queries:

```
INSERT INTO `wp_posts` (`post_author`, `post_date`, ........) VALUES (1,
'2018-07-13 09:09:15',.......)
UPDATE `wp_posts` SET `post_author` = 1, `post_date` = '2018-07-13
09:09:31', ..... WHERE `ID` = 49
```

As we anticipated, only two queries executed in this process. The first one creates the page on screen load and the next one updates the content when the user hits the **Publish** button. So, it's easier to manage pages as a developer, compared to posts.

User creation

Many websites consist of just one or two administrators, with the registration feature blocked for public. However, the need for user registrations is rising in modern websites due the need of personalized content, rather than same content for all users. So, frontend registration becomes a common implementation. Let's track the database usage by creating user from the backend **Users | Add New** section:

```
INSERT INTO `wp_users` (`user_pass`, `user_email`, `user_url`,
`user_nicename`, `display_name`, `user_registered`, `user_login`)
VALUES ('$P$B.NS/td6lI7ug01eNW64p.', 'testuseremail@gmail.com', '',
'testuser', 'john doe', '2018-07-13 09:14:21', 'testuser')
INSERT INTO `wp_usermeta` (`user_id`, `meta_key`, `meta_value`) VALUES (4,
'nickname', 'testuser')
INSERT INTO `wp_usermeta` (`user_id`, `meta_key`, `meta_value`) VALUES (4,
'first_name', 'john')
INSERT INTO `wp_usermeta` (`user_id`, `meta_key`, `meta_value`) VALUES (4,
'locale', '')
INSERT INTO `wp_usermeta` (`user_id`, `meta_key`, `meta_value`) VALUES (4,
'wp_capabilities', 'a:1:{s:10:\"subscriber\";b:1;}')
```

The process starts by inserting a new user to the wp_users table with primary details such as username, email, password, and registered date. The additional details of users goes to wp_usermeta table with key-value pairs. Again, this is different to what we have used as developers, where we store such data in a different table with these keys as columns. We can see many INSERT queries to store details such as names, description, language, and so on. Among these values, locale and wp_capabilities are crucial ones where we define the language for the user and maintain the user roles and capabilities. Developers can use the wp_usermeta table to store custom data required for their websites.

Media uploads

We rarely see only full text-based content in modern websites. Most posts and pages are designed to use images and videos. So, media manager becomes a must user feature for many site owners. Using and developing with the WordPress media uploader could be different compared to building file upload forms from scratch. Let's review the use of database for media uploads using **Media | Add New** section:

```
INSERT INTO `wp_posts` (`post_author`, `post_date`, ...........) VALUES (1,
'2018-07-13 09:16:26',....)
INSERT INTO `wp_postmeta` (`post_id`, `meta_key`, `meta_value`) VALUES (50,
'_wp_attached_file', '2018/07/test.png')
INSERT INTO `wp_postmeta` (`post_id`, `meta_key`, `meta_value`) VALUES (50,
'_wp_attachment_metadata',
'a:5:{s:5:\"width\";i:512;s:6:\"height\";i:512.....')
```

In conventional development, we use a separate table to store the uploaded file details. However, WordPress uses a different approach by considering media as a post type. It might not be the ideal implementation as a large amount of media files could affect the performance of loading important posts and pages. But, we need to get used to the process. So, the main media file details are stored in the `wp_posts` table. Apart from that, two metafields are created in the `wp_postmeta` table to handle path and metadata such as captions, width, height. As a developer, we can use the postmeta table to store many additional data required for media files in your projects.

We used four of the most frequently used scenarios to track database usage. You might have already understood the importance of consistent data and use of database tracking to achieve it. Here, we have tracked the queries in a default WordPress installation. As we use more and more plugins, these scenarios becomes extremely complex. So, I recommend you use this technique to track data for the features of popular WordPress plugins, and understand how we can customize the features without breaking other parts.

Overview of the multisite database structure

Multisite network is a feature that allows creation of multiple sites within the same WordPress installation, while sharing the available resources. Developers moving to WordPress from pure PHP development may be unfamiliar with this concept. The whole database structure changes in multisite in a way that we can't anticipate. So, it's important to get an idea of how multisite database works in case you are planning to develop multisite compatible plugins and themes. The following is a simple illustration of the changes in multisite compared to single site installations:

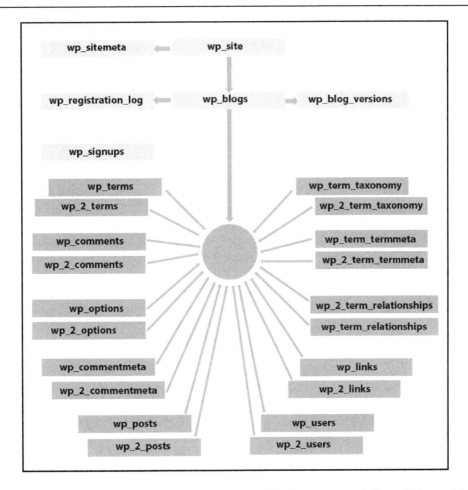

As you can see, six new tables have been added to the database and the existing tables have increased. This image only illustrates how tables are connected in multisite environment. However, this not a precise relationship diagram between the tables. Let's identify the role of six new tables in the preceding diagram:

- `wp_site`: It is the main database table where all your network details are stored. WordPress allows you to create multiple networks in same installation. However, we rarely see real applications with more than one network in the same installation. This means this table will only have one record to store the network details, such as network domain and path.

- `wp_sitemeta`: It stores the options and settings for networks and works similar to the `wp_options` table.

- `wp_blogs`: It is the primary storage location for sites in network. Since you are running a multisite network, this table will contain two more records for site details including domain, path, created dates, and site-specific statuses.
- `wp_blog_versions`: It stores current database version of the sites available in network. WordPress will require certain database versions for its version upgrades. In such cases, this table will be used to track the database version.
- `wp_registration_log`: It stores the admin user details of each site in the network.
- `wp_signups`: It stores the new users added through the registration process of WordPress with the metadata for the respective site. These are also stored in the `wp_users` table of the respective site.

We had a brief introduction to the multisite-specific tables. Let's see how other tables are connected in a multisite environment. Developers who are used to working with conventional database concepts such as normalization may find it tough to understand and get used the WordPress way of handling multisite. Usually, we design database tables with relationships between the necessary tables in way that everything is connected. However, in this scenario, we see some tables not connected with any other tables, while some tables are connected with other tables without table relationships. So, it's important to understand how these tables work within multisites.

The purpose of a multisite network is to share WordPress installation, themes, and plugins. However, we still need different database tables to handle data for each site in the network. WordPress creates multiple versions of the same database table in a multisite network. So, default tables are assigned to the first site of the multisite. The newly created sites in the network will have the same set of tables created with the prefix of `wp_2`, `wp_3`, and so on. The illustration shows that these core tables are connected with the `wp_blogs` table. However, there are no relationships between `wp_blogs` and other tables. Instead, when a site is loaded, WordPress identifies the loaded blog ID and then uses the tables with the prefix of the blog ID. Each site in the network shares WordPress installation, plugins, and themes while using separate database tables with the prefix of blog ID.

In development, a multisite structure may not become a major issue unless you don't follow the recommended ways of accessing the database. However, understanding where the data is stored for each site is important to test and resolve conflicts.

Creating and managing custom tables

A default WordPress database can be extended by any number of custom tables to suit our project's requirements. The only thing we have to consider is the creation of custom tables over existing ones. There are two major reasons for creating custom tables:

- **Difficulty of matching data to existing tables**: Existing database tables are flexible enough to handle many common requirements. However, we need to be wise enough to choose custom tables in certain scenarios. Assume we have a requirement where we need to store user's previous job history. If we consider existing tables, we can only match this requirement to `wp_usermeta` table as key-value pairs. However, it's extremely difficult to implement proper search for these data by using the same metakey with multiple values. In such requirements, we need a custom table to create predefined columns and make user job searching a simpler process.

- **Increased data volume**: The posts table plays a major role in WordPress sites. When it comes to large-scale websites or applications with a sizeable amount of data, it's not recommended to keep all the data in a posts table. Let's assume that we are building a product catalog that creates millions of orders. Storing order details in the posts table as a custom post type is not the ideal implementation. In such circumstances, the posts table will go out of control due to the large dataset. The same theory applies to the existing meta tables as well. In these cases, it's wise to separate different datasets into their own tables to improve performance and keep things manageable.

Now, we can look at the process of working with custom database tables.

Creating custom tables

In pure PHP development, we create the database tables manually before moving onto the implementation phase. With the WordPress plugin-based architecture, it's certain that we might need to create custom tables using plugins in the later stages of the projects. Creating custom tables through plugins involves certain predefined procedures recommended by WordPress. Since table creation is a one-time task, we should implement the process on plugin activation or installation. Let's take a look at the code for creating custom database tables:

```
function create_custom_tables() {
  global $wpdb;
  require_once( ABSPATH . 'wp-admin/includes/upgrade.php' );
  $custom_table = $wpdb->prefix.'user_job_history';
```

```
if($wpdb->get_var("show tables like '$custom_table'") != $custom_table) {
    $sql = "CREATE TABLE $custom_table (
            id mediumint(9) NOT NULL AUTO_INCREMENT,
            time datetime DEFAULT '0000-00-00 00:00:00' NOT NULL,
            user_id mediumint(9) NOT NULL,
            job_title mediumint(9) NOT NULL,
            job_description longtext NOT NULL,
            job_period var varchar(255) NOT NULL,
            UNIQUE KEY id (id
               );";
    dbDelta( $sql );
}
}
```

Firstly, we have to include the `upgrade.php` file to make use of the `dbDelta` function. The next most important thing is to use the prefix for database tables. By default, WordPress creates a prefix called `wp_` for all the tables. We should change the prefix in the installation process covered in Chapter 1, *Introduction to WordPress Development*. It's important to use the existing prefix to maintain consistency and avoid issues in multisite scenarios. Next, we have to check the existence of a database table using the **show tables** query. Finally, you can define your table creation query and use the `dBDelta` function to implement it on the database.

 Check out the guidelines for creating a table creation query at `http://codex.wordpress.org/Creating_Tables_with_Plugins`, as the `dbDelta` function can be tricky in certain scenarios.

We should only use plugin installation/uninstallation to create and delete custom tables to avoid unnecessary queries. Since we have not started plugin development yet, you need to wait for later sections of the book to understand how and where to use this code.

We looked at the necessity of custom tables in WordPress sites. Even though custom tables offer you more flexibility within WordPress, there will be a considerable number of limitations, as listed here:

- WordPress default backups will not include custom tables.
- There are no built-in functions for the accessing database. All the queries, filtering, and validation needs to be done from scratch using the existing `$wpdb` variable.
- User interfaces for displaying these tables' data need to be created from scratch.

Therefore, you should avoid creating custom tables in all possible circumstances, unless they would be advantageous in the context of your application.

Executing basic CRUD operations on existing tables

WordPress provides well-optimized built-in methods for accessing the existing database tables. Therefore, we don't need to write our own queries. Let's see how basic **Create, Read, Update, Delete (CRUD)** operations are executed on existing tables.

Inserting records

All the existing tables contain a pre-built insert functions for creating new records. Some of these functions uses a predefined set of parameters while other functions accepts array of information for inserting the record. Let's take a look at some of the frequently used insert functions:

wp_insert_post	Creates a new post or page in the wp_posts table. If this is used on an existing post, it will update the existing record. Accepts an array type parameter with all post details.
add_option	Creates a new option in the wp_options table, if it doesn't already exist. Accepts key and value as parameters.
wp_insert_user	Creates a new user in the wp_users table. Accepts an array type parameter with all post details.

Updating records

All the existing tables contain a pre-built update method for updating existing records. The following list illustrates a few of the built-in update functions:

update_post_meta	This creates or updates additional details about posts in the wp_postmeta table. Accepts post ID, key, and value as parameters.
wp_update_term	This updates existing terms in the wp_terms table. Accepts term ID and taxonomy as parameters.
update_user_meta	This updates user meta details in the wp_usermeta table based on the user ID. Accepts user ID, key, and value as parameters.

Deleting records

We have similar methods for deleting records in each of the existing tables as we have for updating records. The following list illustrates a few of the built-in delete functions:

`delete_post_meta`	This deletes custom fields using the specified key in the `wp_postmeta` table. Accepts post ID, key, and value as parameters.
`wp_delete_post`	This removes existing posts, pages, or attachments from the `wp_posts` table. Accepts post ID as parameter.
`delete_user_meta`	This removes the metadata matching criteria from a user from the `wp_usermeta` table. Accepts user ID, key, and value as parameters.

Selecting records

As usual, there is a set of built-in functions for selecting records from the existing tables. The following list contains a few of the data-selecting functions:

`get_posts`	This retrieves the posts as an array from the `wp_posts` table based on the passed arguments. Also, we can use the `WP_Query` class with the necessary arguments to get the post list from the OOP method. Accepts an array type parameter with all post details.
`get_option`	This retrieves the option value of the given key from the `wp_options` table. Accepts a key parameter.
`get_users`	This retrieves a list of users as an array from the `wp_user` table. Accepts an array type parameter with all post details.

Most of the database operations on exiting tables can be executed using these built-in functions, and you rarely find scenarios for creating your own queries.

Executing basic CRUD operations on custom tables

WordPress provides a built-in class called wpdb for handling database queries. This class is located inside the wp-includes directory. The wpdb class will be available inside your plugins and themes as a global variable and provides access to all the tables inside the WordPress database, including custom tables. Using this class for queries adds an extra layer of security as well as optimizes the database queries.

 Using the wpdb class for CRUD operations is straightforward with its built-in methods. A complete guide for using the wpdb class can be found at http://codex.wordpress.org/Class_Reference/wpdb.

Basically, there are no built-in methods for accessing custom tables using direct functions, so it's a must to use the wpdb class for handling custom tables.

Inserting records

The wpdb class provides a built-in insert function to insert records to custom database tables. So, we need to use it for better performance, instead of writing INSERT queries from scratch. Let's take look at the syntax of insert function:

```
$wpdb->insert(
  'table',
  array( 'column1' => 'value1', 'column2' => 'value2' ),
  array( '%s', '%d' )
);
```

The first parameter takes the table name. You need to specify the custom table name with the WordPress database prefix. The next parameter uses an array of column names and respective values. The final parameter defines the correct format for the fields defined in the previous array. We can get number of affected rows on success and false as a return value on failure.

Updating and deleting records

These operations works similar to insert, by using the update and delete functions of the wpdb class. Let's take a look at the syntaxes:

```
$wpdb->update(
  'table',
  array( 'column1' => 'value1' ),
  array( 'ID' => 1 ),
  array( '%s' ),
  array( '%d' )
);
```

In this method, clause conditions as an array for the third parameter and format of the columns in where clause as fifth parameter. Other parameters are exactly the same as the insert function:

```
$wpdb->delete( 'table', array( 'ID' => 1 ), array( '%d' ) );
```

In this method, we only have to pass the delete conditions as an array and respective formats of the columns. The preceding query will delete the record with an ID equal to 1.

Selecting records

We can pass the query to various wpdb class functions such as get_results, query, and get_var, and get the result dataset. The following section illustrates the use of these functions:

`$wpdb->get_results( 'select query' )`	This can be used to select a set of records from any database table.
`$wpdb->query('query')`	This can be used to execute any custom query. This is typically used to update and delete statements instead of select statements, as it only provides the affected rows count as the result.
`$wpdb->get_row('query')`	This can be used to retrieve a single row from the database as an object, an associative array, or as a numerically indexed array.

In this section, we had a brief overview of the techniques used for querying the database as well as built-in functions that simplify the database operations. In the upcoming chapters, we will be working with these functions as well as advanced query techniques while developing themes and plugins.

Summary

The goal of this chapter was to understand the role of default database tables and how we can adapt them to our requirements. We started by analyzing the database relationship diagram and identifying connections between tables. We also looked at the role of each database table with commonly used data.

We identified the need for knowing proper database usage of core features, and explored various ways of tracking database usage for each feature. Then, we had a brief overview of database structure in multisites and how it varies from that of a single site database. Finally, we looked at various functions for querying both default tables and custom tables.

In Chapter 3, *Designing Flexible Frontends with Theme Development*, we will be starting the development process by working with child themes, theme templates, and dynamic theme components.

3
Designing Flexible Frontends with Theme Development

The design of a website plays a vital role in attracting visitors. WordPress themes are used as a standard technique for designing the frontend of a site. The availability of thousands of existing themes makes the design process simple as well as flexible. This means that developers have the ability to build custom designs in a rapid process. Building advanced designs via the modification of existing theme files is a common problem in development, and is often realized in the late stages of site development. Developers should have the ability to turn default WordPress themes into amazing frontends and also build custom themes, while being compatible with the WordPress core and theme upgrades.

In this chapter, you will gain knowledge of what should be in a theme and how you should use the theme files hierarchy to build flexible designs using custom templates. You will also learn to extend themes by using child themes, actions, filters, and page templates. From there, you will learn the process of understanding and modifying the templates of various themes in existing sites. Understanding how different theme components fit into your design and modifying these components in existing sites without breaking the theme is the highlight of this chapter.

In this chapter, we will cover the following topics:

- Understanding the role of themes in development
- Tracking and understanding theme components in existing sites
- Using child themes to extend existing themes
- An in-depth overview of the theme template hierarchy
- Extending theme features using actions and filters
- Techniques for conditionally changing theme design

By the end of this chapter, you will have the ability to understand the role of themes and knowledge to build highly customizable theme templates to design modern websites.

Technical requirements

You will be required to have WordPress 4.9.8 installed to follow this procedure. Even if you have a later version of WordPress, the described examples should work with no significant problems.

The code files of this chapter can be found on GitHub:
`https://github.com/PacktPublishing/WordPress-Development-Quick-Start-Guide/tree/master/Chapter03`

Check out the following video to see the code in action:
`http://bit.ly/2EPpNIR`

Introduction to WordPress themes

A WordPress theme is a set of files, created using a predefined structure and features, to act as the presentation layer of the website. In simple terms, the presentation layer should contain the HTML needed to generate the layout and all the data passed by the models. WordPress is built to create content management systems, and hence it doesn't focus on separating the presentation layer from its business logic.

Themes contain template files as a mix of both HTML code and PHP logic. As a developer, you need to have knowledge of both designing layouts and applying logic to work with themes.

The themes in your WordPress site are located in the `wp-content/themes` directory, with each theme using its own folder. A theme is identified by the predefined set of comments used in the `style.css` file. If this file is not available or the comment is broken, WordPress will not list it as a theme, even though the theme files have been placed in the `wp-content/themes` directory.

Installing and configuring themes

The process of installing a WordPress theme is super simple, even for a person who has no prior experience with CMS. WordPress includes a few basic themes upon initial installation and activates the latest theme on your site. The Twenty Seventeen theme is the one activated by default in the latest version of WordPress.

Let's go through the process of installing a theme:

1. First, you have to log in as administrator and go to the **Appearance | Themes** section. You will see a list of available themes, with the first one being the active theme. You can change the theme by clicking the **Activate** button of other available themes in the list.

2. Once the new theme has been activated, the previous one will be automatically deactivated. Usually, we will not be using the existing themes unless your site needs basic features. Therefore, we need a way to install new themes.

3. We can install themes by using the **Add New** button in the **Appearance | Themes** section. You will get a list of free themes from the WordPress theme directory, as shown in the following screenshot:

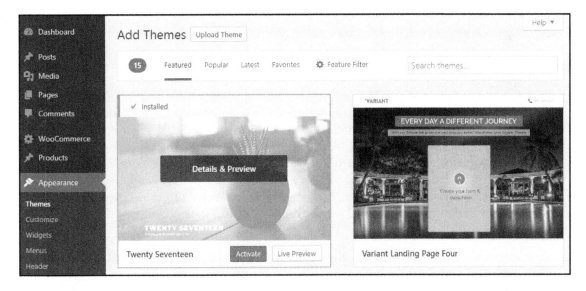

4. You have two options: installing a theme from the free theme directory or uploading a theme that's not available in the directory. The first option only requires you to click the **Activation** button of the theme in the list. The other option requires you to click on the **Upload Theme** button and upload a .zip file with a valid WordPress theme. After installation, you can activate the theme from a separate screen.

The files for the new theme will be located in the `wp-content/themes` directory, with a new directory by the theme name. Once a new theme has been installed, you will see changes in the Customize, Widgets, and Menus sections of the **Appearance** menu. The theme-specific settings and components will be added to these menu items.

We will be using the default Twenty Seventeen theme throughout this chapter. Since it's a free, built-in theme, you won't find a separate options panel. In advanced premium themes, you will find an options panel in a separate menu item, where you can configure the theme's features and layouts.

This kind of basic installation is good enough that you can now dive into the development aspects of a theme. We will start by understanding how we can use a theme in development.

Understanding the role of themes in development

The ability to choose an existing theme among thousands of free and premium themes is one of the reasons for the success of WordPress as a CMS. Using an existing theme dramatically reduces both development time and cost, as opposed to designing the site from scratch.

The primary intention of a theme is to function as the presentation layer of the site. However, WordPress has evolved into a state where a basic theme, designed to act only as a presentation layer, no longer works. As a result, developers are including more and more advanced functionalities and logic within their themes to compete with other themes. In modern sites, the developer's role may involve customizing theme design, building themes from scratch, and even creating application-specific themes. Therefore, we need to be aware of the type of development involved in a theme. Let's take a look at some of the most common tasks as a developer:

- **Customizing post and page designs**: This is the most common task developers face in the beginning of their developer role. There are millions of websites that have been created with WordPress, and a high percentage of them are created by non-technical site owners who are using existing themes and plugins. So, when there is a need for a change in theme, owners have no option other than to look for a third-party developer. In such scenarios, you will be asked to modify the existing theme designs to match a client's requirements. Therefore, developers need to be familiar with various types of modern themes and design techniques.
- **Creating page templates**: This is the next step for a developer, where clients ask you to create different types of landing pages to promote their products, services, and other businesses.

- **Integrate UI components**: Modern websites are filled with interactive components such as sliders, galleries, accordions, graphs, and so on. Most of these are generated from open source libraries. Many premium themes have built-in support for these types of components. But in scenarios where your site is using a basic theme, you may be asked to integrate these components to make them attractive and deliver lots of information in a limited space. Therefore, you need to be aware of the techniques for integrating these libraries into themes.
- **Converting designs into a theme**: This will require you to build a theme from scratch. In the old days, we got a PSD from the designer, and the developer's role was to turn it into HTML. With WordPress, you need to go the extra step and convert the HTML into a WordPress theme. It's a very difficult process unless you understand the WordPress template hierarchy, theme functions, and the necessary WordPress conventions.

The preceding list goes over some of the tasks involved in working with themes in sites intended to function as a basic CMS. However, modern WordPress sites go beyond the norm by creating full-fledged web applications. In such applications, we can see the use of application themes.

What are application-specific themes?

General-purpose WordPress themes mostly use a standard set of theme files, with the primary intention of providing awesome blog posts and page features. On the other hand, application-specific themes use a lot more application-specific files, which are intended to build application-specific features. These files include application-specific features, business logic, and templates. The advantage of such themes is the ability to use them right away in a site, as opposed to developing these features on top of a generic theme. However, the limitation of application themes is the inability to switch themes, as most features are bound to the theme. Let's take a look at some of the common application theme types to understand the concept of application themes:

- **Buddypress**: This is a plugin that allows you to add social networking features to WordPress. Nowadays, BuddyPress-specific themes are built to extend basic social networking capabilities. The functionality of a BuddyPress theme includes user management, user group management, user activities, user messaging, and so on. You can check out the amazing features of BuddyPress specific-themes at `https://themeforest.net/category/wordpress/buddypress`.

- **Real estate**: These types of themes are built for creating property listings and selling. Apart from the basic posts and page templates, such themes contain various advanced templates and features for property maps, agent management, property comparison, and searching. You can check out the features of real estate-specific themes at `https://themeforest.net/category/wordpress/real-estate`.

- **LMS**: These types of themes are built for learning management systems where there are teachers, students, and courses. Apart from basic theme features, these themes include templates and features for managing courses, instructors, students, exams, and grades, with advanced searching features for all of the preceding data. You can check out the features of LMS-specific themes at `https://themeforest.net/category/wordpress/education?term=lms`.

After looking at the use of application-specific themes, you will understand that such themes contain the functionality of an entire plugin or maybe an entire application. This might not be the ideal implementation according to development best practices. However, we have to get used to building or using such themes in order to provide cost-effective solutions.

As you may have noticed, your role as a developer has a very wide scope in regard to themes. More often than not, you will have to take responsibility for the design part, along with the functionalities of the theme. It's important to understand how theme components work together to build the design and functionality of the site.

Understanding built-in theme components

The design of any WordPress frontend screen consists of many components on top of the template files. These components act as the location placeholders for the site data. By understanding these components, you can let administrators change the content and locations dynamically based on various needs.

Getting started with developing themes

We discussed the development tasks involved in themes in the preceding section. Building a theme from scratch is a process with a very wide scope and hence not feasible to discuss in this type of book. Therefore, we will focus on customizing existing themes while providing the necessary knowledge to build themes from scratch. There are two ways of adding or modifying features in an existing theme:

- Building and customizing features of a design by modifying template files
- Extending theme features through available filters and actions

Both of these techniques require us to modify the files of an existing theme. In most sites, we will be using existing, free, or premium themes that have developed by third-party developers. So, it's obvious that we will receive updated versions of the theme with more features, bug fixes, and improved code. The theme update process wipes out all of the changes that have been made to core theme files. This means that we need a way to customize a theme without losing the changes on theme updates. This is where the concept of a child theme is used.

What is a child theme?

A child theme is a sub-version of a theme, inheriting its features, design, and styles. We call the main theme the parent theme. Based on its name and purpose, you may think that a child theme is part of a parent theme. However, a child theme has its own directory inside the `wp-content/themes` directory, and relates to the parent theme through a few lines of comments. The child theme doesn't get updated with the parent theme and hence we can use it for custom development.

Creating a child theme

Developers who are new to WordPress may assume that this is a considerable process involving many steps and configurations. However, it's a straightforward process that takes less than a minute. Let's create a child theme called `WPQuickStart` for the existing **Twenty Seventeen** theme.

The first step is creating a directory in the `wp-content/themes` directory and naming it `wpquickstart`. Next, we need to create a `style.css` file inside the `wpquickstart` directory and add the following comment:

```
/*
Theme Name: WPQuickStart
Theme URI:
Description: Twenty Seventeen Child Theme
Author: Rakhitha Nimesh
Author URI: http://example.com
Template: twentyseventeen
Version: 1.0.0 */
```

The highlighted line in the code defines the directory as a child theme and defines the parent theme. You should use the directory name of the parent theme for the **Template** setting. The final step of this process is to create a `functions.php` file in the `wpquickstart` directory and add the following code to load the parent theme styles:

```
add_action( 'wp_enqueue_scripts', 'wpquickstart_enqueue_styles' );
function wpquickstart_enqueue_styles() {
    wp_enqueue_style( 'twenty-seventeen-style',
get_template_directory_uri() . '/style.css' );
    wp_enqueue_style( 'wpquickstart-style',
get_stylesheet_directory_uri() . '/style.css',
        array('twenty-seventeen-style')    );
}
```

The preceding code includes the `style.css` file of both the parent and child themes. We have added a dependency to the child theme style file by passing `twenty-seventeen-style` to the dependency array. As the child theme's `style.css` file is dependent on the parent theme, it will load after the `style.css` of the **Twenty Seventeen** theme. Therefore, we override the necessary parent theme styles using the `WPQuickStart style.css` file.

In just three steps, our child theme is ready to function with all of the features of the parent theme. The other files follow the opposite process, with the exception of the `functions.php` file. If a template file is available in the child theme, it will be loaded instead of the parent file template. On the other hand, missing template files in the child theme will be loaded from the parent theme.

Modifying parent themes with a child theme

Now, the most important thing to know is how a child theme can be used to implement the two techniques discussed in the preceding section. Let's start by using template files.

Building and customizing designs by modifying template files

We created a child theme to customize the designs of parent themes without losing the changes on theme updates. This can be achieved by either modifying the entire template of the parent theme or part of the template in the parent theme. Let's learn this by using an example template design change. Consider the following screenshot for our requirements:

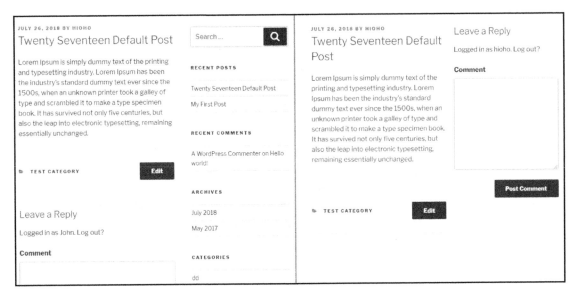

The screen on the left displays the default single post design of the **Twenty Seventeen** theme. Let's assume that we want to change the post template to remove the sidebar and display the comment form in a way that the user can add comments while reading the post. So, we have to change the left screen to match the screen on the right.

In order to achieve our requirement, we have to override the parent file template. So, we need to copy the `single.php` file of the Twenty Seventeen theme to the root folder of the WPQuickStart child theme. We don't need the sidebar for the new design and hence the following line needs to be removed from the `single.php` file we created in our child theme:

```
<?php get_sidebar(); ?>
```

Instead, we need to add the comment form to the same location. The comment template is already loaded inside `single.php` using the following code, after the post content:

```
if ( comments_open() || get_comments_number() ) :
  comments_template();
endif;
```

We need to remove this code from the existing location of the `single.php` file and add it to the location where we had the sidebar. Consider the following code, where we have placed the `comments` code within a container element called `wpquickstart-comments`:

```
<div id="wpquickstart-comments" >
  <?php if ( comments_open() || get_comments_number() ) :
        comments_template();
      endif; ?>
</div>
```

Finally, we need to change the CSS class of the element with the `primary` ID from `content-area` to `wpquickstart-content-area`. Now, we can apply the CSS to reduce the size of the post content elements and get the comments to the right of the post content. Add the following CSS to the `style.css` file of the child theme:

```
.wpquickstart-content-area{
    width:50% !important; float:left;
}
#wpquickstart-comments{
    width: 45%;     float: left;     padding: 0 3%;
}
#wpquickstart-comments #comments{
    padding-top: 0 !important;
}
```

Now, you can refresh the browser to check the new design with the comment form on the right side. This is a very basic example of how we can change the designs of parent themes for our needs. By using a few lines of styles and moving the existing elements, we were able to create a new design in minutes. In real site development, you can turn simple designs into advanced, feature-rich designs by using the same process.

Extending theme features through available filters and actions

We already discussed the importance of using child themes to customize and extend theme templates. Using the WordPress filter and action hooks is another way of customizing theme features. We will mainly use these hooks to extend the functions provided by the theme. However, we can use some of the filter and action hooks to change parts of templates without needing to replace them completely.

 In WordPress, an action is a PHP function that is executed at specific points in a process. A filter is a function that is used to modify the existing data or features in a process. Even though actions are intended to do something before or after an event, they are used frequently to add content to templates. More about actions and filters will be covered in upcoming chapters.

Once we choose a theme, we can explore the actions and filters within the theme to understand its extendable features and locations. The simplest way to identify these actions and filters is to use the directory or project search feature in your code editor. Most quality code editors provide this feature by default. You should use the term `apply_filters` to search for filters in the theme, and `do_action` to find out the actions defined in it. You may find a small number of these hooks in free themes and hundreds in premium themes. These hooks consist of built-in WordPress hooks as well as theme-specific hooks. As a developer, you need to have a thorough knowledge of the common built-in WordPress hooks in themes. Let's take a look at some of the common filters and actions used in themes:

- `the_content`: This is the most commonly used filter in themes, intended to modify the post content. We can either modify the entire post content or add dynamic content before or after a post. Usually, this is used to display additional data for posts such as related posts, advertisements, and social sharing buttons. Consider the following code for adding custom content after each post. This code should be placed in the `functions.php` file of the child theme:

```
add_filter( 'the_content', 'wpquickstart_add_custom_text_single_posts' );
function wpquickstart_add_custom_text_single_posts( $content ) {
    if ( is_single() && in_the_loop() && is_main_query() ) {
        return $content . "Custom Text After Post";
    }
    return $content;
}
```

- The post content is passed as a parameter to this function. Here, we use the is_single template tag to make sure that the custom content is only applied to individual posts, and not to archives. The other two conditions restrict this text from applying to posts outside the main query and loop. This is a very basic illustration of the functionality of the the_content filter. You can add more content and different conditions to handle various requirements.

- the_permalink: This filters the display of the permalink for the current post. You can use code similar to the preceding example for modifying a post link.

- the_title: This filters the title of the post. Used for modifying a post title based on certain conditions.

- comment_form_default_fields: This filters the fields of a comment form. By default, the comment form contains fields for comment, name, email, and website. The fields are passed as an array type parameter to this filter. You can use this filter to add new fields or remove existing fields from the comment form. The following code removes the website field from the comment form using this filter:

```
function wpquickstart_remove_website_field($fields) {
    unset($fields['url']);
    return $fields;
}
add_filter('comment_form_default_fields',
'wpquickstart_remove_website_field');
```

- wp_nav_menu_item_custom_fields: The name suggests that this as a filter, but it's actually an action executed in WordPress. The process of adding custom fields to menu items is one of the common tasks for features such as menu item-specific CSS and menu item restrictions. In such cases, we can use this action to add custom fields, as shown in the following code:

```
add_action( 'wp_nav_menu_item_custom_fields',
'wpquickstart_menu_button_fields', 10, 4 );
function wpquickstart_menu_button_fields( $item_id, $item, $depth, $args )
{      ?>
  <div class="fusion-menu-options-container">
  <div class="option-details">
    <h3><?php _e( 'Menu Class', 'wpquickstart' ); ?></h3>
    <p class="description"><?php _e( 'Add custom css class.',
'wpquickstart' ); ?></p>
  </div>
  <div class="">
    <input type="text" id="wpquick-menu-class" name="wpquick-menu-class"
value="" />
  </div>
```

```
        </div>
<?php } ?>
```

- The preceding code will add a new text field named `Menu Class` to menu items in the backend menu.

These are some of the frequently used ones, among hundreds of possible WordPress actions and filters. You should explore these hooks by using various WordPress themes in order to identify the necessary ones for your implementations.

The filters and actions discussed in the preceding section are used for common WordPress purposes and hence can be used in any theme. Theme-specific actions and filters, on the other hand, are designed for advanced theme features. Most of these actions and filters cannot be used in other themes. We can easily identify theme-specific hooks by looking at the prefix used for hook names. The **Twenty Seventeen** theme uses `twentyseventeen_` as the prefix for theme-specific hooks. Let's consider one of the filters that's available in the Twenty Seventeen theme to understand the use of theme-specific hooks:

```
apply_filters( 'twentyseventeen_content_width', $content_width );
```

This filter is used to customize the width of the page based on page layout. Let's see how we can implement this filter to modify the width:

```
add_filter( 'twentyseventeen_content_width', 'wpquickstart_content_width'
);
function wpquickstart_content_width($content_width){
  if(is_page()) {
    $content_width = "800";
  }
  return $content_width;
}
```

In the preceding code, we changed the width of pages in the **Twenty Seventeen** theme by using the theme-specific filter. We can add more conditions to change the width and display different types of layouts.

Steps for extending theme-specific hooks

Now, you should have a brief understanding of built-in hooks in themes, as well as theme-specific hooks. Let's take a look at the basic steps for customizing themes using these hooks:

1. Execute a directory search on the theme and identify the hooks by tracking the `apply_filters` and `do_action` functions.

2. For the filters, check whether more than two parameters have been passed to the `apply_filters` function. The second parameter will be the variable you will be filtering, and additional parameters will be used to support the filtering process.

3. If the `apply_filters` function contains two parameters, you can implement it by using following code:

```
add_filter( 'filter_hook_name', 'filter_implementation_function_name'
);
    function filter_implementation_function_name ($param1){
        // Modify $param1 based on your preferences
        return $param1;
    }
```

4. If the `apply_filters` function contains more than two parameters, you can use following code:

```
add_filter( 'filter_hook_name',
'filter_implementation_function_name',10,3 );
    function filter_implementation_function_name ($param1,$param2,$param3){
        // Modify $param1 based on your preferences and help of $param2
and $param3
        return $param1;
    }
```

5. In the preceding code, 10 will be the priority. The number 3 will be the number of parameters used in the `apply_filters` function, after the hook name.

6. For actions, check whether more than one parameter has been passed to the `do_action` function. These parameters will be used to support the execution of our custom action code.

7. Use the following code to implement the actions:

```
add_action( 'filter_hook_name',
'action_implementation_function_name',10,2 );
    function action_implementation_function_name ($param1,$param2){
        // execute some code related to action - Ex: send emails, save
data to database
        echo 'Custom Content' ; // you can add content to location where
action hook is executed
    }
```

8. You should change 2 based on the number of parameters. If the hook contains only one parameter, you can omit both 10 and 2.

In this section, we have looked at two techniques for modifying or extending theme features. You should check the requirements of the site and decide whether you can do certain customizations with existing hooks or whether you need a complete replacement of template files in child themes.

Working with the WordPress theme template hierarchy

A WordPress theme can be built with just three files: **style.css**, **index.php**, and **comments.php**. However, the complete template hierarchy can support quite a large number of sub-templates, flexible enough to cater for the advanced requirements of many sites. More often than not, developers will be working on less than ten files in this hierarchy. However, the knowledge of the complete template hierarchy may come handy in projects with advanced requirements. Let's take a look at the following diagram, which consists of the types of pages used in WordPress to handle the initial request:

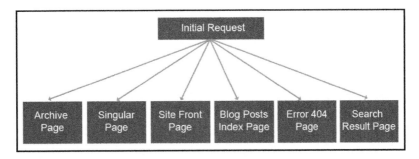

There are six paths to handle the user request based on the loaded content. **Archive Page** and **Singular Page** are the most complex yet flexible among these, and have a tall structure. Let's identify the main purpose of each of these pages before moving into the complete template hierarchy:

- **Archive Page**: This is usually used to display the posts list, category posts, tag posts, author posts, and custom post types, with a short summary about the post
- **Singular Page**: This is used to display individual posts, pages, or custom post types
- **Site Front Page**: This is used to display the home page of your site
- **Blog Posts Index Page**: This is used to display the list of posts on your site
- **Error 404 Page**: This is used when WordPress can't find a matching template for the request
- **Search Result Page**: This displays the search results that contain a list of posts and pages

You can find more details about template hierarchy at `https://developer.wordpress.org/themes/basics/template-hierarchy/`. Now, we need to go through the complete hierarchy for each of these page types to get the knowledge to handle advanced application requirements. Let's start with the **Archive Page**.

Archive Page hierarchy

This path is divided into six sub-types, and WordPress will use one of these sub-types for any given request with a collection of post data. Let's consider the following diagram for the Archive Page's hierarchy:

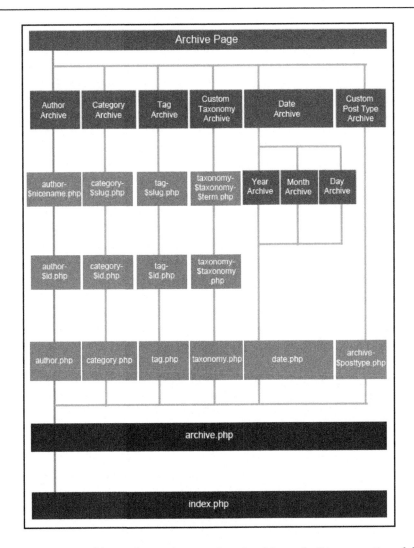

We use the `archive.php` file as the main template in this path. It's an optional file for a theme, with the `index.php` file handling the archives when this template is missing in a theme. However, almost all of these themes will include the `archive.php` file for handling the collection of data. Let's take a look at the various types of Archive Pages, starting with Author Archive.

Author archive pages

In WordPress, posts are created by an administrator or users with post creation capabilities. In most themes, you will see a linked author name alongside the post title. Once you click on the link, you will be redirected to a page with all the posts that have been created by the specified user. This is the Author Archive page, and it's usually handled by the `archive.php` file. Let's take a look at the author archive page of the Twenty Seventeen theme.

Basically, we have the display name of the author and the description. This might be good enough for basic WordPress sites with blogs and one or two authors. In situations where you have a large number of writers with the primary site feature being publishing articles, this might look modest. Instead, such sites requires you to have a well-designed profile, including a profile image, website details, and social account details. The following screenshot is a preview of a modified author template from a popular theme:

As you can see, this site uses a complete user profile as well as a modified post list with two columns. We can't build such a design using `archive.php` without complicating the template with lots of conditions. Instead, we can leverage the additional templates in the author archive path, as shown in the preceding diagram. There are three templates in the author archive path, as follows:

- `author.php`: This is the main template for customizing the author archive. Many themes, including premium themes, use `archive.php` to generate the author archive, instead of a separate template. Therefore, we can add our own `author.php` file to the child theme and design a separate author archive. This template is executed before `archive.php` and `index.php`.

- `author-$id.php`: This is one of two dynamic templates that's executed before the `author.php` template. The ID of the user is used as part of the template name and hence this template will only be loaded for a single user. Since this is a dynamic template, you won't find it in any of the themes. This is something a developer should create to cater for the specific requirements of a site. Creating a theme template for each author is not practical, unless you have a limited and fixed number of authors. Therefore, you will rarely find requirements to use this kind of template in development.

- `author-$nicename.php`: This is similar to `author-$id.php` and is executed before the preceding template. This template uses a WordPress nicename instead of ID.

In scenarios where you need a custom author archive page, you should copy the content of the `archive.php` page into the `author.php` file and change the design as needed. More about author templates and the implementation of author data is available at `https://codex.wordpress.org/Author_Templates`.

Categories, tags, and custom taxonomy archives

Taxonomy is a term used by WordPress to group things into different sections. If you have already worked with WordPress posts, you should be familiar with **Categories** and **Post Tags** in the post creation screen. These are two built-in taxonomies that are assigned to normal posts by default. On the other hand, custom taxonomies are the grouping types we create for certain post types based on the requirements in different sites. We can assign one or more taxonomy values to posts or custom post type items. Once posts are assigned, we get an archive page with a list of posts for the specific taxonomy.

Categories, tags, and custom taxonomies work in the exact same way, with similar template hierarchies. The `archive.php` file is used to load these three types by default, by using taxonomy title and description. In the author archive, we needed a way to display complete author details with an attractive design. In this case, we don't need to focus on such details, as taxonomies rarely use additional details. Instead, we might need to change the design and display of posts in taxonomy archive pages. We can use the `category.php`, `tag.php`, and `taxonomy.php` templates in such scenarios, similar to the way we used `author.php`. These templates need to be added to child themes based on your requirements as most of the themes only use the `archive.php` file for all three types.

Similar to author archives, each of these three types also has two dynamic sub-templates that use a taxonomy ID or slug. However, we rarely use them as the template needs to be created dynamically based on the taxonomies we use in development.

Date Archive pages

This is another type of archive page where we can see a list of posts for year, month, or date. We are using the **Twenty Seventeen** theme and hence you will see a widget in the sidebar called **Archives** with a list of values, such as August 2018, July 2018, and so on. Once you click on one of these links, it will load the posts that were created in that month. The URL of the site may look similar to `http://www.example.com/2018/07`. We can check yearly archives by removing 07 from the URL and daily archives by adding the date after 07. One again, `archive.php` is used by default to handle all three of these archive pages.

Now, if you consider our archive page diagram, you will notice the use of the `date.php` file to separate the date archives from the `archive.php` file. This template works similar to the author and taxonomy templates that we have discussed so far. Even though it's not used frequently, we can add the `date.php` file to our child theme and display any additional information about each year, month, or date.

Custom Post Type Archive

The use of custom post types is common in modern WordPress sites. Unlike a normal blog post, custom post types can contain a considerable amount of data and design requirements. Therefore, it may not be feasible to use `archive.php` to load the list of custom posts in most scenarios.

Instead, we can observe the preceding diagram to identify the use of additional template files. Unlike the previous paths, we only have one dynamic template for custom post archives, called `archive-$post_type.php`. The post type variable should be replaced by post types in your sites such as product, topic, and forum. Even though this is a dynamic template type, we can create and add this template to child themes, since custom post types in a site are fixed in most scenarios. In this case, WordPress will only load archive.php when it can't find a template with `archive-$post_type.php`. Nowadays, many premium themes comes with built-in custom post type support and hence you will find such templates within the theme files. Let's take a look at the following screenshot for use as the archive page:

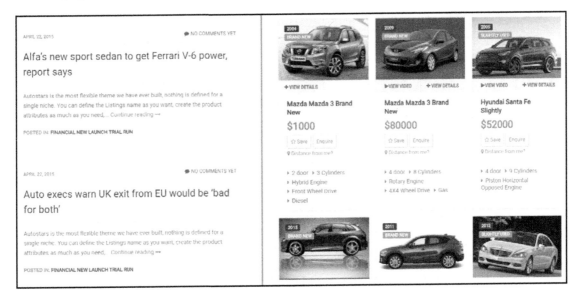

The screen on the left displays a normal blog post archive, which is displayed using the `archive.php` file. The screen on the right displays a custom post type, with a completely different design and various pieces of data, in a user-friendly manner. We need `archive-$post_type.php` to build such designs as it's not possible to generate both screens using the same `archive.php` file.

Singular Page Hierarchy

This path is divided into two sub-types for displaying the data for individual posts or pages. Let's consider the following diagram for the **Singular page** hierarchy:

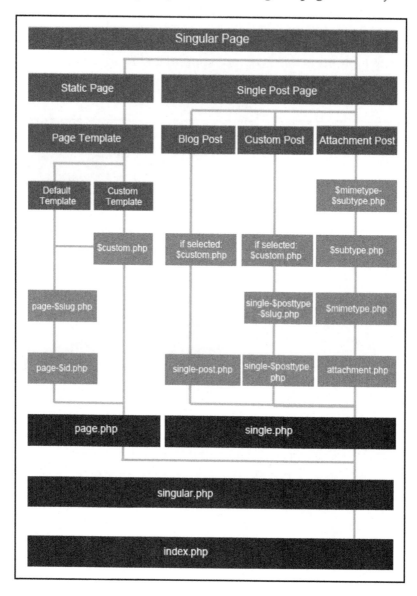

In the archives, we displayed a collection of posts with summarized details. In this path, we need to display the complete data for an individual post or page. We use the `single.php` file as the main template in this path. It's an optional file for a theme, with the `index.php` file handling the posts and pages when this template is missing in a theme. However, almost all of the themes will include the `single.php` file for individual post data. Let's take a look at the various types of Singular Pages, starting with the Static Page.

Static Page Hierarchy

In WordPress, pages are used to manage the structure of the website and contain timeless content. Usually, we call pages static, even though they're not as same as the pages of pure HTML websites we had in the old days. However, the content doesn't change often and hence is considered static compared to posts. In a basic site, you will find WordPress pages for contact, about, services, and so on. This path is divided into two types called **Custom Template** and **Default Template**. Let's start with **Default Template** so that we can understand the need for custom templates.

By default, WordPress pages are handled by either `page.php`, `singular.php`, or `index.php`. Most themes contain a separate `page.php` file for handling pages and hence `singular.php` and `index.php` may not be used.

We can build most of our page designs with the `page.php` file. However, there are two other optional templates preceding `page.php` in cases where you want to handle different pages with a different design:

- `page-$slug.php`: This uses the slug to identify the page and provide a separate design. This template can only be used to design one page.
- `page-$id.php`: This uses the page ID to provide a separate design for chosen pages. This template can only be used to design one page.

Many sites contain a limited number of pages, and the design of these pages is usually different from one another. So, it's possible to use different page templates by specifying the ID or slug. However, these two templates might not be used in modern sites as the same functionality can be achieved with custom page templates, which will be discussed in the next section. The default template works for most sites where the page design is simple and only intended to provide content to the user.

The custom page templates, on the other hand, are templates varying from the default design, and are used to change the look and feel of one or more pages in the site. This template is loaded before the page.php template. Unlike other templates in the hierarchy, there is no predefined naming pattern for page templates. Instead, we can name it whatever we like and specify it as a template using PHP comments in the template file.

Creating and using custom page templates

The process of creating a new page template is relatively simple. First, we need to create a file on the root folder of the theme. Let's name the template fullwidth.php. Next, we need to add the following comment to the top of the fullwidth.php file, as follows:

```
/* Template Name: WPQuickStart Full Width */
```

The preceding comment will register this as a page template, and WordPress will load it as an option in the page creation screen. In the **Twenty Seventeen** theme, page design contains two columns where the title is displayed on the left and the content is displayed on the right. The left column takes almost half of the page and hence is not ideal for some pages in websites. Therefore, our full width template will remove the left column and increase the width of the content section to 100%.

First, we have to copy the content from the page.php file and add it to our fullwidth.php template. Next, replace the following line with the content from the twentyseventeen/template-parts/post/content.php file:

```
get_template_part( 'template-parts/page/content', 'page' );
```

Next, we have to remove the complete header tag to omit the left column. Then, we need to increase the width of the <div> element containing the **entry-content** class to 100%. Finally, add the page title within the **entry-content** div element. Now, we have a full width page template ready.

Now, we can go to **Pages** | **Add New** from the admin section to create a new page. The available page templates of your theme will be listed, as shown in the following screenshot:

The Template setting allows us to assign a page template for any given page. Therefore, we can use such templates when multiple pages require the same design. In the default template section, we discussed the availability of the `page-$slug.php` and `page-$id.php` files. With this technique, we have to create templates for each and every page we need. We also have to manually modify the templates when we remove or change the existing pages. Custom page templates don't have these limitations and we can use one template to design multiple pages. We can also quickly change the template from the page creation section. So, we should prefer custom page templates over the dynamic page types that are available in the default path.

In their basic form, we use page templates to change the structure of pages. We already changed the structure of the page by introducing a full width template. The most basic types of templates include two columns, three columns, full width, sidebar on the right, and sidebar on the left templates. These are very basic types of templates compared to what we get in modern premium themes. These modern themes include templates such as portfolios with lists, grids and galleries, contact forms, home page templates with various sliders, and so on.

This is a just a list of template types, and you need to check out these template designs in order to understand the real power of page templates. You can find these types of templates in many premium themes. I recommend that you visit `https://themeforest.net/category/wordpress` and check out the page types provided by the modern themes. You will be amazed by the innovative use of page templates.

It's very important to know how to build a page template from scratch. Basically, you can add anything after the **Template Name** comment. As you are starting WordPress development, you can use the various functions from the `page.php` file in your template and build on top of them. Once you are experienced, you should create advanced templates from scratch without needing any code from existing templates.

Single Post Page hierarchy

In the preceding section, we discussed pages as static elements. On the other hand, posts are highly dynamic and provide time critical information. Usually, the post list page changes frequently, with the new posts being displayed at the top of the list. In this path, we are considering the display of the complete details for individual posts or custom post types.

By default, WordPress posts are handled by either `single.php`, `singular.php`, or `index.php`, depending on the availability of the preceding template files in the hierarchy. Most themes contain a separate `single.php` file for handling posts and hence `singular.php` and `index.php` may not be used. The `single.php` template is quite similar to `page.php`. However, posts have options such as categories, tags, featured images, and pagination for other posts. So, including these details changes `single.php` from `page.php`.

This path is divided into three types called **Attachment Post, Custom Post**, and **Blog Post**. Let's start with **Attachment Post**-specific templates.

Attachment Post hierarchy

In WordPress, files uploaded to the media library or assigned to posts are considered attachments. The diagram shows templates going up to seven levels for attachments. However, we rarely use these templates unless the primary feature of the site is managing attachments. Therefore, the `single.php` template will be responsible for handling attachments in most themes. We are not going to discuss the optional templates due to their lack of use.

You can go to **Media | Library** and click on one of the attachments. Then, you can click the **View Attachment Page** link to view the attachment using the `single.php` file. If your site requires that you change the default template, you should add the `attachment.php` file to the child theme and try out the custom designs.

Blog post hierarchy

The default post in WordPress is often known as a blog post, as it's intended to provide content for blogs. By default, the `single.php` file is responsible for handling the template for blog posts. In the archives section, we understood the difference between the normal post list and the custom post type list with regard to advanced features. Similarly, we need even more specific templates for custom post types, and hence using `single.php` for all three types may not possible. In such scenarios, we can make use of the `single-post.php` template, which was designed exactly for normal blog posts. The content of the `single-post.php` file will be similar to `single.php`, and we can add more elements and styles to change the design.

We can also find the optional `$custom.php` template in the blog post path. This is a variation of page templates, where we can specify templates for specific post types. This feature was introduced in WordPress version 4.7.

Creating and assigning page templates for posts

The process of creating post-specific templates is similar to the process we used earlier. We can just create a template file with the preferred name in the root folder of the theme and add the following comments to the top of the file:

```
/* Template Name: Featured Post
Template Post Type: post, product */
```

In this template, we have to add an additional comment called **Template Post Type**, with the list of supported post types. Based on our comment, this template will be available for both normal blog posts and the product custom post type. The process of assigning a template to a post is the same as the process we used for pages.

Custom post hierarchy

This is the path for custom post types that are used in the website, with `single.php` being the default template. Usually, custom post type designs differ considerably from the blog post designs, and hence the use of the dynamic `single-$post_type.php` template is almost guaranteed. We have to create a new template inside the root folder of the theme and name it with the slug post type. These templates are frequently used in premium themes and hence you can look for templates with the **single-** preference.

Apart from the main template, we also get the two preceding templates by using the slug of the post and using post templates, as we discussed in the previous section. The use of `single-$post_type-$slug.php` will not be essential as the same functionality can be achieved by using the `$custom.php` template with additional benefits. Let's take a look at the following screenshot so that we can understand the difference between a normal `single.php` template and a custom designed `single-$post_type.php` template:

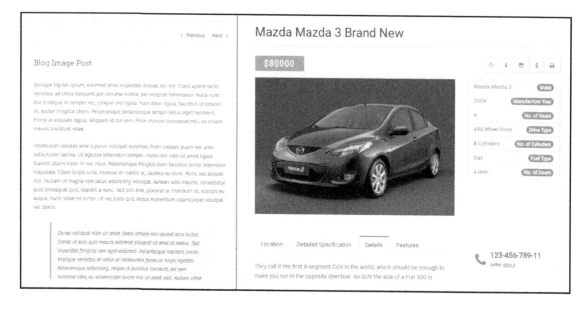

The screen on the left displays a normal blog post using the `single.php` design. The screen on the right contains advanced designs for the `Vehicle` custom post type with the use of the `single-vehicle.php` template. You can clearly see the difference in designs and the need for the `single-$post_type.php` template in custom post types. In WordPress site development, you will need the skills to build advanced templates for custom post types and hence it's very important to know these additional templates and their code.

Other Pages in the template hierarchy

So far, we have discussed the hierarchy of the two main starting template types of WordPress. There are four other page types with limited depth that play a lesser role than the archive and singular page types. Let's take a look at the following diagram to understand the hierarchy of these four types:

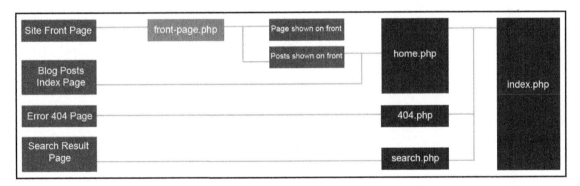

Site Front Page template path

In basic themes, the front page of the site is handled by `index.php`, where all of the blog posts are shown as a list. Unless your primary site functionality is blogging, it will require a separate template for the front page's design. According to the template hierarchy, `home.php` can be used to design the front page of the site. This template is available in most premium themes and contains very advanced designs. There is also an optional template in this path called `front-page.php`. However, it's not available in most themes and hence you may not have to use it in common development tasks.

Apart from using either the `home.php` or `front-page.php` templates, we can also use any default page as the homepage of our site. This is handled by a setting in the WordPress backend. We can use WordPress' **Settings** | **Reading** | Your homepage displays setting to change the front page, as shown in the following screenshot:

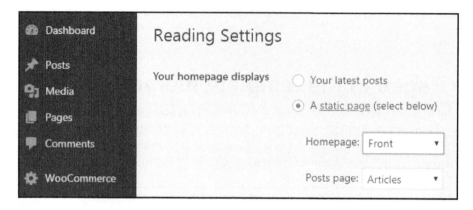

By default, this setting will use the **Your latest posts** option. It's a common technique to change this setting to **A static page** and use custom pages.

Blog Posts Index Page template path

This path defines the template used for the main blog page, where a list of normal posts is displayed. By default, this is handled by the `index.php` file and loads as the home page of the site. We have the ability to create any page and use it as the blog post index by using the setting explained in the preceding section. This template path is straightforward and generally doesn't change based on different scenarios.

Error 404 Page template path

This path is used when WordPress is unable to find a suitable template within the template hierarchy or within any template modification hooks. Most themes have a built-in 404 template containing a `content not found` message. It's essential to have this template in a theme in order to help the user with a meaningful message and provide links to other important content on your site.

Search Result Page template path

WordPress has a built-in search feature, and the search results usually contain posts and pages. These results are similar to the archive page, with searched text on the top. By default, this path is handled by the index.php file. However, there can be scenarios where the search results page needs to differ from the normal archive page. The need for highlighting search tem in content, are some of the instances where we need a separate design. In such scenarios, we can use the search.php file, which includes the same content as the index.php file, and modify it according to the client's custom requirements.

In this section, we had an extensive walkthrough of the complete WordPress theme template hierarchy. You might be exhausted by all of the theoretical aspects of templates. However, knowing about these templates in depth is crucial for building advanced site designs as well as customizing existing sites, where you will need to work with new themes all the time.

Conditionally changing template design and content

The main purpose of the theme is to provide consistent layouts for your site. We can only use one theme, as mixing different layouts from different themes creates contrasting designs, confusing the end user. Instead, we can conditionally change the designs within the theme without losing consistency.

Now, you may be wondering, what are consistent layouts? Basically, the elements in the design should be similar across all screens. Let's say we have a form in a page built with a UI component library. Then, it should be stated that forms on other parts of your site should use the same UI component library. If you use different UI elements in other parts of the site, users may feel confused. Similarly, every other element in the design needs to be consistent. However, this doesn't mean that we can't change the design in different parts of the site. More on this will be discussed in the following sections.

What is conditional template design?

In site development, we may have to change the design and content in different sections in order to do the following:

- **Match user preferences**: Many modern sites allow users to choose content preferences. Therefore, the user has various options, such as choosing which components are displayed on any given screen, filtering content from certain categories, and even the layout and color scheme.
- **Display only relevant content for a post/page**: Usually, we have a sidebar filled with many widgets. In some scenarios, this content may not be directly related to the main content. Let's assume that we have normal articles and another post type called books. In books, we may have a sidebar widget for displaying information such as ratings, ISBN, number of pages, and paper type. This is not relevant to normal articles and hence needs to be removed conditionally.
- **Highlight different sections in various content types**: Different content types require content-specific layouts. Let's assume we have normal articles and electronic products on our site. For normal articles, we display the title, image, and content. This style is not going to work for products as we need a way to attract customers. Therefore, we need to highlight product features by using image galleries, image sliders, or expandable tabs. All in all, we need to conditionally change the layout to highlight content based on the content type.

We already discussed the WordPress template hierarchy. The built-in template hierarchy provides many template types for conditional changes. It's important to know the possibilities for template and content changes without requiring major effort as a developer. We can apply conditional changes from basic styles to headers, footers, sidebars, menus, and even entire templates.

There are several ways to conditionally change the design based on the type of change. In this section, we are going to discuss two simple techniques.

Adding conditions to theme files

This is the simplest way to start as a developer. In this technique, we modify the existing theme files, add the conditions, and load different elements and content within those conditions. We already discussed the disadvantages of changing core theme files. Here, we need to implement this technique within the child theme. You can implement these techniques in the Twenty Seventeen child theme we created earlier in this chapter.

Let's understand this technique by creating conditional headers for our site. Usually, pages on a WordPress site are static and provide information about the site. About us, services, and contact are some of the common uses of such pages. On the other hand, posts or custom post type pages are highly dynamic and filled with various pieces of content such as promotions, advertisements, social sharing options, and so on. So, there are scenarios where we need different headers for posts and pages. Let's keep the header for pages as it is for now and modify the header for posts with advertisements on top. Consider the following screenshot for the default header section of the **Twenty Seventeen** theme:

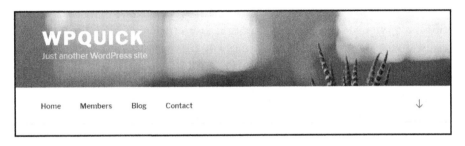

First, you need to copy the `header.php` file of **Twenty Seventeen** to the root directory of the child theme. Next, you can define the conditions to change the header section for posts. The following code adds an advertisement bar to the top of the header section for the normal post template:

```php
<?php if(is_single()) { ?>
   <div id="wpquick-article-ads" style="padding:20px;text-align:center;font-size:20px;background:red;color:#FFF;"> GET MEMBERSHIP WITH 30% DISCOUNT
</div>
<?php } ?>
```

The preceding code should be added right after the `<header>` tag of the `header.php` file in the child theme. Now, you can view a single post and the header will contain the dynamic advertisement bar, as shown in the following screenshot:

This technique can be used effectively to conditionally change templates in scenarios where you have a limited number of different conditions. However, it's not feasible for handling complex conditions as it complicates the template file.

We can use the same process to conditionally change other important parts of the site. Let's a take quick look at the steps involved in changing each of those parts:

- **Footer**: We need to copy the `footer.php` file from the parent theme to the child theme. Then, we follow the same process for adding/removing content based on the necessary conditions.
- **Sidebar**: We need to copy the `sidebar.php` file from the parent theme to the child theme. Then, we follow the same process for loading different sidebars or adding static content to the existing sidebar template based on the necessary conditions.
- **Menu**: Usually, the menu is generated by the `wp_nav_menu` function, which is located in the `header.php` file of the theme. In this case, we are using the **Twenty Seventeen** theme and hence you can find this function inside the `template-parts/navigation/navigation-top.php` file. You can copy this template and modify it to load different menus based on the necessary conditions.

In this section, we looked at the process of conditionally changing the header of the site. You can extend this technique to make major design changes in headers, as well as use other conditions such as front page, category pages, specific pages, and so on. You can find a list of available template tags for adding various types of conditions at `https://codex.wordpress.org/Template:Conditional_Tags`.

Conditionally loading template files

In this technique, we use existing WordPress filters to dynamically change the template based on custom conditions. WordPress executes a filter called `template_include`, just before loading the default template, based on the hierarchy we discussed earlier. In the template hierarchy section, we changed the template by using the preceding templates in a given path. The use of this filter allows us to change any template in any given path. Let's take a look the following code to understand the implementation of this technique:

```
add_filter( 'template_include', 'wpquickstart_conditional_template', 99 );
function wpquickstart_conditional_template( $template ) {
    if ( is_page( 'portfolio' ) ) {
        $new_template = locate_template( array( 'portfolio-page-
template.php' ) );
        if ( !empty( $new_template ) ) {
```

```
                return $new_template;
            }
        }
    return $template;
}
```

The location of the default template is passed as the parameter to this filter. In this scenario, we check whether the page with the name `portfolio` is loaded. If the condition is matched, we return a dynamic new template instead of the default template. The preceding code will look for the template in the root folder of the theme. The advantage of this method is the ability to use different conditions on different template paths at once and load the necessary templates. We can also use this technique to load dynamic templates based on conditions such as URL parameters, the logged in user or user role, and the referrer of a request.

As a developer, you must be aware of this technique. There may be sites that use this technique in the `functions.php` file of the theme, as well as with custom plugins. If you are not aware of this technique, you will have to waste considerable time going through the template hierarchy to find out the template that is loaded.

Summary

The frontend of an application is the main interaction point for users and hence the possibility of requesting frontend changes is relatively high. Therefore, it's important to use the existing features of a theme to make templates as flexible as possible. In this chapter, we looked at the importance of a theme and its components in development. Then, we started extending existing themes with the use of child themes, actions, and filters. Next, we had an in-depth overview of the theme template hierarchy in order to build new themes as well as customize existing themes in a flexible way. Finally, we looked at the techniques for conditionally changing the design to cater for advanced site requirements.

In `Chapter 4`, *Building Custom Modules with Plugin Development*, we will be looking at the process of building different types of WordPress plugins and adding the features, beyond the functionality of a them.

Building Custom Modules with Plugin Development

4

Enormous free plugin base and plugin-based architecture are the keys to success of WordPress as a CMS. Plugins allow developers to build independent features as well as connect with the modules developed by other developers. We can use plugins to build quality sites with the code written by the top WordPress developers in the world, without spending a single dollar. From the developer's perspective, plugins allow you to reach and help thousands of users while being able to promote your skills as a developer. Anyone who has basic programming knowledge can create plugins to meet application-specific requirements. However, it takes considerable effort to develop quality plugins that can be reused across a wide range of projects.

In this chapter, you will learn about the concept of plugins and how they are different from your theme. You will also go through the life cycle events of a proper plugin while creating a post attachments plugin to illustrate the use of these events. The primary concepts in plugin development such as data validation, sanitization, and nonce will be introduced. Understanding how to leverage existing WordPress features to build plugins that can be added or removed without affecting the other parts is the highlight of this chapter.

In this chapter, we will cover the following topics:

- Understanding the role of plugins in development
- Creating a basic plugin from scratch
- Exploring the life cycle of a plugin
- Developing a post attachment plugin
- Identifying the advantages of custom plugin development
- Guidelines for building quality plugins

By the end of this chapter, you should be able to understand the role of plugins and have the necessary knowledge to build a basic plugin from scratch using the recommended practices.

Technical requirements

You will be required to have WordPress 4.9.8 installed to follow this procedure. Even if you have a later version of WordPress, the described examples should work with no significant problems.

The code files of this chapter can be found on GitHub:
`https://github.com/PacktPublishing/WordPress-Development-Quick-Start-Guide/tree/master/Chapter04`

Check out the following video to see the code in action:
`http://bit.ly/2Py2szO`

Understanding the role of plugins

A plugin is a set of functions dedicated to work as an independent solution, while extending or adding new features to WordPress. In WordPress, plugins are similar to the Apps we use in iOS and Android. We have the ability to use or remove any plugin without affecting WordPress's core features. Also, plugins allow us to separate independent features into their own plugins, making them easier to maintain. The `wordpress.org` plugin base has over 50,000 free plugins, and sometimes you don't have to develop anything for WordPress websites. You can just use a number of plugins and integrate them properly to build advanced features.

The role of plugins is vital for the development of a site. In `Chapter 3`, *Designing Flexible Frontends with Theme Development*, we discussed the role of a theme, and the features beyond the scope of a theme. Basically, any feature beyond the scope of a theme should be developed with plugins. However, there are scenarios where we will also use plugins to develop theme-specific things like templates and styles so that they are compatible with multiple themes. In most scenarios, plugins should either use their own styles and designs or default to the styles of the theme. It's not ideal to develop plugins focusing on a specific theme as it's almost impossible to switch to another theme at later stages.

In development, building plugins can range from just a few lines of code with filter implementations to advanced modules with thousands of lines of code. Let's take a look at some of the common types of development tasks with plugins:

- **Building reusable blocks**: WordPress sites are mostly built by non-technical site owners and hence building the blocks of simple features is a common task. These blocks allow the client to add the feature anywhere in the site without needing a developer. We can use shortcodes or widgets to provide features as reusable blocks. In modern sites, page builders are used frequently to build the page's design. Therefore, we can also develop components for page builders that are to be used as reusable blocks.
- **Modifying built-in features**: This is a must for many sites, especially for extending the backend features and customizing the backend display. Since these are built-in features, we can't modify the WordPress file to customize them. Therefore, we need to choose actions and filters of built-in features and implement them with the use of plugins.
- **Data capturing and displaying**: This is another common type of requirement, especially for sites that go beyond basic blogs. In these kinds of tasks, we need to create custom forms in the frontend, and either use backend features to store the data or create our own data storage. Built-in custom post types and custom build forms are used to handle such requirements.
- **Integrating UI components**: Modern websites are filled with interactive user interface components that are designed to display substantial data in a limited space. These components are mostly powered by open source JavaScript libraries. So, integrating these libraries and letting administrators add data to these components is another common requirement.

These are some of the challenges you face when working on a specific WordPress site. The process of building plugins to handle these types of requirements is essential for WordPress developers and hence we will be covering them in upcoming chapters. However, if you are planning to develop your own plugin, the challenges and possibilities are enormous. We can explore the WordPress plugin directory to understand what a plugin can do and the scope involved.

WordPress plugin types based on features

As you explore, you will understand that the roles of plugins may vary from one another. So, it's important to identify these different types of plugins in order to face the challenges in extending different WordPress modules. Here, we are going to choose some of the popular plugins of different plugin types and discuss how they interact with WordPress's frontend and backend. This is purely a personal preference and hence you may want to categorize them differently after exploring the plugin directory:

- **Yoast SEO** (https://wordpress.org/plugins/wordpress-seo/): This plugin is used to improve the SEO of the site by adding necessary content to pages. This type of plugin has interfaces in the backend, where we can add content or settings. However, these plugins work under the hood in the frontend as we can't see any content. The examples for this type includes plugins from caching, analytics, and translation categories.
- **WordPress Importer** (https://wordpress.org/plugins/wordpress-importer/): This plugin imports data into the WordPress database from files. These types of plugins don't have any features in the frontend or backend interfaces. Instead, these plugins are used to provide functionality by changing database values. The examples for these types of plugins include Duplicate Post and All-in-One WP Migration.
- **WooCommerce** (https://wordpress.org/plugins/woocommerce/): This plugin is used to simplify the online shopping process by creating and selling products. These types of plugins have interfaces in the backend to add content as well as interfaces in the frontend to display the content. Apart from that, these plugins contain extensive data processing. This is the most common type of plugin you will get for development tasks. The examples for this type of plugin include BuddyPress and bbPress.
- **Meta Slider** (https://wordpress.org/plugins/ml-slider/): This plugin adds elegant image sliders to the frontend of the site. These types of plugins have backend interfaces for adding content and frontend interfaces for displaying the content inside modern UI elements. However, no data processing is involved. The examples for this type of plugin include Easy FancyBox and Max Mega Menu.
- **Admin Menu Editor** (https://wordpress.org/plugins/admin-menu-editor/): This plugin allows you to change the menus and the related settings. These types of plugins allow you to add, change, and remove built-in backend features to suit your needs. There is no interaction with the frontend or data in such plugins. The examples for this type of plugin include Admin Columns and Simple Page Ordering.

- **Easy Google Fonts** (`https://wordpress.org/plugins/easy-google-fonts/`): This plugin allows you to use Google Fonts for the content of the site. These types of plugins often don't have functionality related to the backend or frontend. Instead, they connect third-party services with WordPress. The examples for this type of plugin include AddToAny Share Buttons and Google Doc Embedder.
- **Advanced Custom Fields** (`https://wordpress.org/plugins/advanced-custom-fields/`): This plugin acts as a framework, letting developers and clients build forms using existing components. These types of plugins interacts with both the backend and the frontend. However, these plugins don't provide site-specific features. Instead, the administrator decides which elements are displayed to the user and how the data is processed. Examples of such plugins include Elementor Page Builder and Pods Custom Content Types and Fields.

The types of plugins we can build is enormous and can't be covered here, even if we were to have a complete chapter dedicated to them. Therefore, we have chosen a few plugins that contain the most popular types of development tasks.

Creating your first plugin

The process of developing a simple plugin is not complex. It follows the same process we used for themes, where we used PHP header comments. First, you have to create a new directory inside `wp-content/plugins`, with a preferred name. In this example, we are going to name it `wpquick-after-post-content`. Once the plugin directory has been created, we can create the main plugin file, which is `wpquick-after-post-content.php`. You can use the preferred name for the main plugin file. Now, we have to add the following header comments section to define it as a plugin:

```php
<?php
/*
Plugin Name: WPQAPC After Post Content
Plugin URI: http://www.wpexpertdeveloper.com/wpquick-after-post
Description: Add dynamic content after the post
Version: 1.0
Author: Rakhitha Nimesh
Author URI: http://www.wpexpertdeveloper.com
*/
```

The plugin definition comment is similar to the theme definition, where Theme Name and Theme URI are being replaced by Plugin Name and Plugin URI. Once the comment has been added, this directory becomes a plugin and you can refresh the backend plugins list to reflect the plugin's details. Now, you can add any PHP code within the main plugin file or sub-files to begin development with WordPress. The only thing that differs from usual PHP development is the use of WordPress hooks. We will be introducing the necessary hooks throughout this chapter.

Let's add some functionality to the plugin. We have named this plugin After Post Content. The functionality is to add dynamic content after each post in the site. In Chapter 3, *Designing Flexible Frontends with Theme Development,*we added a dynamic advertisement bar to the header section. Here, we will be displaying the same advertisement, after the post content. Consider the following code for the implementation of this feature:

```
add_filter( 'the_content', 'wpqapc_file_attachment_display' );
function wpqapc_file_attachment_display( $content ){
  global $post;
  if( is_singular( 'post' ) ){
    $after_content = '<div id="wpquick-article-ads"
style="padding:20px;text-align:center;font-
size:20px;background:red;color:#FFF;">GET MEMBERSHIP WITH 30%
DISCOUNT</div>';
    return $content . $after_content;
  }
  return $content;
}
```

This code is added to the main plugin file, just after the header comments section. Usually, we have to modify the post template to add such content in pure PHP development. In WordPress, everything is hooked into an action or a filter, and hence we can use them without modifying the template files. Here, we have used the the_content filter with a callback function. We already discussed the use of filters in Chapter 3, *Designing Flexible Frontends with Theme Development*. This filter is used to modify the post/page content and is included in all of the properly coded themes. The default post content is passed to this filter and plugins can alter this content by implementing this hook.

In this scenario, we have used the `is_singular` function for the conditional check. This function is used to check if we are viewing the single page of any given post type. Once the condition is matched, we add the dynamic advertisement bar after the existing post content. Now, you can create and view a new post in the frontend. The content we added will be displayed in a similar fashion as to what's shown in the following screenshot:

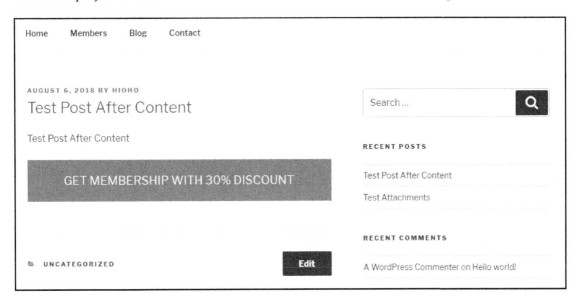

We have created a simple plugin in a very short time span. WordPress plugins can range from a few lines of code like this one, to advanced systems with thousands of lines of code. So, as we can see, developing WordPress plugins is not hard. It's always a good option to separate even a few lines of codes into a separate plugin, assuming that the functionality can be useful for many sites. In this example, we only added a fixed bar to each and every post. In real world implementations, we will have to change these advertisements as well as have the ability to add them to each post from the backend.

Exploring the life cycle of a plugin

A product life cycle is a series of events or stages that occur from the start to the completion of the product or process. WordPress plugins contain life cycle events, from initial activation to uninstallation. It's important to understand all of these events to keep the plugin working and make the data consistent, even after exiting the plugin. Many developers are aware of only a few of these events, leading to low quality plugins.

In this section, we are going to look at the life cycle of a plugin and how we can manage each of the events in the cycle. Consider the following diagram for a basic illustration of events in a plugin:

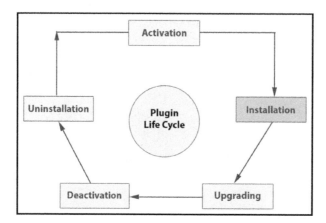

As you can see, the life cycle of a plugin has five events, apart from its functionality. A plugin starts the cycle via an activation event. The cycle is completed with either deactivate or uninstall events, until it starts the cycle again with activation. Let's understand these five events:

- **Activation**: This is a built-in event that's fired by clicking the Activate button from the WordPress plugin list or installation screen. This can be used for executing certain actions upon activation as well as to initialize the plugin data and settings. Ideally, the initialization tasks should be done through a separate installation process since plugin activation is not a one-time event. However, a limited number of plugins offer a separate installation process, as it's a plugin-specific event. Therefore, most developers will use WordPress's built-in activation process to initialize the plugins with necessary condition checks. Adding rewrite rules, creating/modifying database tables, adding default settings. and creating demo data are some of practical functions that are executed in the activation process.
- **Installation**: This is not a built-in event, and most WordPress plugins use the activation event for installation. However, we may need a step by step installation process like WordPress for complex plugins. With this, we can implement our own installation process by using custom code after the activation. You can install WooCommerce to check how the plugin-specific installation process is handled with custom screens.

- **Upgrading**: This is a built-in event for plugins in the WordPress plugin repository and is used just after the version upgrade has completed. However, this event is not available for other plugins unless we build a custom upgrade process to get the files from our own server. Therefore, we need to handle this by combining existing WordPress hooks and conditional checks in scenarios where we don't have a custom automatic upgrade process. This event can be used for adding default values for additional settings in new versions, altering database tables, converting existing data to a new format, and so on.

- **Deactivation**: This is a built-in event that's fired by clicking the Deactivate link from the WordPress plugin list. This action should be used to execute certain tasks before the plugin is deactivated. Often, developers misunderstand the use of this action and tend to use it as an uninstallation process. Deactivation is a temporary event and hence you should not delete plugin data within this hook. Ideally, this event should be used for functions such as removing rewrite rules, clearing the cache, and temporary database values.

- **Uninstallation**: This is also a built-in event that's fired by clicking the Delete link from the WordPress plugins list. This is the proper event to handle uninstallation and must be used to clear plugin-specific data. Many plugins don't have an uninstallation process, leaving the plugin data in the database. Once a plugin is deactivated, the plugin data doesn't affect the site's features. However, this data affects the site's performance, and also makes it prone to conflicts with plugins that will be used in the future. Therefore, it's important to implement the uninstall event for a plugin as well as instruct the user on what happens upon uninstallation.

In the next section, we will be developing a plugin while using the most important and mandatory life cycle events of a plugin.

Developing a post attachments plugin

In the two preceding sections, we discussed the steps for building a basic plugin and the life cycle events. In this section, we will be developing a plugin, while covering the implementation of life cycle events and critical features in plugin development. Let's summarize the requirement of the plugin.

The use of blog posts and displaying dynamic content after the post is common in most WordPress sites. We already looked at the process of adding content after the post, in the first plugin we developed. Now, we are going to extend the feature to allow attachment downloads after the post. In some sites, it's essential to allow users to download files related to the post. This plugin will allow the administrator to add files to a post from the backend and let users download these files by displaying them after the post's content.

Let's start the development of our plugin by creating a new directory called `wpquick-post-attachments` inside the `wp-content/plugins` directory. Then, we need to create the main plugin file inside the new directory as `wpquick-post-attachments.php`. As usual, we need to add the plugin header comments section to this file in order to let WordPress list it as a plugin. You can use the plugin header comments from the previous plugin with a modified name and description.

Now, we have to identify the tasks involved in the development process of this plugin:

- Creating a custom table to store attachment details of each post
- Adding a file field in the post creation screen to upload attachments
- Uploading and saving the attachments in a custom table
- Displaying attachments after post content with a download feature

Let's start the development process by adding these features within the plugin life cycle events we discussed.

Creating settings upon plugin activation

The activation process of a plugin is handled by the built-in `register_activation_hook` function. In this scenario, we are developing a simple plugin to illustrate the importance of concepts in plugin development. Here, we will be using the built-in activation event to initialize the settings and data for this plugin, instead of creating separate installation process. Add the following code to the `wpquick-post-attachments.php` file, after the header comments section:

```
register_activation_hook( __FILE__, 'wpqpa_activate' );
function wpqpa_activate(){
  global $wpdb;
  $table_attachments = $wpdb->prefix . 'wpqpa_post_attachments';
  $sql_attachments = "CREATE TABLE IF NOT EXISTS $table_attachments (
            id int(11) NOT NULL AUTO_INCREMENT,
            file_name varchar(255) NOT NULL,
            user_id int(11) NOT NULL,
            post_id int(11) NOT NULL,
```

```
            file_path longtext NOT NULL,
            updated_at datetime NOT NULL,
            uploaded_file_name varchar(255) NOT NULL,
            PRIMARY KEY (id)
            );";

    require_once( ABSPATH . 'wp-admin/includes/upgrade.php' );
    dbDelta( $sql_attachments );
    $default_headers = array('Version' => 'Version');
    $plugin_data = get_file_data(__FILE__, $default_headers, 'plugin');
    update_option( 'wpqpa_version',$plugin_data['Version'] );
}
```

We use the `register_activation_hook` function to register a custom function to be executed upon the activation process. The first parameter takes the path of the main plugin file, while the second parameter is used to define the function name. Here, we have used a function called `wpqpa_activate`.

We start the plugin activation process by creating a custom table to store the post attachment path and other necessary details. We already discussed the process of creating custom tables and the use of the `dbDelta` function in Chapter 2, *Managing Database Structure, Storage, and Retrieval,* and hence the explanations will not be repeated in this section. Apart from table creation, we can also save initial data or the settings required to run the plugin. In this scenario, we are capturing the plugin version from the header comments section by using the `get_file_data` function and saving it to `wp_options` table with a plugin-specific key called `wpqpa_version`.

We used the activation process to generate the necessary configurations in the database. Before moving into the development of these features, we need to specify the necessary paths to access the other files in the plugin. So, let's add some constants to the main plugin file by using the following code:

```
if ( ! defined( 'WPQPA_PLUGIN_DIR' ) ) {
  define( 'WPQPA_PLUGIN_DIR', plugin_dir_path( __FILE__ ) );
}
if ( ! defined( 'WPQPA_PLUGIN_URL' ) ) {
  define( 'WPQPA_PLUGIN_URL', plugin_dir_url( __FILE__ ) );
}
```

First, we have to use the `defined` function to check whether a constant with a given name is already defined in order to prevent errors. Here, we have added two constants to define the URL to the plugin file inside the plugin directory and the full directory path. These two constants are used in upcoming sections to load scripts, styles, and PHP files for the plugin. Now, we can move into the process of building the features of the plugin.

Implementing post attachment uploads

The post creation screen is designed to let developers extend features by using custom meta boxes. In this scenario, we need a way to let the administrator upload files to a post. So, we need to define a custom meta box for displaying the input elements, as shown in the following code:

```
add_action( 'add_meta_boxes_post', 'wpqpa_post_attachments_meta_box' );
function wpqpa_post_attachments_meta_box( $post ){
  add_meta_box( 'wpqpa-post-attachments', __( 'Post attachments', 'wpqpa'
  ),
  'display_post_attachments_meta_box', 'post', 'normal', 'high' );
}
```

The `add_meta_boxes_post` action is used to register a new meta box for normal posts. Inside this action, we can create a new meta box by using the `add_meta_box` function.

> If you are registering a meta box for a specific post type, it's recommended that you use the `add_meta_boxes_{post_type}` action. In scenarios where the meta box is registered for multiple post types, you can use the generic `add_meta_boxes` action.

The first three parameters of this function are required and used for unique meta box ID, meta box title, and callback function, respectively. In this scenario, we are calling a function in the main plugin file and hence we can just use the function name. However, if the callback function resides within a PHP class, you need to use the following syntax to call the function on an object of the class:

```
$wpqpa = new WPQPA();
add_meta_box( 'wpqpa-post-attachments', __( 'Post attachments', 'wpqpa' ),
array($wpqpa, 'display_post_attachments_meta_box') , 'post', 'normal',
'high' );
```

The remaining three parameters in the preceding code are used for screen, context, and priority, respectively. Let's take a look at the use of those three parameters:

- **Screen**: This parameter specifies the WordPress screen ID or IDs as an array to display the metabox. Each screen in WordPress has a specific ID to let developers build features for specific screens. Here, we have used **post** as the screen since we are only displaying the metabox for normal posts. You can check the available screen IDs of the admin screens by going to `https://codex.wordpress.org/Plugin_API/Admin_Screen_Reference`.

- **Context**: This parameter defines the location within the screen. We have three options for the post screen: normal, advanced, and side. The default value is **advanced** and displays a metabox under the post editor. However, if a *normal* metabox is created, it will display before the metaboxes with **advanced** context. The **side** option moves the metabox to the side column, along with the **Publish** buttons.
- **Priority**: This parameter defines the location of the metabox within a context. We have four values called high, core, default, and low. The **high** value places the metabox on top within the context while the priority will get lower as we move to the **low** option.

Next, we need to complete the implementation of the callback function before we can check the new metabox on the post screen. Let's consider the following code for the implementation of the `display_post_attachments_meta_box` function:

```
function display_post_attachments_meta_box( $post, $metabox ){
  global $wpdb;
  $display = '<div class="wpqpa-files-panel" >
    <div class="wpqpa-files-add-form" >
      <div class="wpqpa-files-msg" style="display:none" ></div>
      <div class="wpqpa-files-add-form-row">
      <div class="wpqpa-files-add-form-label">'.__("File
Title","wpqpa").'</div>
      <div class="wpqpa-files-add-form-field">
      <input type="text" class="wpqpa-file-name" name="wpqpa_file_name" />
      </div>
      </div>
      <div class="wpqpa-files-add-form-row">
      <div class="wpqpa-files-add-form-label">'.__("File","wpqpa").'</div>
      <div class="wpqpa-files-add-form-field">
      <input type="file" class="wpqpa-file" name="wpqpa_file" />
      </div>
      </div>
    <div class="wpqpa-clear"></div>
  </div>';
  $display .= wp_nonce_field( "wpqpa_attachment", "wpqpa_nonce", true,
false );
  echo $display;
}
```

This function automatically receives post object and metabox details as parameters. Most of the code is self-explanatory as it contains the container elements and the necessary HTML fields. However, the last line is very important as a developer. WordPress uses a technique called **nonce** to increase the security of your code. Let's take a look at the definition of nonce, which has been extracted from the official codex:

> *"A nonce is a "number used once" to help protect URLs and forms from certain types of misuse, malicious or otherwise. WordPress nonces aren't numbers, but are hashes made up of numbers and letters. Nor are they used only once, but have a limited "lifetime" after which they expire. During that time period, the same nonce will be generated for a given user in a given context. The nonce for that action will remain the same for that user until that nonce life cycle has completed."*

In short, nonces are used to validate the user's request and keep the integrity of the submitted data. It's a must to use nonce validations in plugin development, especially when you are developing plugins for public use. The `wp_nonce_field` function is used to add a hidden field with a nonce value. The first parameter to this function is an action name that will be used in the verification process, and the second parameter is the name of the HTML hidden field. We can use the `wp_nonce_field` function without any of these parameters, but it's strongly recommended to use both options. The following is a sample output that's been generated from the use of the `wp_nonce_field` function:

```
<input type="hidden" id="wpqpa_nonce" name="wpqpa_nonce"
value="bff32cce02">
<input type="hidden" name="_wp_http_referer" value="/wp-
admin/post.php?post=9&action=edit">
```

This nonce value will be used later in the data saving process for verification. So far, we have added the necessary HTML for displaying file upload input fields. However, these elements might display all over the place without the necessary styles. Therefore, we need to create a directory called `css` inside our plugin directory and add a CSS file as `wpqpa.css`. Then, we need to include the CSS in the file by using recommended WordPress actions. Consider the following code for including the CSS file:

```
add_action( 'admin_enqueue_scripts', 'wpqpa_load_scripts',9 );
add_action( 'wp_enqueue_scripts', 'wpqpa_load_scripts',9 );
function wpqpa_load_scripts(){
  wp_register_style( 'wpqpa_css', WPQPA_PLUGIN_URL . 'css/wpqpa.css' );
  wp_enqueue_style( 'wpqpa_css' );
}
```

In WordPress, we need to use `admin_enqueue_scripts` action for adding script and style files to the backend, and use the `wp_enqueue_scripts` action for the frontend. In this scenario, we are displaying the same files list in both the frontend and the backend. Therefore, we use both actions to load the CSS file we created. First, we have to register style files by using the `wp_register_style` function with a unique key and path. Then, we use the `wp_enqueue_style` function to add the styles file to the page. More details and advanced uses of script and style loading will be discussed in upcoming chapters. The CSS styles for this plugin are not discussed in this chapter. You can use the source files for this chapter to understand and modify them.

Now, we can take a look at the modified post creation screen with our metabox, as shown in the following screenshot:

The custom metabox is displayed under the post editor. However, in a single site, we could be using many plugins with custom metaboxes. Therefore, you can't get the metabox to the exact location we need unless you are willing to change the code of such plugins.

Uploading attachments and saving attachment data

The next step in the process is uploading and saving the file that's been selected by the administrator. In this scenario, we add the **File** and **File Title** inside the metabox by using the defined fields. Then, the administrator needs to hit the post's **Publish** or **Update** button to save the attachment along with the post.

 Ideally, the attachment details should be uploaded and saved using AJAX in order to support multiple files without needing to update the post. In this scenario, we have used a normal form submit as we have not introduced AJAX yet and we need to understand the process of handling normal POST requests.

Let's take a look at the attachment saving process using the following code, which has been added to the main file of our plugin:

```
add_action( 'init', 'wpqpa_save_private_attachment_files' );
function wpqpa_save_private_attachment_files(){
  global $wpdb;
  if( ! isset( $_POST['wpqpa_file_name'] ) ){
    return;
  }
  $file_name = isset($_POST['wpqpa_file_name']) ?
sanitize_text_field($_POST['wpqpa_file_name']) : '';
  $file_nonce = isset( $_POST['file_nonce'] ) ? ( $_POST['file_nonce'] ) :
'';
  $post_id = isset( $_POST['post_ID'] ) ? (int) ( $_POST['post_ID'] ) : 0;
  $user_id = get_current_user_id();
  // Remaining code
}
```

Usually, developers can access POST request data directly within any file of the site. However, WordPress uses an event-based architecture and hence we need to implement proper hooks to access this data. Accessing the request data outside a proper WordPress event can lead to conflicting or the unavailability of data. Therefore, we use the init action to access the POST data, as the user request is fully loaded by the time it reaches the init action. More about action execution process will be discussed in Chapter 5, *Extending Plugins with Addons, Filters, and Actions*.

The `init` action will be executed for each and every request and hence we need to make sure that we use our custom code only when necessary. Therefore, we check the availability of the `wpqpa_file_name` field in the user request and return without executing the custom code when it's not available. Then, we have to grab the necessary data from the POST request. Here, we need three values for the file name, nonce, and post ID.

You may have noticed the use of a function called `sanitize_text_field`. This function is used to remove unnecessary tags, spaces, line breaks, and characters from text field submissions. You should never trust incoming data; that's why you should use `sanitize_text_field` before recording it. We should always validate and restrict user input values to improve the security of the code and prevent conflicts in the database. WordPress uses a three step process to secure data by validating, sanitizing, and escaping:

- **Sanitizing**: At this stage, we have to grab the user submitted data and make sure that it contains the accepted values. WordPress provides a set of functions for cleaning the user input and making it secure. The `sanitize_text_field` is one of the functions among thirteen sanitizing functions. The available functions and their use are explained at `https://codex.wordpress.org/Validating_Sanitizing_and_Escaping_User_Data#Sanitizing:_Cleaning_User_Input`.

- **Validating**: At this stage, we validate the cleaned input values from the previous stage. The intention of this step is to check whether user submitted data matches with the accepted values. Unlike sanitization, there are no specific functions for validation. We can use our own conditions with both PHP and WordPress functions for validation. Validating data types, string lengths, data formats, and empty values are some of the common uses of this step.

- **Escaping**: This step is used when displaying data to the user. The intention of this step is to secure the data to be displayed. WordPress provides a set of built-in escaping functions based on different data. We will be discussing the use of escaping in upcoming chapters. The available escaping functions and their use is explained at `https://codex.wordpress.org/Data_Validation#Output_Sanitation`.

You should choose the necessary functions from these three sections for validating the user data, depending on the type of fields used in a form and the accepted values.

The next step in the process is validating input data and uploading the attachment. Consider the following code, which is placed after the input data capturing code:

```
if ( ! isset( $_POST['wpqpa_nonce'] ) || ! wp_verify_nonce(
$_POST['wpqpa_nonce'], 'wpqpa_attachment' ) ) {
  $result_upload = wpqpa_process_file_upload();
  // Upload code section 1
```

```
}else{
  // Handle error for invalid data submission
}
```

First, we need to validate the user request by using the nonce value that we added in the custom meta box. We start by checking the existence of the nonce value by using the `isset( $_POST['wpqpa_nonce'] )` condition. Then, we can use the `wp_verify_nonce` function to verify the submitted nonce value. The first parameter to this function takes the value of the nonce field and the second parameter takes the action name of the nonce field. Once nonce is successfully verified, we can upload the attachment.

Here, we use a function called `wpqpa_process_file_upload` for handling attachment uploads. The majority of the code in the `wpqpa_process_file_upload` function is not WordPress-specific and hence self-explanatory. You can use the source code files for this chapter to understand the implementation of this function.

Now, we have to revert back to the `wpqpa_save_private_attachment_files` function, where we added the comment *Upload code section 1*. The data generated from the upload file's function is stored in the `$result_upload` variable. Let's continue the implementation to save the attachment details to the custom database table:

```
if( isset( $result_upload['status'] ) && $result_upload['status'] ==
'success' ){
  $file_date = date("Y-m-d H:i:s");
  $uploaded_file_name = $result_upload['base_name'];
  $wpqpa_post_attachments_table = "{$wpdb->prefix}wpqpa_post_attachments";
  $wpdb->insert(
    $wpqpa_post_attachments_table,
    array(
      'file_name' => $file_name,
      'user_id' => $user_id,
      'post_id' => $post_id,
      'file_path' => $result_upload['relative_file_path'],
      'updated_at' => $file_date,
      'uploaded_file_name' => $uploaded_file_name,
    ),
    array( '%s', '%d', '%d', '%s', '%s', '%s' ) );
}else{
  // Handle file upload errors
}
```

First, we check whether the attachment upload has completed by using the status option of the $result_upload variable. Once the condition is matched, we get the file name from the $result_upload variable and define the custom table name in a variable. Next, we use the insert function of the global $wpdb object to save the data to the wpqpa_post_attachments table that was created in the activation event of the plugin. We already discussed the use of the insert function in Chapter 2, *Managing Database Structure, Storage, and Retrieval*, and hence I am not going to explain it in this section.

Now, the code for the attachment upload process is completed. However, you won't be able to upload attachments at this stage. In order to upload files, you need to change the enctype of HTML forms to multipart/form-data. By default, WordPress won't add the enctype attribute to the post submission form. Also it's not possible to manually add it, as the form code is generated within WordPress. So, we need to use the built-in post_edit_form_tag action to add the necessary enctype, as shown in the following code:

```
add_action( 'post_edit_form_tag' , 'wpqpa_post_edit_form_tag' );
function wpqpa_post_edit_form_tag( ) {
  echo ' enctype="multipart/form-data" ';
}
```

Now, the entire process is completed and you should be able to test it by uploading a file with the use of post **Publish** or **Update** buttons. The uploaded attachment data should be reflected in the custom table.

Displaying uploaded attachments

We need a way to display the uploaded files within the post edit screen as well as on the frontend, after the post content. For this, we are going to use a common function called wpqpa_file_attachment_list to generate an attachments list, as shown in the following code:

```
function wpqpa_file_attachment_list( $post ){
  global $wpdb;
  $display = '<div class="wpqpa-files-list" >';
  $sql = $wpdb->prepare( "SELECT * FROM
{$wpdb->prefix}wpqpa_post_attachments WHERE post_id = %d order by
updated_at desc ", $post->ID );

  $files_list = $wpdb->get_results( $sql );
  foreach( $files_list as $file_row ){
    $url = get_permalink( $file_row->post_id );
    $url = wpqpa_add_query_string( $url,
```

```
"wpqpa_file_download=yes&wpqpa_private_file_id =".
$file_row->id."&wpqpa_post_id=".$file_row->post_id );

    $display .= '
        <div class="wpqpa-file-item" id="PF'.$file_row->id.'" data-file-
id="'.$file_row->id.'" >
        <div class="wpqpa-file-item-row" >
        <div class="wpqpa-file-item-name wpqpa-files-list-name"
>'.$file_row->file_name.'</div>
        <div class="wpqpa-file-item-download" ><a href="'.$url.'"
>'.__("Download","wpqpa").'</a></div>
        <div class="wpqpa-clear"></div>
        </div>
        <div class="wpqpa-clear"></div>
        </div>';
    }
    $display .= '</div>';
    return $display;
}
```

This function is placed inside the main plugin file and accepts a post object as a parameter. First, we use the `prepare` function of the `$wpdb` object to securely prepare the SQL query for execution. In this function, we need to assign placeholders to all of the user input data and pass the values as parameters. Once the query has been prepared, we can use the `get_results` function to execute the query and get a list of files that are attached to the specific post.

Next, we use a `foreach` statement to loop through the resulting attachments. Inside the loop, we get the URL of the post by using the built-in `get_permalink` function. Then, we add file-specific query parameters to the URL by using the custom `wpqpa_add_query_string` function. You can check the implementation of this function inside the main plugin file in the source code directory for this chapter. This URL is used to identify the attachment and provides download features in later stages of the implementation. Finally, we add the necessary HTML elements and containers with the attachment information and the download link. The prepared HTML will be returned from this function.

Now, we need to call this function within the `display_post_attachments_meta_box` function and display the attachments list after the file upload fields. After uploading a few files, your screen will look similar to what's shown in the following screenshot:

Here, we have only used **Download** as an action button to keep the implementation simple and useful for this book. Usually, you will need other actions such as edit and delete for attachments.

Displaying attachments in posts

The main requirement of this plugin was to attach files to posts and let users download them from the post page. So far, we have created the background to save and display the attachments. Now, it's time to implement the main requirements by displaying them after the content of each post.

At the start of this chapter, we created a plugin to use the `the_content` filter and add dynamic content after the post. The same technique will be used in this scenario. Let's consider the following code for the implementation of the `the_content` filter:

```
add_filter( 'the_content', 'wpqpa_file_attachment_display' );
function wpqpa_file_attachment_display( $content ){
  global $post;
  if( is_singular( 'post' ) ){
```

```
        return $content . wpqpa_file_attachment_list( $post );
    }
    return $content;
}
```

As usual, we add the `the_content` filter and the callback function to handle the display of attachments. First, we check whether we are actually viewing an individual post by using the `is_singular` conditional function. If the condition is not matched, we return the content, as attachments are only intended for normal posts. Once the condition is matched, we call the reusable function we created earlier to display the list of attachments for the post. The following screenshot previews how attachments are displayed in a single post page:

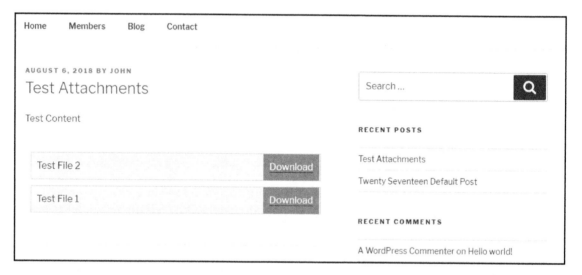

Now, we have come to the final stage, where we need to implement a file download link to complete the plugin.

Implementing the post attachments download

This section is straightforward for developers who have already implemented file downloads with pure PHP. In the preceding section, we created a download link with a few custom parameters. Here, we have to use these parameters to identify attachments. Let's start this implementation by adding a custom download function on the `init` action:

```
add_action( 'init', 'wpqpa_file_attachment_download' );
function wpqpa_file_attachment_download(){
  global $wpdb;
  if( isset( $_GET['wpqpa_file_download'] ) &&
sanitize_text_field($_GET['wpqpa_file_download']) =='yes' && isset(
$_GET['wpqpa_private_file_id'] ) ){

    $wpqpa_file_download = $_GET['wpqpa_file_download'];
    $wpqpa_file_id = isset( $_GET['wpqpa_private_file_id'] ) ? (int)
$_GET['wpqpa_private_file_id'] : '';
    $wpqpa_post_id = isset( $_GET['wpqpa_post_id'] ) ? (int)
$_GET['wpqpa_post_id'] : '';

    if( $wpqpa_file_id != '' && $wpqpa_post_id != '' ){
      $sql = $wpdb->prepare( "SELECT * FROM
{$wpdb->prefix}wpqpa_post_attachments WHERE id = %d AND post_id = %d order
by updated_at desc ", $wpqpa_file_id, $wpqpa_post_id );
      $attachments = $wpdb->get_results( $sql,ARRAY_A );
      if( ! isset( $attachments[0] ) ){
        return;
      }
      $file_link = site_url() . $attachments[0]['file_path'];
      $upload_dir = wp_upload_dir();
      $file_dir = $upload_dir['basedir'] . $attachments[0]['file_path'];
      // Remaining code for file downloads
    }
  }
}
```

As we have already discussed, it's very important to hook every custom function into a suitable WordPress action. In this scenario, we chose the init action since WordPress has finished loading and we need to access data from GET requests. We begin this function by checking the GET parameters in the URL to make sure that it's a request to download post attachments. You should note the use of sanitize_text_field, even for GET parameters, which is intended only for verification. Then, we access the attachment ID and post ID by using URL parameters with the necessary validation. Next, we execute a SQL select query to find the attachment details by using the database functions that were discussed in the previous sections. However, there is a slight difference in the get_results function, and that is that we have used an additional parameter called ARRAY_A. This is used to define the format of the result set. In the previous section, we didn't use this parameter and hence we got a set of objects as a result set. Once we use this option, the results will be provided in an associative array. Next, we check the availability of a matching attachment and use the result set to define the attachment URL and directory path.

Here's one way to write the file download code:

```
$file_mime_type = mime_content_type( $file_dir );
if( $file_mime_type != '' ){
  header( 'Cache-Control: public' );
  header( 'Content-Description: File Transfer' );

  if( isset( $attachments[0]['uploaded_file_name'] ) &&
$attachments[0]['uploaded_file_name'] != '' ){
    header( 'Content-disposition:
attachment;filename='.$attachments[0]['uploaded_file_name'] );
  }else{
    header( 'Content-disposition: attachment;filename='.basename( $file_dir
) );
  }
  header( 'Content-Type: '. $file_mime_type );
  header( 'Content-Transfer-Encoding: binary' );
  header( 'Content-Length: '. filesize( $file_dir ) );
  readfile( $file_dir);
  exit;
}
```

First, we use the file directory path to get the mime type of the file as it's important to keep the integrity of the downloaded file. When the mime type is not empty, we use the necessary PHP headers for file downloading. We uploaded the files with a dynamic name containing a number value based on time. It's not ideal to let users download a file with such a name. Therefore, we use the conditional check to add the original file name stored in our custom table. We revert to using the base name of the file when the original file name is not available in the database. The rest of the code contain the usual PHP headers for file downloads and the readfile function to output the file content. Now, we have completed the functionality of the plugin. You should be able to download the attachments from the list that's displayed after the post content.

Handling plugin version upgrades

The version upgrade process is handled by the built-in upgrader_process_complete hook. We can implement this hook to add whatever data changes are required for the upgrade. We don't have a built-in upgrading event that can handle both plugins from the WordPress directory as well as custom plugins. Therefore, we have to build a custom upgrade process by using one of the existing hooks and conditional checks.

As we have already discussed, the WordPress plugin directory offers an automatic upgrade process. The custom plugins won't have such features by default. Therefore, we need to build an automatic upgrade process for the custom plugin. Many custom plugins don't have such features and hence we have considered such an implementation beyond the scope of this chapter. In such a scenario, users will have to either deactivate the current version and upload the new version or replace the current version files with a new version. So, the upgrade process needs to happen in the initial request after the file's replacement.

Consider the following code, where we used the `wp_loaded` action to handle the upgrade process of this plugin:

```
add_action( 'wp_loaded', 'wpqpa_upgrade_process' );
function wpqpa_upgrade_process(){
  $default_headers = array('Version' => 'Version');
  $plugin_data = get_file_data( __FILE__, $default_headers, 'plugin' );
  $stored_version = get_option('wpqpa_version');
  $current_version = $plugin_data['Version'];
  if ( !$stored_version && $current_version ) {
    update_option( 'wpqpa_version', $plugin_data['Version'] );
  }
  if ( version_compare($current_version, $stored_version ) >= 0 ) {
    update_option( 'wpqpa_max_upload_limit',20 );
  }
  update_option( 'wpqpa_version', $plugin_data['Version'] );
}
```

First, we use the `wp_loaded` hook with a callback function since all of the plugins are loaded when executing this hook. Then, we need to compare whether we are using the old version or the new version of the plugin. So, we grab the current version from the plugin header comments and the stored version from the database. Next, we check if the version is already stored in the database. The unavailability of the version in the database means that we are installing the plugin for the first time and hence we update the version.

The next step is comparing the two versions and seeing if the current version is higher than the installed version. In such a case, we can execute the tasks of the upgrade process. If these values are he same, the version hasn't changed and there is no need for the upgrade process. In this example, we are adding a default value for a new setting. In real world implementations, we can execute tasks such as changing existing data, adding new settings data, and adding database tables or columns.

Handling plugin deactivation

This event is handled by the built-in `register_deactivation_hook` function. The use of this function is similar to the activation hook. This plugin contains basic features and hence we can't find a suitable practical use of the deactivation hook. Therefore, we will not be implementing this event for this plugin.

Uninstalling the plugin to clean the resources

There's a big difference between deactivating and uninstalling a plugin. Cleaning resources should only be done upon deactivation. WordPress provides two methods for implementing the uninstallation process. The first method is using a built-in function called `register_uninstall_hook` to handle the uninstall process. This works similar to the technique we used in activation, through a callback function. The second method is using a file called `uninstall.php` inside the root folder of the plugin. In this plugin, we are going to use the latter technique with the `uninstall.php` file.

 You can view more details about the other technique at `https://developer.wordpress.org/reference/functions/register_uninstall_hook/`.

First, we have to create a file called `uninstall.php` inside the `wpquick-post-attachments` plugin directory. This file runs automatically when deleting the plugin from the plugins section. We can include the code for the uninstallation process directly inside the plugin. This is a basic plugin and hence we only need to delete the plugin-specific settings and custom tables that were created for the plugin. Let's take a look at the implementation of the `uninstall.php` file inside the plugin:

```php
<?php
global $wpdb;
if (!defined('WP_UNINSTALL_PLUGIN')) {
  die;
}
delete_option('wpqpa_version');
$wpdb->query("DROP TABLE IF EXISTS {$wpdb->prefix}wpqpa_post_attachments");
```

First, we need to check the availability of the `WP_UNINSTALL_PLUGIN` constant. This constant is set by WordPress in the process of uninstalling the plugin. If the constant is not available, the request could be an invalid one trying to delete the plugin data. Once the constant is set, we can implement the resource cleaning process. In this scenario, we have deleted the plugin version from the `wp_options` table and the whole `wp_wpqpa_post_attachments` table.

We have completed the simple plugin planned for this chapter by covering the functionality in each life cycle event. Usually, developers often consider the functionality and activation events of a plugin. However, upgrading and uninstalling events are critical in plugin development and hence you must use them with extra caution. Unless these events are handled properly, upgrading can break the entire site's functionality while uninstalling can leave a substantial amount of unused data.

Identifying the advantages of custom plugin development as a developer

WordPress has captured over 35% of sites and the enormous plugin base is continuing to grow at a rapid pace. So, site owners can find existing plugins to build whatever they want. Developers might consider this a risk, since WordPress sites can be built without a developer. This is partially true as the need for basic level developers are declining. On the other hand, the need for quality WordPress developers are emerging more than ever. In this section, we are going to focus on how custom plugin development is important for you as a developer. Let's take a look at the advantages of developing custom plugins:

- **Reusability in many projects**: Among WordPress developers, a higher percentage of development is done for individual clients for site-specific requirements. Therefore, you may feel that you can add features anywhere you want, as it's not going to change over time. However, you can separate non-project-specific features into separate plugins and use them for multiple clients to build rapid and cost-effective solutions.
- **Performance and security**: There are some tools and techniques to measure the performance and security of WordPress plugins. However, the process is not perfect and we won't have time to check each and every piece of code in existing plugins. So, we have no choice other than use existing plugins without knowing the risks. In sites where performance and security is a top priority, custom plugin development is the best solution as you are aware of the security and performance concerns and could improve upon them.

- **Build a community for your profile and work**: In my personal experience, developing a plugin and releasing it to the public for free is the ideal method for exposing you as a developer to the world. There are millions of websites that require developers. However, there are also thousands of developers who are capable of building WordPress solutions. So, this is the ideal way to reach thousands of people that require developers and find potential clients on the way. You will also get other benefits as a substantial amount of people will be discussing your work and help you fix these issues.

- **Generating a consistent income source**: Premium plugin development has become a major business with the evolution of WordPress in recent years. There are developers who have made millions of dollars developing plugins in their spare time and selling them on their own. So, developing plugins could be an ideal solution for making a living without depending on a few clients or needing to find new clients every day.

- **Eliminate the concern of version updates**: This is a major concern for most site owners as they use the services of freelance developers and hence the developer is not available at the stage of upgrading. No matter whether it's free or premium, existing plugins will always release updated versions with more features and fixes. On one hand, upgrading without the proper knowledge is a risk as it could break the existing features. On the other hand, not upgrading could be a security risk. We don't have this concern in custom development, where you build site-specific plugins. Once the site is completed, you don't need to release a new version of the plugin, that is unless you want to add more features or find an incompatibility with WordPress versions.

- **Provides flexibility and consistency in design**: Most basic to intermediate level WordPress sites are built by using existing plugins. The issue with using existing plugins is the flexibility and inconsistency in design. Most plugins are developed for common purposes. Therefore, the design is either very basic to suit any site or fixed without much flexibility. So, using any number of plugins means that the elements generated from plugins will be completely different to the design of the theme. This leads to the tedious process of plugin customization to make the design consistent. On the other hand, custom plugins can be designed to match the theme of the site and keep the consistency of design. Therefore, you can develop custom plugins when it's cost-effective compared to the customization of existing plugins.

These advantages are only a few among the dozens of direct and indirect benefits. You should read WordPress-related blogs and explore the work of popular developers to understand the capacity and potential of plugin development.

Guidelines for building quality plugins

Up until this point, we have looked at the process of building simple plugins with the recommended practices. Most of you will be developing WordPress sites for individual clients and hence the plugins you develop will not have to go through a verification process for quality. However, it's important to build extendable and maintainable plugins that are to be compatible with WordPress version upgrades as well as other third-party plugins. On the other hand, if you are developing plugins for the WordPress plugin directory or premium plugin marketplace, you will have to go through an extensive verification and review process for both the code and features. So, the quality of the plugin needs to match the minimum quality standards.

Let's take a look at some of the common guidelines for building quality WordPress plugins, apart from the need to follow WordPress coding standards:

- **Using built-in WordPress functions**: This is a common problem in WordPress development where developers tend to create their own functions due to a lack of knowledge in WordPress. The power of WordPress comes from its existing modules and hence we should always use the existing functions rather than create our own functions. Also, the existing functions are optimized and coded by expert WordPress developers and hence there is less chance of generating bugs or compatibility issues.

- **Using the necessary hooks in existing features**: Certain hooks are used in core features to let developers customize and extend their functionality. If you are implementing or modifying a core feature, you should include the necessary hooks so that solutions created by other developers are compatible with your solution.

- **Always load built-in libraries**: There can be dozens of plugins inside a single site and often some of these plugins require the same libraries, such as jQuery. So, one developer may build the solution for a specific jQuery version and another one could build for a different version. Including multiple versions of the same library often leads to conflicts. Therefore, you should always check if the library is available within the WordPress core and load the built-in version by using the recommended hooks.

- **Use plugin-specific prefixes**: When working with plugins that come from multiple developers, there is a high chance of generating conflicts in both code as well as data. So, we should always add a unique prefix to our plugin. We should use this prefix on function names, class names, constants, database tables, and even plugin-specific data in common tables such as `wp_options`, `wp_postmeta`, and `wp_usermeta`. However, most of the modern plugins follow the object-oriented style, and hence you may not need to use the prefix for function names.

- **Use hooks for extendable features**: You might be developing a plugin with common solutions after complete research of the requirements. But, more often than not, clients will ask for customization's in all parts in your code. So, it's better to keep your code as open as possible for future changes. Therefore, you should always use filters for values which might change and use actions for places where the process or template can be extended.

These are some of the well-known and recommended guidelines. As you gain experience with plugin development, you can add a lot more guidelines to the preceding list based on user feedback and how other plugins work. Make sure that you use these guidelines as much as possible and release the plugin to the public whenever possible.

Summary

Plugins can be considered the most important aspect of WordPress when it comes to custom development. If we discard the existing plugin base, WordPress will be a just another CMS without major attention from users or developers. As a developer, it's important to know the ins and outs of plugin development to survive in the growing WordPress community. Due to this, in this chapter, we looked at the role of plugins in development by discussing common plugin-related tasks. We chose popular plugins to explain different types of plugins and how they interact with WordPress sites. Next, we looked at the process of creating a basic plugin for WordPress. Most beginner developers are capable of building solutions with PHP and integrating the solution as a WordPress plugin. However, plugins created without the knowledge of complete life cycle events can turn into a nightmare at later stages of the project. Therefore, we looked at the life cycle events of a WordPress plugin and the functionality of each event. Next, we built a WordPress plugin to attach files to posts and let users download them from the frontend. In the process, we covered life cycle events, data validation, sanitization, use of metaboxes, and the concept of nonces. Finally, we looked at the common guidelines for building quality plugins and how plugin development can benefit you as a WordPress developer.

In `Chapter 5`, *Extending Plugins with Addons, Filters, and Actions*, we will be looking at advanced plugin concepts as well as customizing existing popular plugins.

Extending Plugins with Addons, Filters, and Actions

5

uilding sites with WordPress involves using existing plugins or creating your own plugins. You should be able to extend existing plugins with new features as well as make your plugins extendable for other developers. We use addons to extend the functionality of a core plugin. So, it's important to keep your plugins extendable so that you can later use addons to add or remove functionality. On the other hand, using and customizing existing plugins with addons allows you to provide low-cost and quality solutions. So, you need to master the techniques of building addons for customizing plugin features as well as integrating multiple plugins.

In this chapter, we explain the importance of addons while following the step-by-step guide to creating an addon for a plugin. WordPress uses a hook-based architecture and hence the built-in hooks are executed in a predefined sequence. We look at the proper execution of these hooks to prevent unnecessary conflicts. Then, we move into customization techniques for plugins while learning the advance uses of script loading and built-in AJAX features. We will be developing a product files addon for WooCommerce, in order to practically experience the customization process. Finally, we integrate the WooCommerce, MyCred, and BuddyPress plugins to learn the best practices of plugin integrations and their limitations.

In this chapter, we will cover the following topics:

- Introduction to addons development
- Creating a basic addon for the post attachments plugin
- Understanding the WordPress core action execution process
- Customizing third-party plugins
- Identifying techniques for integrating plugins
- Integrating multiple plugins for continuous workflow

By the end of this chapter, you will have the ability to customize third-party plugins using different techniques, and integrate multiple plugins to build a continuous workflow for your site.

Technical Requirements

You will be required to have WordPress 4.9.8 installed to follow this procedure. Even if you have a later version of WordPress, the described examples should work with no significant problems.

The code files of this chapter can be found on GitHub:
`https://github.com/PacktPublishing/WordPress-Development-Quick-Start-Guide/tree/master/Chapter05`

Check out the following video to see the code in action:
`http://bit.ly/2Q8LtBa`

Introduction to addons

In general terms, addons are components that change the behavior of a core component. As a developer, you might be familiar with using browser extensions to support development tasks. In such a scenario, the web browser acts as the core component and the extensions act as the addons that install on top of the web browser. The addons in WordPress follows the same concept. However, WordPress addons itself are plugins that change the behavior of a main plugin. Unlike browser extensions, addons in WordPress don't install on top of a plugin. Instead, they act as separate addon plugins.

Usually, addons are used to add new features to the core component. However, WordPress addons are developed to add, change, or remove features of a core component. Let's take a look at some of the popular plugins with a large addons base:

- **WooCommerce**: This is an eCommerce plugin that allows you to sell physical goods as well as digital products. This plugin has an extensive addons base of over 250 addons in various categories. Payment gateways are the most popular type of addon in WooCommerce with over 75 addons. You can view and learn more about the addons base at `https://woocommerce.com/product-category/woocommerce-extensions/`.

- **Easy Digital Downloads**: This is an eCommerce solution allowing you to sell digital products. This plugin also offers over 100 addons while many of them fall into the marketing category. You can learn more about the addons base at `https://easydigitaldownloads.com/downloads/`.

- **WP Bakery Page Builder**: This is a plugin used for building page using pre-built components. Both WooCommerce and Easy Digital Downloads are free plugins in the WordPress plugin directory. However, this is a premium-only plugin with over 250 addons in various categories. The UI elements is the most popular addon category for this plugin. You can view and learn more about the addons base at `https://wpbakery.com/addons/`.

hese are some of the plugins with a large addons base. The existence of addons means that the plugin is coded with necessary hooks for future extension. You can check more popular free and premium plugins to check the availability of addons. Also, you should check the role of each addon and how it interacts with the main plugin. Once you explore different types of addons, you will understand the types of hooks needed in development and how to add them to keep the code open for extension.

Creating addons for plugins

The process of creating addons is similar to the process we used for plugins. However, the possibility of creating an addon depends on the quality of the code in the core plugin. The core plugin should either provide an API to build addons or necessary hooks for extension. As many plugins don't contain a separate API, most addons are built by using the existing hooks. Let's see how we can create an addon for the post attachments plugin created in the previous chapter. Assume that we have the following requirements to be developed as an addon:

- Restrict attachment file types based on default WordPress user roles. Let's provide PDF file access only for non-subscriber members and all other file types to all users in the site.
- Download counter for attachments. We have to count the number of downloads for all attachments of a post, separately for guest users and logged-in users.

In order to implement such requirements without touching the core plugin files, we need to check the availability of any hooks within the plugin. Unfortunately, we don't have any hooks within the plugin, as it was not planned for future extension. So, we have to make the plugin extendable, by adding the necessary hooks.

Adding a filter hook for restricting attachments

Implementing attachment restrictions requires us to conditionally check the user permissions and hide the attachment for unauthorized users. So, we need a filter that can modify the output of attachments in list. Let's add a filter to the file list code inside `wpqpa_file_attachment_list`. We need to replace the following code:

```
$display .= '
    <div class="wpqpa-file-item" id="PF'.$file_row->id.'"  data-file-
id="'.$file_row->id.'" >
        <div class="wpqpa-file-item-row"     >
            <div class="wpqpa-file-item-name wpqpa-files-list-name"
>'.$file_row->file_name.'</div>
            <div class="wpqpa-file-item-download" ><a href="'.$url.'"
>'.__("Download","wpqpa").'</a></div>
            <div class="wpqpa-clear"></div>
        </div>
        <div class="wpqpa-clear"></div>
    </div>';
```

First, you should remove the preceding code and add the following code to the same location:

```
$file_display = '
  <div class="wpqpa-file-item" id="PF'.$file_row->id.'" data-file-
id="'.$file_row->id.'" >
    <div class="wpqpa-file-item-row" >
      <div class="wpqpa-file-item-name wpqpa-files-list-name"
>'.$file_row->file_name.'</div>
      <div class="wpqpa-file-item-download" ><a href="'.$url.'"
>'.__("Download","wpqpa").'</a>            </div>
      <div class="wpqpa-clear"></div>
    </div>
    <div class="wpqpa-clear"></div>
  </div>';

$file_display = apply_filters('wpqpa_post_attachment_list_item',
$file_display, $file_row);
$display .= $file_display;
```

Instead of directly adding each file HTML code to the `$display` variable, we use a custom filter called `wpqpa_post_attachment_list_item` with file details passed as a parameter. This filter allows us to modify the HTML for each file before it's delivered to the browser.

Adding an action hook for counting downloads

In the preceding section, we looked at the process of using filter hooks to extend plugins. We can also use action hooks to extend plugins through addons. The process of counting downloads should be initialized just after the user clicks the **Download** link and before the file download popup is shown on the browser. So, we need an action hook within those two events. Let's modify the `wpqpa_file_attachment_download` function to include a new action, as shown in the following code:

```
$file_mime_type = mime_content_type( $file_dir );
if( $file_mime_type != '' ){
  do_action('wpqpa_before_download_post_attachment',$attachments[0]);
  header( 'Cache-Control: public' );
  header( 'Content-Description: File Transfer' );
```

The highlighted line shows the modifications added to the existing code. This action allows us to implement additional features before the file is sent to the browser as a download. Now, we have the necessary hooks to create the addon and implement the features.

Creating the attachments addon

As usual, we have to start by creating a plugin directory with a main plugin file, and inserting the header comments to define it as a plugin. We are not going to repeat the code in this section. You can find a directory and files for attachments addon inside the `wpquick-attachments-addon` directory in source codes. We are going to start the development by restricting the PDF files to users with a subscriber role. Let's implement the `wpqpa_post_attachment_list_item` filter we added in the previous section:

```
add_filter( 'wpqpa_post_attachment_list_item',
'wpqaa_post_attachment_list_item' , 10 ,2 );
function wpqaa_post_attachment_list_item( $display, $file_data ){
  $upload_dir = wp_upload_dir();
  $file_dir = $upload_dir['basedir'] . $file_data->file_path;
  $file_mime_type = mime_content_type( $file_dir );

  if($file_mime_type == 'application/pdf'){
    if( !is_user_logged_in() || ( is_user_logged_in() &&
current_user_can('subscriber') ) ) ){
      $display = '';
    }
  }
  return $display;
}
```

Here's what this code does:

1. The callback function has two parameters, with the first one being the HTML for displaying the file link and the second one being the details about the file from database.
2. First, we construct the path of the file by using the WordPress `wp_upload_dir` function and file path captured from our custom table.
3. Then, we use the PHP `mime_content_type` function to get the MIME type of the attachment.
4. Next, we filter the files with the MIME type for PDF.
5. Then, we use the condition to check whether the file should be displayed to the user. The first part of the condition checks if we are logged into the site, as the file needs to be restricted for guest users. The second part of the condition checks if the user is logged in as a subscriber.
6. We restrict the file by emptying the content when one of these conditions is met.

Now, we have implemented one of the addon features using a filter hook. Next, we can implement our second requirement for counting downloads using an action hook. Let's implement the custom `wpqpa_before_download_post_attachment` action using the following code:

```
add_action( 'wpqpa_before_download_post_attachment',
'wpqaa_before_download_post_attachment' );
function wpqaa_before_download_post_attachment( $data ){
  $post_id = $data['post_id'];
  if( is_user_logged_in() ){
    $count = get_post_meta( $post_id, 'wpqaa_member_download_count',true );
    update_post_meta( $post_id, 'wpqaa_member_download_count', $count + 1);
  }else{
    $count = get_post_meta( $post_id, 'wpqaa_guest_download_count', true );
    update_post_meta( $post_id, 'wpqaa_guest_download_count', $count + 1 );
  }
}
```

First, we define the action with a callback function, `wpqaa_before_download_post_attachment`. The attachment data received from the `wp_wpqpa_post_attachments` table is passed as an array type parameter to this function. We use a conditional check to filter the logged in users and guest users. Our requirement is to count the total downloads for attachments of a single file. So, we can use the `wp_postmeta` table to store the download count.

In actual implementations, we may need to count the downloads for individual attachments, instead of the total count for all attachments in a post. In such a scenario, we can't use the `wp_postmeta` table as we can only store data based on post ID. So, we need to have an additional column in the `wp_wpqpa_post_attachments` table to keep and display the download counts for each attachment.

We can get the existing download count for a post using the `get_post_meta` function. Here, we use two keys called `wpqaa_member_download_count` and `wpqaa_guest_download_count` to separate the counts for guests and members. Later, we can use these keys to display the counts along with files.

In just a few lines of code, we have an addon that adds functionality to the core plugin and works independently. So, developing addons for any plugin is simple. However, the core plugin needs to provide the correct actions and filters, as well as developers being capable of finding the appropriate hooks.

The WordPress action execution process

Up to this point, we used some of the built-in actions and filters, while explaining the practical uses. However, you might be still trying to grab the concept, as it's not a practice used in pure PHP development. The process gets even tougher when coping with the lack of knowledge in the action execution process.

What is the action execution process?

WordPress has a set of built-in actions that are executed within the loading process of each and every request. Each of these actions has a sepcific responsibility in the loading process. The actions used for the loading process are executed in a predefined sequence. However, The WordPress Codex specially mentions that we shouldn't rely entirely on the loading process as it can vary based on the other components in the site.

This list may show only the first time each action is called, and in many cases no function is hooked to the action. Themes and plugins can cause actions to be called multiple times and at differing times during a request. This list should be viewed as a guideline or approximation of the WordPress action execution order, and not a concrete specification.

Implementing features using these actions without considering the sequence can often lead to conflicts. In WordPress, execution of these actions in the admin page requests differs from a typical page request. So, we have to be aware of both the frontend action execution process as well as the backend action execution process.

The frontend action execution process

The frontend action execution process starts with the `muplugins_loaded` action, which fires after the must-use and network-activated plugins are completed loading. The process completes by executing the `shutdown` action. There are 40+ actions called in a typical request, where some of them have higher importance in the development tasks. However, some of these actions change based on the request, and hence we can only use this as guidance. Let's take a look at the following illustration to understand the general actions and the order of execution:

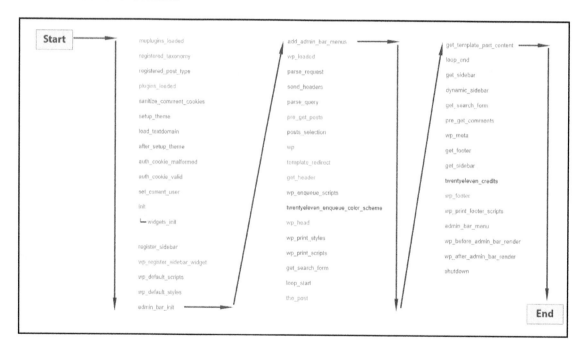

Let's understand the illustration of the loading process. The process begins with the `muplugins_loaded` action and moves downwards until it reaches the `admin_bar_init` action. Then, it starts from the `add_admin_bar_menus` action in the second column and moves downward, and so on. We have highlighted some of the actions used frequently in development. You can learn more about the action execution process at `https://codex.wordpress.org/Plugin_API/Action_Reference`. The order of execution of these actions is very important in custom development, especially when we use the built-in global objects of WordPress.

First, we are going to create a new plugin called **WPQAL Action Loading**, to test the functionality when loading specific actions. The process of creating the plugin is same as the one used in previous occurrences. Therefore, you can check the source codes directory of this chapter to find the implementation for the WPQAL Action Loading plugin. Let's use the preceding illustration and some practical usage scenarios to understand the importance of proper use of actions.

Scenario 1 – Using parent plugin features

This is commonly used in addon development, as we rely on the features of the main plugin. In addon development, we have to use constants, functions, classes, global objects from the main plugin. Unless we use the proper WordPress actions, these features may not be accessible within the addon. Assume that we have an addon plugin that gets loaded before the parent plugin. We can think of the **WPQPA Post Attachments** plugin as the main plugin and WPQAL Action Loading as the addon plugin to check this scenario. The WPQPA Post Attachments plugin is loaded after WPQAL Action Loading plugin. So, we can add the following line of code to main file of WPQAL Action Loading plugin and check the output by refreshing the browser:

```
echo WPQPA_PLUGIN_URL;exit;
```

This is the constant used to define the plugin path of the **WPQPA Post Attachments** plugin and hence it should print the actual path to the browser. Instead, the output will be `WPQPA_PLUGIN_URL`, as string. The problem is we are trying to access a constant not defined when we are trying to access it. So, we need to access such constants, functions, variables when all plugins have completed the loading process. We can refer to the image and find an action called `plugins_loaded`. This action is executed after WordPress has completed loading all active plugins. So, let's take a look at the proper implementation of the preceding code to print the plugin path:

```
add_action( 'plugins_loaded', 'wpqal_plugins_loaded_action' );
function wpqal_plugins_loaded_action() {
  echo WPQPA_PLUGIN_URL;
```

```
}
```

Now, you should see the correct plugin path printed to the browser. You can uncomment the code for *Scenario 1* in the WPQAL Action Loading plugin to test the scenario. To access features from other plugins, we must use `plugins_loaded` or a later action.

Scenario 2 – Accessing the WordPress post object

Usually, we can use the WordPress global `$post` object in the post details page to get the necessary information about a post. Let's assume we want to get the ID of the loaded post within a plugin function to execute some tasks. Let's use the `init` action to print the post ID to the browser while accessing an individual post:

```
add_action( 'init', 'wpqal_init_action' );
function wpqal_init_action() {
  global $post;
  print_r($post->ID);exit;
}
```

We expect the post ID to be printed on the browser. However, we will get an empty output as the `$post` object is not loaded at this stage. So, we have to use an action executed later in the loading process. The global `$post` object is only accessible in the `wp` action and the actions executed afterward. Use the following code to test the process:

```
add_action( 'wp', 'wpqal_wp_action' );
function wpqal_wp_action() {
  global $post;
  print_r($post->ID);exit;
}
```

Now, you can see the ID printed to the browser. You can also test the process by using the actions between `init` and `wp` in the loading process.

Scenario 3 – Accessing the WordPress query object

WordPress executes many database queries in the process of loading a certain post, page or screen. In development, we might need to access the details of the query such as query variables, conditions, and even the complete `sql` query generated from WordPress functions. So, we use the global `$wp_query` variable to access query details as well as make necessary modifications before execution.

Let's try to access the $wp_query variable using the pre_get_posts action that gets executed after the query variable object is created:

```
add_action( 'pre_get_posts', 'wpqal_pre_get_posts_action' );
function wpqal_pre_get_posts_action( $query ) {
  global $wp_query;
  print_r($wp_query);
}
```

Once the post is refreshed, you will see the details of the $wp_query variable with some parameters. But, most of the query conditions and queries are not set at this stage. Even though the query variable object is created, the actual query is not executed at this stage. This action allows us to make the modifications to the query using the $query variable passed to the function. Let's use an action executed later in the process to check the $wp_query details using following code:

```
add_action( 'wp', 'wpqal_wp_action' );
function wpqal_wp_action() {
  global $wp_query;
  print_r($wp_query);
}
```

Now, you will see the complete $wp_query variable with all the query parameters, conditions, and actual SQL queries.

As we experienced in these three scenarios, the action loading process plays a major role in development. We need to use the proper action hooks to access built-in WordPress variables as well as execute certain core WordPress functions. The method of identifying which hook to be used for certain features may not be straightforward. You can define the necessary actions and print the details to the browser without using the exit statements. Then you will see the action execution process and which action is responsible for handling each WordPress built-in variable and method.

The backend action execution process

The backend action execution process starts with the muplugins_loaded action, which fires after the must-use and network-activated plugins are completed loading. The process completes by executing the wp_dashboard_setup action, instead of the shutdown action.

There are six more actions in the backend execution process, compared to the frontend process. Let's take a look at the following image to understand the actions and the order of execution:

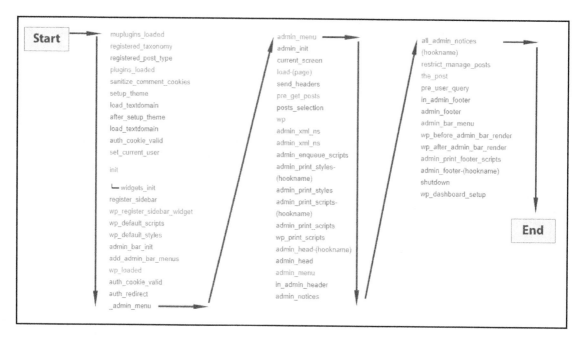

As you can see, the initial part of the loading process is similar to the frontend process. Then, we see some admin-related actions executed for menus, styles, and header sections. So, you can use the same technique we used earlier to understand the execution of each action, its responsibility, and when we should use them.

How to use the priority of actions and filters

We learned the action loading process and how it should be used to grab the proper data and execute the core features. However, developers may still get into trouble, even after knowing the loading process. This is due to the priority of executing actions. As we discussed, these actions can be executed multiple times within a request by WordPress core, theme, as well as other plugins. So, the same action hook will be implemented with different priorities. Consider the following code for using the `pre_get_posts` action:

```
function wpqal_pre_get_posts_action1( $query ) {
    if ( !is_admin() && $query->is_main_query() ) {
        if ($query->is_search) {
            $query->set('post_type', 'post');
```

```
      }
    }
  }
add_action( 'pre_get_posts', 'wpqal_pre_get_posts_action1' );

function wpqal_pre_get_posts_action2( $query ) {
  if ( !is_admin() && $query->is_main_query() ) {
    if ($query->is_search) {
      $query->set('post_type', array( 'post', 'product' ) );
    }
  }
}
add_action( 'pre_get_posts', 'wpqal_pre_get_posts_action2', 20 );
```

In the first part, we use the `pre_get_posts` action to call the `wpqal_pre_get_posts_action1` function and restrict site search to only posts. However, another plugin executes the same action with higher priority number of 20 and changes the searchable post types to both posts and products. So, our implementation doesn't work as expected. So, it's important to consider the action loading process as well as priority when working on a site with many plugins. Before implementing a critical hook, you should check the use of the same hook in other plugins of the site and make sure to use the correct priority to avoid conflicts.

Identifying the extendable features of third-party plugins

As we already discovered in the *Creating addons for plugins* section, not all plugins are extendable. Even within extendable plugins, we have a low to high degree of extendibility in features. So, identifying the extendable features is not an easy task, especially when working with advanced plugins such as WooCommerce, BuddyPress, and bbPress.

In Chapter 3, *Designing Flexible Frontends with Theme Development*, we identified the extendable features of a theme by searching for built-in actions and filters. We can use the same process for plugins, unless each and every hook in the plugin is documented on the plugin site. Let's take a quick look at the extendable features of the popular WooCommerce plugin. Use the code editor to search actions and filters within the WooCommerce directory.

We are using WooCommerce 3.4.4 version, and we get 849 action executions and 1,553 filter executions. So, this means we have over 2,000 locations where we can customize the WooCommerce plugin. In the process of customization, we have to find the necessary hooks with the support of documentation, checking the code files and experiences shared by other developers in development communities such as StackOverflow.

The availability of hooks differentiates from one plugin to another. Sometimes, we find plugins with a limited amount of hooks and popular plugins with thousands of hooks. So, you have to master the process of identifying the hook and how it impacts the plugin to be successful in customizing any plugin.

Customizing third-party plugins

As developers, we prefer building our own solutions compared to using third-party solutions. The main reason for building our own solutions is to gain more control over the features as well as future enhancements. However, the main purpose of using WordPress is to develop rapid low-cost solutions with the use of existing features. It's obvious that you have to work on customizing third-patty plugins at some point in your development career. These third-party plugins are developed to provide standard solutions to common problems. Therefore, these plugins won't fit into the complete requirements of most sites. Often, we have to adapt these plugins by adding, changing, or removing features. In this section, we are going to look at the techniques and implementation of plugin customization using sample scenarios.

Techniques for customizing third-party plugins

As with themes, plugins consists of various types of common customization's. Most site owners and developers misunderstand the meaning of plugin customization. Often, they think of it as a process that completely changes the plugin to suit the needs of your site. However, we may only need a few style changes as the customization. Sometime,s we have quicker and simple ways to customize plugins compared to using advanced processes. So, it's important to understand the different types of customization's and techniques for implementing them. Let's go through some of the common types of customization's.

Customizing look and feel using styles

This is one of the frequently used customization's where you need all plugins to match the styles of the theme. We have three ways of applying style customization's for a plugin:

- **Using theme styles files**: We can add the styles to the `style.cs` file of theme theme and override the plugin styles. This method should be only used in the child theme, when there are minor style changes to the plugin.
- **Using a custom CSS plugin**: There are many existing CSS plugins that allows us to add dynamic custom styles to various parts of the site without needing to create CSS files. These plugins provide a settings section, where we can add the dynamic CSS to be stored in the database and loaded to the site. This technique can be used for minor style customizations of many plugins.
- **Using an addon plugin**: This is the recommended method to keep the styles changes independent from other plugins. In this method, we have to create a simple addon plugin and include a new CSS file. Then, we can override the plugin styles by using new styles for the same CSS classes. We have to use the dependency parameter of the `wp_register_style` function to include the plugin CSS file as a dependency, and load our CSS file after loading the plugin CSS file.

These are the common methods for changing the look and feel of a plugin. However, some plugins may provide you with a setting to add a dynamic plugin-specific CSS or settings to adjust the styles of different parts by modifying values.

Customizing the features with hooks

In the beginning of this chapter, we have seen that the execution of hooks isn't always trivial. WordPress is using hooks all over the place, and this can sometimes make things complex. However, in plugin customization, this solution helps a lot, and we will see the benefit of using such a solution.

We may have to use different plugins every day. So, it's impossible to learn each and every feature of the plugins we us on different projects. Instead, we can look for files or classes that implement the customized feature. Then, we can search for possible hooks that supports our customization. Once the necessary hooks are found, we implement them based on the guidelines. Implementing a hook makes sure that the complete process for the feature is executed. If hooks were not available, we have to go through complete plugin files and classes to identify the location for the customization's. Also, we have to go through follow-up code to check if it affects our customization or possible future modifications.

Let's consider an example from a popular WooCommerce plugin. Assume we want to execute certain code after the user completes product payment. So, we can just search for a payment success hook and its implementation. WooCommerce executes the `woocommerce_payment_complete` action after the payment. Therefore, we can implement it using the following code to execute any kind of custom code on completion of the payment:

```
add_action( 'woocommerce_payment_complete', 'wpaql_payment_complete' );
function wpaql_payment_complete( $order_id ){
  // Custom code
}
```

As you can see, within few lines of code, we have customized WooCommerce without spending too much time or getting in-depth knowledge of WooCommerce. Let's assume there are no such hooks in WooCommerce. In such a case, first we have to find the `WC_Order` class and the `payment_complete` function used to handle the payment process. Then, we have to go through each and every line of code within the `payment_complete` function to understand the location for the completion of payment. You can already see the difficulty in the second process compared to the method of using hooks. So, we should always look for possible hooks to customize the plugins. There are two types of feature customization's in plugin development:

- **Customizing existing features**: Sometimes, we want to change or remove the existing features of a plugin. In such cases, we can implement an existing hook and change existing data or settings using the parameters passed to the function. Sometimes, we may want to go one step further by completely changing a feature with our own implementation. In such a case, we can remove the existing hook using the built-in `remove_action` or `remove_filter` functions. Then, we add the same hook with our own implementation.
- **Adding new features**: In customization's, a high percentage of tasks are involved in adding new features, compared to modifying existing features. In this method, we implement the existing hooks similar to the previous section. However, we use our own code and add new features on top of existing features, rather than modifying the existing ones.

We discussed different types of customization's in plugins. In the next section, we are going to customize a plugin by implementing a real-world requirement.

Building the WooCommerce product file manager

The process of changing or adding a new feature using hooks is the most common type of customization for third-party plugins. These hooks allow us to build advanced features without spending much time. In this section, we are going to implement a real-world use case to understand the hook-based customization process in detail. So, we have chosen to customize WooCommerce.

 Assume we want to provide files related to each WooCommerce product. These files may contain product specifications, user guides, or any information related to the product. So, we need a way to upload these files while creating or editing a product. Then, we have to list them in the frontend product page as a separate tab. This might seem like an uphill task for developers not familiar with WooCommerce. However, the implementation is quite simple once we find out the necessary WooCommerce hooks. Also, another purpose of this implementation is to reuse the code from the post attachments plugin and learn the use of AJAX, instead of normal form submissions.

Let's start the implementation by creating a new plugin called **WQWPF Product Files** with the same process. You can find the plugin files inside the source codes directory for this chapter. Consider the initial code for the plugin:

```
register_activation_hook( __FILE__, 'wqwpf_activate' );
function wqwpf_activate(){
  global $wpdb,$wp_roles;
  $table_product_files = $wpdb->prefix . 'wqwpf_product_files';
$sql_product_files = "CREATE TABLE IF NOT EXISTS $table_product_files (
      id int(11) NOT NULL AUTO_INCREMENT,
      user_id int(11) NOT NULL,
      post_id int(11) NOT NULL,
      file_path longtext NOT NULL,
      updated_at datetime NOT NULL,
      uploaded_file_name varchar(255) NOT NULL,
      PRIMARY KEY (id)
    );";
  require_once( ABSPATH . 'wp-admin/includes/upgrade.php' );
  dbDelta( $sql_product_files );
}

if ( ! defined( 'WQWPF_PLUGIN_DIR' ) ) {
  define( 'WQWPF_PLUGIN_DIR', plugin_dir_path( __FILE__ ) );
}
if ( ! defined( 'WQWPF_PLUGIN_URL' ) ) {
  define( 'WQWPF_PLUGIN_URL', plugin_dir_url( __FILE__ ) );
```

```
    }

    add_action( 'plugins_loaded', 'wqwpf_plugins_loaded_action' );
    function wqwpf_plugins_loaded_action() {
      if( class_exists('WooCommerce')){
        // All actions and filters need to be added here
      }
    }
```

The initial part of the code is similar to the code we used in WPQPA Post Attachments plugin, with the exception of removing the `file_name` column from the custom table for product files. This will be an addon for WooCommerce and hence we need to check whether WooCommerce is activated before executing any addon functions. Therefore, we use the `plugins_loaded` action to check the availability of `WooCommerce` class. We can use constants, classes, or functions to check the availability of a core plugin. When `WooCommerce` class is available, we add all the actions and filters related to the addon, so that they are executed only when `WooCommerce` is available. Now, we can start building the required functionalities for customization.

Adding the file upload field to WooCommerce products

The first step in the development process is to provide an interface to let administrators upload files to products. We can implement this by using the metabox technique we used while building the post attachments plugin. However, we are trying to understand plugin customization and hence we are going to integrate this feature into WooCommerce. In the WooCommerce product creation screen, we can find a meta box called **Product Data** with various tabs such as **General**, **Inventory**, **Shipping** and so on. We are going to add a new tab to the meta box as **Product Files**. First, we have to look for actions or filters that let us modify the **Product Data** tabs. You can find a filter called `woocommerce_product_data_tabs` for customizing the tabs. Let's use the following code to add a new tab using this filter:

```
    add_filter( 'woocommerce_product_data_tabs', 'wqwpf_custom_product_tabs' );
    function wqwpf_custom_product_tabs( $tabs ) {
      $tabs['wqwpf_files'] = array(
            'label'      => __( 'Product Files', 'wqwpf' ),
            'target'     => 'wqwpf_file_options',
            'class'      => array( 'show_if_simple' ),
      );
      return $tabs;
    }
```

This filter is dependent on WooCommerce and hence the `add_filter` line should be placed inside the `wqwpf_plugins_loaded_action` function. The existing tabs are passed as a parameter to the callback function of this filter. We add a new tab with a unique key and assign the necessary options. The `target` setting contains the ID of the HTML element that is used to display the content for this tab. The tab content will be added in next stage. The `class` setting defines an array of classes assigned to this tab. Here, we have used `show_if_simple` as the class. So, our tab will be only visible for Simple WooCommerce products. We need to add more classes in case we want to make the tab available for other product types.

 In this scenario, we added a new tab. We can also use this filter to remove existing tabs by using the `unset` function on `$tab` array elements, or change the settings of existing tabs by using the proper array key.

The next step is adding a file field to the tab for uploading files. We can find another action hook called `woocommerce_product_data_panels` for adding tab content. Let's use it to add the file field, as shown in the following code:

```
function wqwpf_product_files_panel_content() {
  global $post;      ?>

  <div id='wqwpf_file_options' class='panel woocommerce_options_panel'>
    <div class='options_group'>
      <div id="wqwpf-product-files-msg"></div>
      <p class="form-field _wqwpf_product_files_field show_if_simple"
style="display: block;">
        <label for="_wqwpf_product_files"><?php _e('Product Files','wqwpf');
?></label>
        <input type="file" name="wqwpf_product_files"
id="wqwpf_product_files" />
        <input type="hidden" id="wqwpf_product_file_nonce"
name="wqwpf_product_file_nonce" />
        <input type="button" name="wqwpf_product_file_upload"
id="wqwpf_product_file_upload"  value="<?php echo __('Upload','wqwpf'); ?>"
/>
      </p>
    </div>
  </div>
    <?php
}
```

In this code, we have added a file field to upload files, a button to initialize the upload process, and a hidden field to keep the nonce value. The structure of the HTML is copied from the other available tabs. The most important part is understanding how this tab content connects with the tab we created earlier. We have used `wqwpf_file_options` as the ID of the main container for the tab. We used the same ID as the `target` setting for our new tab. So, once the tab is clicked, WooCommerce will use the target setting to find the container and display it to the user. The following screen previews the new tab after using the custom code:

The new tab for **Product Files** is added between the **Inventory** and **Shipping** tabs. Now, we are ready to start uploading files.

Adding scripts for uploading files

In `Chapter 4`, *Building Custom Modules with Plugin Development*, we created a plugin to upload attachments to posts. However, we had to select a file and upload files one by one while updating the post for each file. This is not ideal in situations where we have many files to be uploaded. Instead, we have to use AJAX and let the user upload multiple files without refreshing the browser. Before moving into the process of uploading files, we need to add the necessary scripts to the plugin. First, you have to create a new directory inside `wpquick-woo-product-files` as `js`, and create a new file called `wqwpf-admin.js`. Next, we can add the script to the plugins, as shown in the following code:

```
add_action( 'admin_enqueue_scripts', 'wqwpf_admin_load_scripts',9 );
function wqwpf_admin_load_scripts(){
  wp_register_script( 'wqwpf_admin_js', WQWPF_PLUGIN_URL . 'js/wqwpf-
admin.js', array('jquery') );
  wp_enqueue_script( 'wqwpf_admin_js' );
  $custom_js_strings = array(
      'AdminAjax' => admin_url('admin-ajax.php'),
      'Messages' => array('fileRequired' => __('File is
required.','wqwpf') ),
      'nonce' => wp_create_nonce('wqwpf-private-admin'),
  );
  wp_localize_script( 'wqwpf_admin_js', 'WQWPFAdmin', $custom_js_strings );
}
```

We can use the preceding code to learn some of the important techniques in script loading. Let's list the important parts of script loading:

- **Registering and enqueuing scripts**: Until this point, we only learned how to include CSS files. So, we can now move onto loading scripts with the `wp_register_script` function. Here, we are including a script in admin side and hence we have to use the `admin_enqueue_scripts` action to use a callback function for including scripts. The first line of the preceding code should be placed inside the `wqwpf_plugins_loaded_action` function, as it depends on the existence of WooCommerce. Inside the callback function, we can use the `wp_register_script` function to register a custom script for WordPress. The parameters of this function include a unique key for the script, a path to the script, and dependent script files. The script is only registered at this stage and not included in the browser. Then, we use `wp_enqueue_script` wherever we want to include the script to the browser using the key used in script registration.

- **Defining script dependencies**: We can define dependent scripts using the third parameter of the `wp_register_script` function. In this scenario, our script is coded using **jQuery**, and hence it's a dependency. So, we add jQuery as the key to dependency array. WordPress has a set of built-in scripts with specific keys. We need to use these keys without loading these libraries from our own plugins or external sources. The list of available script libraries can be found at `https://developer.wordpress.org/reference/functions/wp_register_script#core-registered-scripts`. You can use the key in the **Handle** column to load these dependencies. Once we define `script 2` as a dependency of `script 1`, the second script will be loaded before the first script. Apart from using core script files, we can also use custom script files as dependencies. Consider the following line of code:In this code, we are registering a script of another plugin with **jQuery** and `wpwpf_admin_js` scripts. So, both of these files will be loaded before loading the script with `upme_admin_js` as the handle.

```
wp_register_script( 'upme_admin_js', WQWPF_PLUGIN_URL . 'js/
wqwpf-admin.js',
array('jquery','wqwpf_admin_js') );
```

- **Localizing scripts**: Sometimes, we need to add necessary settings and dynamic data to specific scripts. WordPress allows us to add such data by using the `wp_localize_script` function. This function uses three parameters, starting with script handle, variable name, and the data. Once used, these data will be added inline to the browser, before loading the script file. Therefore, these data will be accessible within the specified script and the other scripts loaded after that defined script.

In this implementation, we are going to use AJAX, and hence we add the AJAX url to the script by using the `admin_url('admin-ajax.php')` function. More about AJAX will be discussed later in this section. Next, we add the necessary data using preferred array keys. Here, we are only adding messages as an array. We also add a nonce value to the script to verify the AJAX request from the server side. Once the page is loaded, you can use **View Source** option to check this data loaded before the `wqwpf_admin_js` script. Now, we have completed the script loading process and hence we can move into uploading product files.

Uploading files to products

In this section, we are going to upload files for products using AJAX requests. Before diving into AJAX, we need to complete the initial script with necessary data retrieval and validation. Add the following code to the `wqwpf-admin.js` file of our plugin:

```
jQuery(document).ready( function( $ ) {
  $('#wqwpf_product_file_upload').click(function(e){
      e.preventDefault();
      var file_form = $('#post');
      var file = file_form.find('#wqwpf_product_files').val();
      var post_id = $('#post_ID').val();
      var msg_container = file_form.find('#wqwpf-product-files-msg');
      msg_container.removeClass('wqwpf-message-info-
error').removeClass('wqwpf-message-info-success');

      var err = 0;
      var err_msg = '';
      if(file == '' ){
        err_msg += '' + WQWPFAdmin.Messages.fileRequired + '<br/>';
        err++;
      }
      if(err != 0){
        msg_container.html(err_msg).addClass('wqwpf-message-info-
```

```
error').show();
    }else{
        // AJAX request for uploading files
    }
  });
});
```

Here's what this code does:

1. First, we define a callback function for the `click` event of the **Upload** button, within the jQuery `ready` function.
2. Inside the `click` event, we need to capture the file and the post ID. We can't add our own form as the metabox is inside the WordPress form for creating posts. So, we use the form with the ID **post**, to capture the values of form fields.
3. Next, we retrieve the container element used to display messages and reset the CSS classes.
4. Then, we start the validation process for fields. Here, we have only filed field and hence checking for empty value is the only required validation.
5. Finally, we check for any errors and display the error message by adding the necessary CSS classes and enabling the message container.

In the previous section, we used the `wp_localize_script` function to add the data to the scripts. In this section, we are using it to add the error message using the following line:

```
WQWPFAdmin.Messages.fileRequired
```

In this line, `WQWPFAdmin` is the variable name we used earlier and `Messages` is the sub-key of the main array. The `fileRequired` option in the `Messages` array will contain the actual message. Similarly, we can access the other data using respective keys. Now, we need to implement the AJAX request when the validation is completed without errors. Before that, we are going to have a brief introduction to AJAX.

Introduction to AJAX in WordPress

AJAX is an abbreviation for Asynchronous JavaScript And XML. This technology allows us to sent and retrieve data without refreshing the browser. So, the execution of repetitive tasks such as multiple file uploading can be simplified by using AJAX. Usually, we use a direct URL to execute AJAX requests. However, WordPress offers a built-in interface for executing AJAX requests and it's recommended to use this technique without using our own AJAX handlers.

WordPress uses a file called `admin-ajax.php` for handling requests, and the file is located inside the `wp-admin` directory. This file contains the necessary code for built-in core AJAX requests as well as code for supporting custom requests through *actions*. The action is responsible for handling the AJAX request and providing the output. Let's consider the following code:

```
add_action( 'wp_ajax_sample_action', 'wqwpf_sample_action' );
add_action( 'wp_ajax_nopriv_sample_action', ' wqwpf_sample_action ' );
function wqwpf_sample_action(){
  // Get data from client side request, process and return the output
}
```

The preceding code defines how we should use AJAX in WordPress. Each different AJAX request has an action name. We have to use the `wp_ajax_{action name}` or `wp_ajax_nopriv_{action name}` action to define the handling function for each request. The action with the `wp_ajax` prefix is used for requests when the user is already logged into the site. The action with `wp_ajax_nopriv` is used for guest users of the site. So, you have to define one or both of these actions depending on who is allowed to execute the request.

Now, we have the basic knowledge about AJAX in WordPress and the method for handling the request from the server side. So, we can get back to the file uploading process by implementing the AJAX call to upload files. The following code should be added to the `else` statement of the `click` event in the `wqwpf-admin.js` file:

```
msg_container.html('').hide();
var formObj = file_form;
var formURL = WQWPFAdmin.AdminAjax+'?action=wqwpf_save_product_files';
var formData = new FormData();
var file_data = $('#wqwpf_product_files').prop('files')[0];

formData.append('post_id', post_id);
formData.append('file_nonce', WQWPFAdmin.nonce);
formData.append('file_data', file_data);
jQuery.ajax({
  url: formURL,
  type: 'POST',
  data:  formData,
  mimeType:'multipart/form-data',
  contentType: false,
  cache: false,
  dataType : 'json',
  processData:false,
  success: function(data, textStatus, jqXHR){

    if(data.status == 'success'){
```

Checking the impact with other plugins

Usually, we use at least a few plugins in every website, and some sites may contain dozens of plugins. Some of these plugins may have existing integrations between them. Let's assume we need to implement a new feature by integrating two or more plugins. In such scenarios, it's not sufficient to check the data, hooks, and integration points of those two plugins. We have to also check the impact by other existing plugins, or the impact on other existing plugins not involved in the integration.

Let's consider the same scenario discussed in the *Checking the feasibility of integrations* section. We integrated two plugins to redirect the user to a private page of the content restrictions plugin after login. Assume we have a third plugin not involved in the integration. This plugin is used to change the login redirection URL based on user role. Consider the following integration in the third plugin:

```
add_filter('wpquick_login_redirect_url','wpquick_user_role_redirect_url',20
);
function wpquick_user_role_redirect_url($url){
  // Get the role of the user being logged in
  if($role == 'subscriber'){
   $url = "Subscriber redirect URL";
  }
  return $url;
}
```

The URL modification hook in user role based redirection plugin has a higher priority value, and hence is executed later than the hook used in the previous scenario. Therefore, the logged-in user will be redirected to the user role specific page, instead of the private page of the content restrictions plugin. So, our integration completely falls apart.

We can prevent such issues by considering how other plugins use the data, and the hooks related to our integration process. In this scenario, we could prevent this situation by using a higher priority value for the hook in the first scenario:

```
add_filter('wpquick_login_redirect_url','wpquick_content_restriction_redire
ct_url',30);
```

This line of code is executed after the filter code in the role-based redirection plugin, and hence our integration works without issues. However, now you must also check how our integration affects the functionality of the role-based redirection plugin.

Implementing multiple plugin integrations

Up to this point, we looked at the methods used in plugin integrations and important considerations. Now, it's time to integrate a few plugins to understand their practical usage. We are going to integrate three popular plugins to illustrate the process. Let's identify the plugins used for this integration and their functionality:

- **WooCommerce**: This is the most popular eCommerce plugin. The main functionality is selling physical and digital goods. These days, it's also being used for selling services, bookings, and memberships by modifying the features through addons.
- **MyCred**: This is a point management plugin where you can allow users to earn points by doing various tasks in a site such as commenting, viewing content, publishing content, registering on the site, and so on. Then, you can reward these users by providing benefits with the use of these points.
- **BuddyPress**: This is a plugin used to build online communities in your site. The default features include user management, groups, messages, activities, friends, and notifications. Many people use this plugin to build mini-social networks.

Now, we can take a look at the requirement for integrating these three plugins.

Assume that we have a point system in our site using **MyCred**. Users can earn points through various tasks and spend those points to get wide range of benefits. In this scenario, we assume users only get points by purchasing products from the **WooCommerce** store. The points will be given for *completed orders* based on order value. Once the user reaches a specific number of points, the user will be added automatically to a private **BuddyPress** group.

Before starting the implementation, we need to create a new plugin called **WPQPI Plugin Integrations** in a new plugin directory called `wpquick-plugin-integrations`. The process for creating the main file and using header comments to define the plugin will be the same as previous scenarios.

Assigning points for completed orders

We have to start the implementation by connecting WooCommerce and MyCred plugins to award points for completed orders. First, we need to find the ways for tracking the completion of a WooCommerce order. The simplest way is to use a search engine to check the availability of **order complete hook**, or go through the documentation of the WooCommerce plugin. We can find an action called `woocommerce_order_status_completed` for handling tasks after the completion of order. Let's take a look at the implementation of order complete hook:

```
add_action( 'woocommerce_order_status_completed', 'wpqpi_payment_complete'
);
public function wpqpi_payment_complete( $order_id ) {
    // Execute code after the order is successfully completed
}
```

We can define the action using the `add_action` function with a specific callback function. The order ID is passed as a parameter to this function, and hence we can execute any tasks based on order details. The next task is to identify how we can add points in MyCred using custom code.

We have few tasks to be implemented before we can add points to orders. First, we have to add a new hook to enable points for WooCommerce orders. MyCred points are added through built-in and custom hooks. The available hooks can be viewed by visiting the **Points | Hooks** section in WordPress admin. You need to go through the MyCred documentation to find the necessary hooks for adding custom MyCred hooks. So, let's create a new hook for enabling points for WooCommerce orders:

```
add_filter( 'mycred_setup_hooks', 'wpqpi_woocommerce_hooks', 10, 2 );
function wpqpi_woocommerce_hooks( $installed, $point_type ) {
   $installed['wpqpi_woo_purchase'] = array('title' => __( 'Points for
WooCommerce Purchases', 'wpqpi' ), 'description'  => __( 'User will get
points for completing product purchases.', 'wpqpi' ), 'callback' => array(
'WPQPI_WooCommerce_Hooks' ) );
   return $installed;
}
```

The `mycred_setup_hooks` filter is used to add custom hooks to MyCred, or remove existing hooks. In this scenario, we add a new hook called `wpqpi_woo_purchase` for awarding points for WooCommerce purchases. The array defines the name of the hook, the description, and the PHP class to implement the point awarding procedure.

We have added a custom class called `WPQPI_WooCommerce_Hooks`. Once this code is added, you will see a new hook named **Points for WooCommerce Purchases** in the **Available Hooks** section. You can drag the hook to **Active Hooks** section to make it work, as shown in the following screenshot:

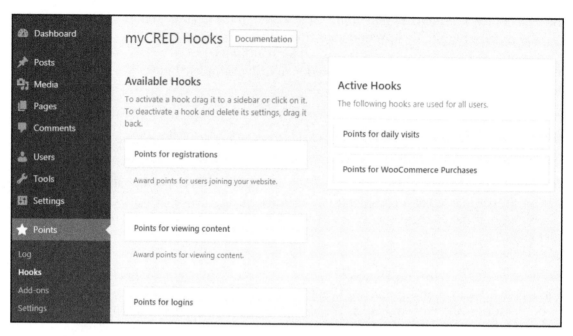

The next step is to implement the class to award points for WooCommerce purchases. So, we need to implement the `mycred_load_hooks` action to load the hook set up in the previous section. Let's take a look at the implementation of the `WPQPI_WooCommerce_Hooks` class inside the `mycred_load_hooks` action:

```
add_action( 'mycred_load_hooks', 'wpqpi_load_custom_taxonomy_hook', 10 );
function wpqpi_load_custom_taxonomy_hook() {
  class WPQPI_WooCommerce_Hooks extends myCRED_Hook {

    public function __construct( $hook_prefs, $type ) {
      parent::__construct( array(   'id'       => 'wpqpi_woo_purchase',
'defaults' => array( 'creds'   => 1,  'log'      => '%plural% for purchasing
a product' ) ), $hook_prefs, $type );
    }

  }
}
```

Inside the hook, we just define the class by extending the myCRED_Hook core class of MyCred plugin. Then, we add the class constructor with unique ID and default settings. The settings include the number of points awarded by default and the text for the log entry of awarding points. This class executes a built-in function called run, while loading the hooks. This will be the point of integration where we define the WooCommerce order completed hook. Let's see how we can implement the run function after the class constructor:

```
public function run() {
    add_action( 'woocommerce_order_status_completed', array( $this,
'wpqpi_payment_complete') );
}
```

We can define any number of actions in the loading process of the MyCred hook created earlier. Here, we have the woocommerce_order_status_completed action and the callback function ready to be executed on successful orders. Now, we can move into the process of awarding points by implementing the wpqpi_payment_complete function, as shown here:

```
public function wpqpi_payment_complete( $order_id ) {
    $order = wc_get_order( $order_id );
    $total = $order->get_total();
    $credits = (int) $total / 10;
    $user = $order->get_user();
    $user_id = $user->ID;
    $this->core->add_creds( 'wpqpi_woo_purchasing', $user_id, $credits,
$this->prefs['log'], 0, '', $m );
}
```

First, we use the $order_id parameter to load the order details using the wc_get_order function. Next, we get the order total by calling the get_total function on the $order object, and divide it by 10 to generate the number of MyCred points for the order. Next, we get the ID of the user who purchased the products by using the get_user function on the $order object. Finally, we call the MyCred add_creds function to add the points to the user for the order.

The add_creds function has three required parameters and some optional parameters. The first three parameters are used respectively for the reference ID, user ID, and number of points to be awarded. The other parameters are not important for the scenario used in this book. Now, the two plugins are integrated to award MyCred points to the user on successful WooCommerce order completion. We have used an event of one plugin to integrate with another plugin by modifying the data of the second plugin.

Adding users to BuddyPress private groups

In the previous section, we completed the first part of the integration with MyCred and WooCommerce. The next step is to complete the integration by connecting MyCred with BuddyPress groups. As we discussed, the requirement is to assign users to a BuddyPress private group once they reach specific number of MyCred points. So, we have to look for a way to add users to a BuddyPress group. We can either check for the documentation or use a search engine to find the appropriate implementation. BuddPress provides a function called `groups_join_group` to add users into a group. Let's use that function to modify the `wpqpi_payment_complete` function and add users to groups:

```
public function wpqpi_payment_complete( $order_id ) {
    // Existing code for adding MyCred points
    $balance = mycred_get_users_balance( $user_id );
    if($balance > 100){
      groups_join_group(1, $user_id);
    }
}
```

First, we use the built-in `mycred_get_users_balance` function to receive the available points of the user. Then, we call the BuddyPress `groups_join_group` function with the group ID and user ID once the user balance has reached the limit we specified.

 We have simplified the code in this scenario to illustrate the process of plugin integration. In an ideal scenario, we have to implement a lot more permission checks before we add a user to a group, and points to a user.

In this implementation, we only award points for WooCommerce orders, and the user can only use points to join the group. Therefore, we can implement the points checking process within the same function. When we award points for multiple tasks, this balance checking code needs to be implemented in all of these tasks.

Now, we have completed the integration and made three plugins work together for our requirements. Similarly, you can use existing hooks and functions to connect the necessary plugins for your requirements. However, I strongly recommend not to custom-integrate a large number of plugins in a single site, as it's hard to manage on plugin updates.

Summary

The process of customizing and extending plugins is crucial for building websites in a rapid process. So, we started extending plugins by creating an addon for the post attachments plugin developed in the previous chapter. Next, we looked at the WordPress core action execution process and its importance using sample scenarios. Then, we moved into the process of using various techniques for customizing plugins, while modifying WooCommerce product features. Finally, we looked at the different types of integrations between plugins, while integrating popular plugins to understand the process.

In Chapter 6, *Practical Usage of WordPress APIs*, we will be exploring the built-in WordPress APIs, while learning how to use them practically in plugin development.

Practical Usage of WordPress APIs

6

The use of application programming interfaces is common in modern websites. We use APIs such as Google Maps, Google Analytics, and Facebook to leverage the functionality of third-party services. Basically, APIs are created by developers to enable their features to other developers and platforms. Similarly, WordPress APIs let us use core features in a standard way to change and extend the functionality. We can also use these features to create our own APIs on top of WordPress and expose them to third-party services and platforms.

In this chapter, we are going to explore the available APIs, their functionality, and their use in development. We will be focusing more on three APIs that play a major role in custom development and yet have not been introduced in previous chapters. Developers often use WordPress shortcodes to provide pieces of reusable functionality, and the clients are familiar with using these shortcodes. So, we look into the techniques of creating shortcodes as well as identifying limitations. Next, we look at the importance of the Rewrite API in development tasks for building features without affecting the core features. Finally, we look at the REST API usage for enabling features to third-party developers through a standard interface.

In this chapter, we will cover the following topics:

- A brief overview of WordPress APIs
- Introducing Shortcode API
- Creating custom shortcodes
- Understanding the usage of shortcodes
- Managing custom routes with Rewrite API
- Building remote connections with REST API

By the end of this chapter, you should understand the API functions required for your development tasks. Also, you should be able to build reusable features with shortcodes and expose your features to third-party applications using REST API.

Technical Requirements

You will be required to have WordPress 4.9.8 installed to follow this procedure. Even if you have a later version of WordPress, the described examples should work with no significant problems.

The code files of this chapter can be found on GitHub:
`https://github.com/PacktPublishing/WordPress-Development-Quick-Start-Guide/tree/master/Chapter06`

Check out the following video to see the code in action:
`http://bit.ly/2EQa24y`

A brief overview of WordPress APIs

WordPress API is a set of sub APIs that works together, allowing developers to build on top of core features. The individual APIs cover one or more core features, while some of the APIs can be used beyond WordPress's core features. The REST API, Rewrite API. and Shortcode API are some of the ones we can use for WordPress's core features, as well as custom features. The use of WordPress APIs reduces your workload as a developer, compared to building your own functions. Let's take a look at the advantages of using APIs in WordPress:

- **Use of actions and filters**: WordPress API functions executes the necessary actions and filters within the process, allowing developers to customize the features. Using our own custom functions omits these actions and filters. Therefore, it will be difficult to combine or use many plugins together, as some of the plugins might be relying on these hooks within API functions.
- **Input validation and security**: The built-in API functions are developed and tested by the best WordPress developers in the world. Therefore, validation of the data and security in the process is highly reliable. Using custom built functions instead of API functions increases the workload of the developer to implement these security features and validations.
- **Efficiency**: The built-in API functions are optimized to provide better performance when interacting with database as well as working with core

Structure of a shortcode

In this section, we are going to understand WordPress shortcode by considering the perspective of different user types. As a developer, it's important to understand all the three user perspectives to build and use shortcodes in development tasks. Let's take a look at the following diagram:

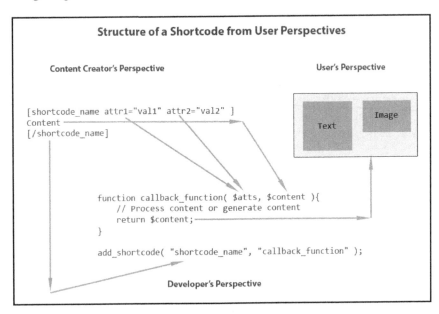

The preceding diagram is based on the three user perspectives involved in the process of using shortcodes.

 The use of content is optional for a shortcode. We can find many self-enclosing shortcodes that generate the output without using any content.

Let's understand each of these three user perspectives.

Developer's perspective of a shortcode

The developer is responsible for building the shortcode, unless you only plan to use the shortcodes available in the WordPress core. The shortcode needs to be created using the API functions and registered with WordPress using a plugin or theme. The preceding diagram shows the basic syntax of a shortcode from a developer's perspective.

Content creator perspective of a shortcode

Usually, the site administrator creates the content for most of the sites. However, you may also have other user roles or specific users with permission to create content. These users are responsible for using the shortcodes with necessary attributes and content in the site development process. The previous diagram illustrates the main syntax of a shortcode, where these users will use inside posts or pages.

They can use the shortcodes offered by WordPress core, theme, or plugins on the site. It's not a must for the content creator to know the source of the shortcode. However, the knowledge of whether a shortcode is generated from a theme, plugin, or WordPress core becomes handy in scenarios where you want to switch the theme or a plugin. Lack of knowledge in the source of the shortcode may lead to conflicts or even a complete breakdown of the site in such scenarios. These users are not aware of the source code of a shortcode, unless they want to explore the code inside theme or plugins.

User's perspective of a shortcode

The user is anyone who visits the site, including guests and members. They will only see the output generated from the shortcode. These users are not aware of the existence of a shortcode, as the shortcode is not visible on the browser view or the page source. Also, the shortcode output doesn't have any predefined IDs or classes, and hence it's not possible for these users to track a shortcode from the frontend.

Now you should have a basic idea of how WordPress shortcode is created and used to generate dynamic output. More details on the creation and use of a shortcode will be discussed in upcoming sections.

Using built-in shortcodes

WordPress core contains set of built-in shortcodes mainly focused on adding various content types to posts and pages. The content creators can use these shortcodes directly on posts, pages, or any supported location without the need for any modifications. Let's take a look at the existing shortcodes:

- **Audio**: It used for embedding and playing audio files
- **Caption**: It used for adding captions to content. Mainly used for images
- **Embed**: It used for embedding content from different sites supported by WordPress
- **Gallery**: It used for displaying image galleries by passing the image ID's

- **Video**: It used for embedding and playing video files
- **Playlist**: It used for displaying collection of audio and video files

As you can see, these shortcodes don't use the main data of a WordPress site, such as posts, comments, users. So, we will have to work with shortcodes from external plugins or create custom shortcodes to cater for the functionality involving the WordPress database.

Building custom shortcodes

The process of building custom shortcodes is not as complex as many people think. The minimal implementation of a shortcode requires only few lines of code as shown in the diagram in the last section. A shortcode consists of four main parts:

- **Opening and closing tags**: Opening and closing tags are similar to HTML, WordPress shortcodes have opening and closing tags using square brackets. These tags are used by content creators to add the functionality into posts or pages. On the other hand, developers need to use this `tag` to register a shortcode as a unique element. Some of the shortcodes don't have a closing tag and use a self-enclosing opening tag.
- **Attributes**: Attributes is a collection of data and settings required to process the functionality within the shortcode function and return the output. The list of attributes starts after the shortcode name in the opening tag. Each attribute has a key and values, as shown in the structure of a shortcode image. The attributes should be separated by one or more spaces. Inside the shortcode, developers can access the passed attributes using the array keys of the attributes variable.
- **Content**: Content is the content we add between the opening and closing tags of the shortcode. Once content is used, shortcode will act as a WordPress filter where we retrieve, process, and return the modified content. We can also define shortcodes without content by using a self-enclosing opening tag.
- **Output**: Output is the return value by the shortcodes based on the passed attributes and content. The output will be either content modified within the shortcode or the content will be used to capture and display site data. Many developers tend to print the shortcode output directly to the browser using PHP `echo` statements. However, shortcodes should always return the output instead of printing directly to the browser.

Now we can move on to the process of creating custom shortcodes using these parts.

Creating custom shortcodes

In this section, we are going to consider two scenarios to build custom shortcodes and explain the different kinds of uses of a shortcode. Let's list the two requirements for building shortcodes for each one:

- Restricting the content based on a user's role
- Displaying a list of posts with attachments

Let's get started.

Restricting content using a shortcode

This scenario explains the creation of a shortcode using all the four shortcode components discussed in the previous section. Basically, we need a shortcode that accepts content and displays the output only to authorized users, while providing a custom output for unauthorized users. Let's consider the shortcode needed for this scenario:

```
[wpquick_restrict_content  role=subscriber]  Content to be protected
[/wpquick_restrict_content]
```

The previous shortcode has one attribute for specifying the user roles not authorized to view the content and the content to be protected within the opening and closing tags. Now we have to match the previous shortcode with the code used in the *Structure of a shortcode* diagram. Consider the following code for the implementation of this shortcode:

```
add_shortcode( 'wpquick_restrict_content',
'wpquick_restrict_content_display' );
function wpquick_restrict_content_display( $atts, $content ){
  $sh_attr = shortcode_atts( array( 'role' => '' ), $atts );

  if( $sh_attr['role'] != '' && ! current_user_can( $sh_attr['role'] ) ){
    $content = __('You don\'t have permission to view this
content','wqsa');
  }
  return $content;
}
```

In this case, a callback function accepts attributes and content for the shortcode. WordPress provides a function called shortcode_atts to merge the passed attributes with default attributes and make an array of attributes required for processing the shortcode. It's a good practice to define the allowed attributes and default values inside the shortcode_atts function as an array. In this case, we are passing a value for the role parameter, and hence it will override the default parameter.

If we don't specify a value for a attribute, `shortcode_atts` will look for the default value. Next, we access the attributes using `$sh_attr` array and apply the conditions. Finally, we return the original content or a message based on the conditions. This is the most basic code required to build a shortcode.

Displaying posts with attachments

This scenario explains a different use of a shortcode from both a developer's perspective as well as a content creator's perspective. Here, we need to display the list of posts with at least one attachment. Unlike the previous scenario, we are not retrieving and modifying the content. Instead, we are generating dynamic content based on the shortcode attributes. Let's take a look at the shortcode needed for this scenario:

```
[wpquick_attachment_posts/]
```

As you can see, there is no closing tag, and the closing part is done within the opening tag. These types of shortcodes are called as *self-enclosing* shortcodes. We don't use any content in such shortcodes. In this case, we are displaying all the posts with attachments, and hence shortcode attributes are not required. If we were displaying posts with attachments for a specific category, the shortcode would have looked as follows:

```
[wpquick_attachment_posts category='1' /]
```

Now we can implement the previous shortcode by matching it with the syntax we used in our shortcode diagrams:

```
add_shortcode( 'wpquick_attachment_posts',
'wpquick_attachment_posts_display' );
function wpquick_attachment_posts_display( $atts, $content ){
  global $wpdb;
  $post_attachments_table = $wpdb->prefix.'wpqpa_post_attachments';
  $sql = "SELECT P.post_title,P.guid from $post_attachments_table as PA
inner join $wpdb->posts as P on P.ID=PA.post_id group by PA.post_id ";

  $result = $wpdb->get_results($sql);
  $html = '';
  if($result){
    foreach ( $result as $key => $value ) {
      $html .= '<a href="'. $value->guid .'">'. $value->post_title
.'</a><br/>';
    }
  }
  return $html;
}
```

In this case, we have no attributes, and hence we query the custom table by joining it with a posts table to generate the result. The $content variable will be empty, as we are not passing any data by using opening and closing tags. Finally, we return the HTML string to display the list of posts.

Understanding the usage of shortcodes

We discussed the techniques of building shortcodes in previous section. Now we need to understand the techniques of using these shortcodes in different parts of the site. Let's take a look at the different locations where we can use shortcodes:

- **Posts and pages**: This is the most common use of a shortcode, where the content creator directly adds the shortcode to the post or page editor. Then, WordPress executes the shortcode and displays the result in the frontend post or page.
- **Widgets**: We can use shortcodes inside WordPress widgets to provide dynamic content similar o the posts and pages. However, we have to use additional code depending on the widget we use. The WordPress **Text widget** allows you to add shortcodes directly to the content editor and display the output on the frontend. Sometimes, you may want to use the shortcodes with HTML elements and hence need to use the **HTML widget** instead of the **Text widget**. The HTML widget doesn't support shortcodes by default. So, we have to use the following code in the functions.php file of the theme or within any plugin to execute the shortcode:

```
add_filter( 'widget_text', 'do_shortcode' );
```

WordPress has a filter called widget_text that gets executed on the content of all widgets. We can use this filter to change the content as required. So far, we used add_filter statement with a callback function. Here, we also have a callback function called do_shortcode. However, you might be wondering why the implementation is missing. The do_shortcode function is built into WordPress, and hence we can directly call it without adding an implementation for the function. This function executes any shortcodes within the content.

- **Template Files**: Sometimes, we may need to call shortcodes inside a header, footer, or any template file. This becomes handy when you are customizing existing themes to integrate the features of other plugins. In such scenarios, adding the shortcode to the template file won't work. We have to use a PHP script and execute the shortcode using `do_shortcode` function. Consider the following code for using a shortcode inside a template file:

```php
<?php echo do_shortcode('wpquick_attachment_posts'); ?>
```

We need to also use the `echo` statement to print the output to the browser, as it's not automatically printed as in previous scenarios.

- **Plugins and themes**: Sometimes, we want to integrate the shortcode features with other plugins or themes. In such cases, we can directly call the shortcode instead of replicating the code for the shortcode. Assume we want to display the posts with attachments after the content of each post. In this scenario, we can internally call the shortcode within our plugin and generate the list of posts with attachments instead of writing a separate function or duplicating code. Consider the following statement for using a shortcode within a theme or a plugin code:

These are some of the common methods and locations for using shortcodes.

Tips for using shortcodes

The shortcode is a simple and flexible way of adding reusable functionality to a site. However, there are pros and cons of using shortcodes. As a developer, you need to understand when to use shortcodes and how to build quality shortcodes. The following tips will help you improve the shortcodes, as well as avoid unnecessary issues:

- **Filtering shortcode output**: Usually, we create some content within the shortcode and directly return the content as output. There are some plugins that use a filter on the output of a shortcode. It's a great way of adding more flexibility where the developers can control the shortcode output of other plugins.
- **Using nested shortcodes**: We can add shortcodes inside other shortcodes to get an output. However, when using nested shortcodes, you need to use `do_shortcode` in the main shortcode to execute the shortcodes within its content.

- **Validating shortcode attributes**: Attributes are added by the content creators and hence need to be considered as user input. Since we shouldn't trust any kind of user input, validation is a must for attribute values.
- **Using unique shortcode names**: Many plugins use generic shortcode names such as [product], [event], and so on. This may lead to conflicts with multiple plugins, and hence you should always use a plugin-specific prefix to make it unique.

- **Overuse of shortcodes**: Shortcode is an easy way of adding a bunch of content. However, using too many shortcodes inside posts or pages can lead to maintenance nightmares in later stages. As the post or page is dependent on shortcodes, it will be difficult to change the content.

We have covered the process of creating and using shortcodes. Now it's time to take a look at plugins that use shortcodes and identify various uses and developing techniques.

Managing custom routes with Rewrite API

The default WordPress URL structure uses query parameters to load the necessary posts and pages. So, the URL of a post will look like http://www.example.com/?p=130. This is not ideal, as its difficult to remember the post ID and search engines won't give a higher preference to such URLs. Therefore, we need a better URL structure that doesn't use query parameters and gives a SEO-friendly URL. So, we use the WordPress permalinks section to change the URL structure. Then, WordPress will internally convert those SEO-friendly URLs to the default URL structure. We can access the permalinks settings section from **Settings** | **Permalinks**. Let's choose *Post Name* as the URL structure for our site. Then, the preceding URL will be converted to http:// www.example.com/sample-post/.

As you can see, this is a much more user and SEO-friendly URL structure. Once the permalinks are set up, all the WordPress core features in the frontend will use this structure. However, in custom development, we may need custom URL structures to handle the functionality. In such cases, we can use Rewrite API to define our own routes and manage the functionality without interfering with default WordPress features.

What is Rewrite API?

WordPress Rewrite API is a set of functions that allows you to manage custom routes using tags, rules and endpoints. Let's identify the functions used for implementing with Rewrite API:

- `add_rewrite_rule`: This function is used to register new rewrite rules to WordPress for generating custom templates.
- `add_rewrite_tag`: This function is used for registering new query variables. We need to use it with `add_rewrite_rule` to create rewrite rules for custom templates.
- `add_rewrite_endpoint`: This function is used to create extra rewrite rules for WordPress core components.
- `flush_rewrite_rules`: This is used to remove rewrite rules and then recreate rewrite rules.

In this section, we are going to create and manage custom rules using these functions except `add_rewrite_endpoint`. You can view more details about rewrite endpoints at `https://codex.wordpress.org/Rewrite_API/add_rewrite_endpoint`.

Understanding the need for custom routes

The use of custom routes becomes vital in developing plugins that goes beyond the default WordPress features. We are going to consider two scenarios to understand the need for custom rewriting:

- Assume we have a shortcode that is used to display user profile details and we use it inside a WordPress page called **Profile**. So, the URL of the page will be `http://www.example.com/profile`. Now, we need to use the same page to display user details of each user. Currently, it's not possible, since we don't have a way to identify the user when accessing this page. So, we need to modify the URL in a way that we can identify each user. Let's assume we have a URL like `http://www.example.com/profile/john123` with the username after the page. Then, we can use the username component to identify the user and display the profile details. In this scenario, we have to use Rewrite API functions to match the URL with necessary query parameters and execute our functionality.

- As we already discussed, adding shortcodes to such an important functionality can become an issue when the administrator deletes or removes the shortcodes by mistake. So, relying on posts or pages to handle such functionality can be considered as a risk. In such cases, we can avoid risk by using custom URLs that don't use posts or pages. Assume we want to display a login form at `http://www.example.com/user/login` and registration at `http://www.example.com/user/register`. By default, these URLs will redirect to the *404 Not Found Page* when you don't have a post or page called *user*. So, we need to use Rewrite API to register custom routes and manage these URLs to offer custom features without interfering with core WordPress features.

In this section, we are going to implement the second scenario, as handling custom URLs without posts or pages is the ideal solution for custom features.

Creating the routing rules

We can use `add_rewrite_rule` function to register new custom routes with WordPress. This function can be implemented within many actions in WordPress. However, we usually use `init` action to handle the rewrite rules. Let's add a custom rewrite rule to handle the scenario of user login and registration:

```
add_action('init','wqraf_manage_user_routes');
function wqraf_manage_user_routes() {
  add_rewrite_rule( '^user/([^/]+)/?',
'index.php?wpquick_action=$matches[1]', 'top' );
}
```

You can find the code for this section inside the `wpquick-rewrite-api` plugin in the source codes directory. The `add_rewrite_rule` function accepts two required and one optional parameters. Let's take a look at the parameters and their role:

- `regex`: This is the first parameter that matches the URL to the rule using a regular expression.
- `redirect`: This is the second parameter that specifies the URL to request when current URL is matching the regular expression. As you can see, we pass the request to `index.php` with custom parameters that uniquely identify our functionality.
- `after`: This optional parameter decides when to use this rewrite rule. If a `top` value is used, the rewrite rule will take precedence over other default WordPress rewrite rules. If a `bottom` value is used, preference will be given to existing rules.

Now, you might think we can access `wpquick_action` using `$_GET` query parameters and implement the functionality for both login and registration. However, you won't get `wpquick_action` as a `$_GET` parameter. WordPress doesn't allow you to use any type of variable in the query string. It will check for query variables within the existing list, and all other variables will be ignored. So, we have to specify the custom query variables before we can actually use them in code.

Adding query variables

WordPress has over 40 params registered to be used in queries. Let's check the existing query variables before adding custom query variables. Add the following code to main file of `wpquick-rewrite-api` plugin and open the home page of your site:

```
add_filter( 'query_vars', 'wqraf_manage_user_query_vars' );
function wqraf_manage_user_query_vars( $query_vars ) {
  echo "<pre>";print_r($query_vars);exit;
}
```

You will see all the existing query parameters as an array. Now we need to create our own query parameters to handle user login and registration. So, we add the following code to the `wpquick-rewrite-api` plugin:

```
add_filter( 'query_vars', 'wqraf_manage_user_query_vars' );
function wqraf_manage_user_query_vars( $query_vars ) {
  $query_vars[] = 'wpquick_action';
  return $query_vars;
}
```

The `query_vars` is a built-in filter that allows us to add or remove query variables before the request is processed. In this scenario, we add a new query parameter called `wpquick_action` to the existing query parameters array.

> WordPress core and other plugins registers considerable number of query variables. So, it's better to use a unique name with a prefix to avoid conflicts with query parameters in other plugins.

Now we have the ability to access `wpquick_action` variable from the URL. In this scenario, I used the `query_vars` filter to add new query variables and for the purpose of identifying built-in query variables. Rewrite API provides a function called `add_rewrite_tag` to implement the same functionality, and it's the recommended way. So, we can remove the `query_vars` filter from our plugin and change the `wqraf_manage_user_routes` function as following to get the same functionality:

```
function wqraf_manage_user_routes() {
   add_rewrite_rule( '^user/([^/]+)/?',
'index.php?wpquick_actions=$matches[1]', 'top' );
   add_rewrite_tag('%wpquick_actions%', '([^&]+)');
}
```

The first parameter takes the **action name** surrounded by a `%` and the second parameter defines a `regex` to validate the value. Adding rewrite tags is relatively easy compared to using `query_vars` filter.

We modified the WordPress rewrite rules by adding a new rule. So, we have to flush the rewrite rules before the new rule takes effect. There are two ways to flush rewrite rules. First, we can visit **Settings | Permalinks** section to automatically refresh the rewrite rules. However, this is not ideal in development, as the user needs to manually go into the **Settings** section. So, we need a way to flush the rewrite rules automatically within our plugin, without needing an input from the user.

Flushing the rewriting rules

We can easily flush the rewrite rules by calling WordPress `flush_rewrite_rules` function inside the `init` action. However, it will flush the rewrite rules on every request, generating unnecessary performance overhead. So, we need to use activation handler of the plugin to flush the rules. Let's see the following implementation inside the activation handler:

```
register_activation_hook( __FILE__, 'wqraf_activate' );
function wqraf_activate(){
   flush_rewrite_rules();
}
```

Now go to the admin panel, deactivate the plugin, and activate the plugin again. Then, go to the URL `http://www.example.com/user/login` and check whether it works. Unfortunately, you will still get the 404 error for the request. You might be wondering what went wrong. Let's go back and think about the process to understand the issue. We flushed the rules on plugin activation. So, the new rules should persist successfully. However, we define the rules on the `init` action, which is only executed after the plugin is activated. Therefore, new rules will not be available at the time of flushing. So, we have to update the function as follows to get it working:

```
register_activation_hook( __FILE__, 'wqraf_activate' );
function wqraf_activate(){
  wqraf_manage_user_routes();
  flush_rewrite_rules();
}
```

Now deactivate and activate the plugin again. Then, go to the URL `http://www.example.com/user/login`. This time, you won't get the 404 errors, as the rewrite rule is added and flushed properly. Now we are ready with our routing rules for user functionalities.

Displaying content for custom routes

We have to build a custom route to manage the login and registration of the site. Now we need to access the custom query variable from the custom route and generate the screens for login and registration. Consider the following code for the implementation of login and registration forms:

```
add_action( 'template_redirect', 'wqraf_front_controller' );
function wqraf_front_controller() {
  global $wp_query;
  $wpquick_action = isset ( $wp_query->query_vars['wpquick_action'] ) ?
$wp_query->query_vars['wpquick_action'] : '';
  switch ( $wpquick_action ) {
    case 'register':
      echo "<h1>REgistration Form</h1>";exit;
      break;
    case 'login':
      echo "<h1>Login Form</h1>";exit;
      break;
  }
}
```

WordPress executes the `template_redirect` action just before deciding which template to load. So, we can use this action to intercept the request and load our own template. First, we access the `wpquick_action` value using the `$wp_query` global object. This variable will contain either register or login in this scenario. Then, we use a `switch` statement to filter the action and load the necessary template. Here, we are only printing a title for explanations. You have to generate the login or registration forms instead of the title.

> Since we are intercepting the request, our content will be loaded instead of the WordPress template. Here, it will only print the title without the header, footer, or other parts of the WordPress template. So, you have to generate a complete template by including header, footer, content area, and sidebars.

We have looked at the process of using Rewrite API functions to create custom routes and load custom templates for your plugins. This will become handy when developing advanced plugins with non-WordPress specific screens.

Building remote connections with REST API

WordPress REST API is gaining popularity over the old XML-RPC API and becoming a standard in site development. The API allows developers to connect WordPress sites with other sites as well as third-party applications. Modern sites are moving towards JS Framework-based frontends to optimize performance as well as to simplify the user experience. In such scenarios, developers can use WordPress as the backend for the core functionality and expose the data through the REST API to build frontends without using WordPress. The REST API could well be the future of development with WordPress.

The REST API was initially introduced in a external plugin for testing. Finally, it was included in WordPress core in WordPress 4.7, and now it fully supports REST API endpoints for all the major data models in WordPress.

Let's identify some of the common terms used in REST API operations:

- **Route**: This is a well-defined URL that can be mapped to an HTTP method
- **Endpoint**: The process of matching a specific route to a HTTP method
- **Request**: The call to an API endpoint with the necessary data
- **Response**: The data provided by an API to a specific request
- **Schema**: This is used to structure API data and provide info on the available properties and input parameters for API requests

Introducing core REST API endpoints

WordPress provides built-in API endpoints for working with most of the main core features. The documentation defines the endpoints, attributes, and example requests, simplifying the learning curve for developers. In this section, we are going to look at the core REST API endpoints and the use of test requests to understand the process. You can check all the available endpoints and additional information in WordPress REST API documentation at `https://developer.wordpress.org/rest-api/reference/`. The WordPress REST API is enabled by default. You can check whether an API is enabled on your site by accessing `http://www.example.com/wp-json` in the browser. If the API is enabled, you will get a large JSON string with the available settings and endpoints.

Understanding and testing Core API endpoints

We have to identify and understand the use of API endpoints, arguments, and return data formats to build features with API functions. Testing API requests is the best way to understand the process. We can use an existing tool to simplify the API request testing process. There are many such tools and we are going to use the Postman extension of Google Chrome browser.

Postman is a tool that simplifies the process of managing APIs by offering features such as testing API requests, building API documentation, and monitoring API usage. This tool also provides many additional API-related features in both free and PRO versions. The free extension is more than enough to work with basic API testing for your projects. You can use the PRO version for advanced features such as team colloboration, creating mock servers and integrations with many third-party APIs.

You can install the extension in your chrome browser from `https://www.getpostman.com/`. Once installed, you will get a standalone app, as shown in the following screenshot:

Now we are ready to test API requests with WordPress REST API. Mainly, we use HTTP `GET` and `POST` requests in development tasks. However, this tool provides the ability to use various HTTP request types, such as `PUT` and `DELETE`. The REST API contains endpoints that allows us to directly use GET requests as well as `POST` requests which requires authentication. So, we are going to check both types of requests.

Let's start by testing a GET request. Basically, these endpoints exposes the existing data in WordPress. First, you have to enter the URL of the endpoint in **Enter request URL** field and select the HTTP request as GET. The endpoint needs to be added after the `http://www.example.com/wp-json/` section in the URL. So, the request for accessing the list of posts via REST API looks similar to the parameters shown in the following screenshot:

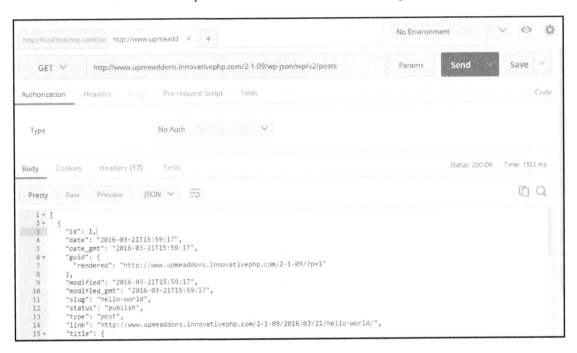

The screen on the bottom displays the result of the request in the format we choose. We have to choose JSON as the result type, since successful API requests returns JSON data. Since we are using GET requests, the **Type** was also set as **No Auth**.

Now we can move forward to testing POST requests for retrieving data for display as well as modifying the database through API requests. Testing POST requests require more work compared to using GET requests. These requests always require some authentication and return an error when valid authentication is not available. So, first. you have to add the URL in **Enter request URL** and select the method as POST. Next, go to **Authorization** tab and select **Basic Auth** as the type. Then add the **Username** and **Password** of a user in your site with post creation and edit capabilities.

Generally, POST requests need additional parameters and values. Here, we are trying to create a post, and hence you can add the post details as key-value pairs in the **form-data** section of **Body** tab. Finally, click on the **Send** button to send the API request. However, you will get the following error message instead of creating the post:

```
{ "code": "rest_cannot_create", "message": "Sorry, you are not allowed to
create posts as this user.", "data": { "status": 401 } }
```

You might be confused why it's returning a permission error even when we have provided basic authentication details. WordPress considers Basic Auth as an unsafe way of handling REST API requests, and, hence, **Basic Auth** is disabled by default. So, we have to use a plugin called **JSON Basic Authentication** by the WordPress API Team. This plugin is included in the source code folder for this chapter. Once this plugin is activated, you can send the request again and will see the response and form parameters, as shown in the following screenshot:

We can use this technique to validate multiple parameters with different conditions and make sure requests only contain the data in requested formats. Now we can move into the implementation of the `wqra_list_post_attachments_handler` function for handling the request to the new route:

```
function wqra_list_post_attachments_handler($data){
  global $wpdb;
  $data = $data->get_params();
  $post_id = isset($data['id']) ? $data['id'] : 0;
  $post_attachments_table = $wpdb->prefix.'wpqpa_post_attachments';
  $sql  = $wpdb->prepare( "SELECT * from $post_attachments_table where
post_id = %d ", $post_id);
  $result = $wpdb->get_results($sql);
  $post_attachments = array();
 if($result){
    foreach ($result as $key => $value) {
      $post_attachments[] = array('ID'=> $value->id, 'file_name' =>
$value->file_name, 'file_path' => $value->file_path);
    }
  }

  return rest_ensure_response(($post_attachments));
}
```

The REST API request object is passed to this function as a parameter. So, we use the `get_params` function of the `$data` object to retrieve the available parameters in the request. Next, we capture the post ID using the `id` attribute of the `$data` object. Next, we execute a custom query on the `wpqpa_post_attachments` table. The result will contain the file attachments for the given post. Then, we traverse through the results and assign the attachment details in to an array. Finally, we use the `rest_ensure_response` function to pass the attachment data in JSON format to the response.

 There are also some disadvantages in using custom routes and endpoints, in situations where we have the ability to use existing routes and endpoints. We need to implement our own pagination and sorting for custom endpoints while WordPress provides them by default for existing endpoints. We can use user permission checks by default in WordPress core endpoints while we need to pass additional nonce parameters to check user permissions.

Now we can call this new route and retrieve the file attachments list for a given post.

Building the REST API client

The API client is the user or service that uses the data provided by the REST API. We use the client to access the REST API of another site. The client site could be WordPress or a non-WordPress site. The client can also be implemented in a different programming language without using PHP. Let's identify the usage of API clients. In this chapter, we going to look at the process of building REST API client to access our data from external sites, as it's the most important use of an API.

REST API client from external site

This is where the REST API is used to its maximum potential, even though we use it to build functionality of the same site. The main intention of creating a REST API is to provide access to third-party WordPress and non-WordPress based applications. So, the API client can be implemented in any programming language. In this section, we will be building a PHP based API client for accessing REST APIs of other applications with the support of CURL.

Let's add the API client implementation with CURL. You should place this code in a PHP file and access it from a source external to your application:

```php
function wpquick_rest_api_client( $url, $post_data = '' ){
  $api_route = $url;
  $ch = curl_init( $api_route );
  $headers = array(
    'Authorization:Basic YWRtaW46dTh1OHU4dTg='// <---
    );
  curl_setopt( $ch, CURLOPT_HTTPHEADER, $headers );
  curl_setopt( $ch, CURLOPT_SSL_VERIFYHOST, false );
  curl_setopt( $ch, CURLOPT_RETURNTRANSFER, 1 );
  curl_setopt( $ch, CURLOPT_POST, true );
  curl_setopt( $ch, CURLOPT_SSL_VERIFYPEER, false );
  if( $post_data != '' ){
    curl_setopt( $ch, CURLOPT_POSTFIELDS, $post_data );
  }
  curl_setopt( $ch, CURLOPT_VERBOSE, 1 );
  $return = curl_exec( $ch );
  echo "<pre>";
  print_r( $return );
  exit;
}

$post_data = array();
$post_data = json_encode( $post_data );
$api_route
```

- **Built-in templates**: Building templates and displaying the data requires a considerable development effort. By default, custom post types use the built-in templates of the theme, and hence we don't require any effort to display the data in basic form. Even with advanced requirements, we can just duplicate the default template and adjust it with minimum effort to include our design elements or custom data.

These reasons may give you an idea about how custom post types became such a valuable feature in WordPress. Now, it's time to understand the process of using and developing custom solutions with these features.

Building an object-oriented plugin

Up to this point, we created several plugins in previous chapters. However, we used the procedural approach, where we define the necessary hooks and functions directly inside the main plugin file or sub-files. As the website or application gets complex, we will have a hard time managing the development with the procedural method. So, we need a way to use best development practices and modularize the code into necessary classes. In this section, we are going to look at the basic structure for creating a plugin with object-oriented concepts. Let's consider the following code for the OOP-based plugin structure:

```
if( !class_exists( 'WPQuick_CPT' ) ) {
  class WPQuick_CPT{
    private static $instance;
    public static function instance() {
      if ( ! isset( self::$instance ) && ! ( self::$instance instanceof
WPQuick_CPT ) ) {
        self::$instance = new WPQuick_CPT();
        self::$instance->setup_constants();
        self::$instance->includes();

        add_action( 'admin_enqueue_scripts',array( self::$instance,
'load_admin_scripts' ),9);
        add_action( 'wp_enqueue_scripts',array(
self::$instance,'load_scripts' ),9);
        self::$instance->model_property= new WQCPT_Model_Property();
      }
      return self::$instance;
    }
    public function setup_constants() {
      if ( ! defined( 'WQCPT_PLUGIN_DIR' ) ) {
        define( 'WQCPT_PLUGIN_DIR', plugin_dir_path( __FILE__ ) );
      }
    }
```

```
      public function load_scripts(){ }
      public function load_admin_scripts(){ }
      private function includes() {
         require_once WQCPT_PLUGIN_DIR . 'classes/class-wqcpt-model-
   property.php';
      }
   }
}
```

WordPress doesn't provide a recommended method or boilerplate to build the plugins using the object oriented method. So, it's the choice of the developers to use a technique that better suits them. The preceding structure is used by some of the exciting plugins, and it's also my personal preference as well. So, you can use it as a guide and build a better solution that suits your style.

We begin by checking the availability of the main plugin class and define the main class for the plugin. We will be using the main class to handle all other files as well as classes. Then, we define a variable to hold the instance of the class and use the instance function to generate an object from this class. This static function and the private instance variables make sure that we only have one instance of our plugin class. The instance function acts as the initialization point of our plugin, and hence we can include the necessary function calls, class initialization, and hooks inside this function.

We have two function calls to the setup_constants and includes functions, inside the instance function. These functions respectively define the constants required for the plugin features and add the plugin files using the PHP require_once function. As we develop complex plugins, we can have many such functions to separate these kinds of basic configurations for the plugin. Then, we can define all the action and filter hooks intended to be used throughout the plugin for configuration purposes. Here, we have used two actions for including the scripts and styles on the frontend and the backend of the website.

The next section should consist of the object creation for the main classes of the plugin. In this scenario, we only have one class, even though we will need many classes in advanced plugin development. We need to use the self::$instance object as we are within the static function. Finally, we return the instance of the main class.

```
    ),
    'hierarchical' => true,
  )
 );
}
```

We start the function by defining the taxonomy and the necessary labels, similar to the custom post types. Then, we can call the `register_taxonomy` function with the necessary parameters to create the taxonomy for property types. Let's take a look at the parameters in detail:

- `taxonomy`: This is the first parameter, where we have to pass the name for the taxonomy. We can only use lowercase letters and characters. We have specified it as `wqcpt_property_type`, with a prefix to make it unique from other plugins.
- `object type`: This is the second parameter, where we have to assign the post types that will use this taxonomy. In this scenario, we have specified `wqcpt_property` as the post type. We can use an array in scenarios where we have multiple post types. However, using a taxonomy in multiple post types makes archive pages as a mix of different post type entries. It might be difficult to handle archive pages with multiple post types due to different designs and data. So, it's ideal to use separate taxonomies for each post type, unless all post types contain similar design and data in archive pages.
- `arguments`: This is the third parameter where we can pass different settings from the list of available options. In this scenario, we have used the **labels** for property listing types and **hierarchical** options. The **hierarchical** setting defines whether the taxonomy should act as a **tag** or **category**. The default value is `false`, making it act as a **tag**. We have used it as a **category** by setting it to **true**. There are many other settings similar to the custom post type registration process. You can view more details about all the available arguments at https://codex.wordpress.org/Function_Reference/register_taxonomy.

The choice of category against tag for taxonomies depends on your requirements. Generally, we use categories when we want to have different sub-levels as well as when have a fixed set of primary options. Tags don't provide sub-levels and usually use a dynamic set of values to explain the data. In this scenario, property listing types have predefined options such as Sale, Rent, and Mortgage. Therefore, we choose category over tags for property listing types.

Once this code is used, you will see a new taxonomy added to the **Property** menu. You can create properties and assign property listing types to categorize the properties based on your needs. In real-world requirements, you have to match the taxonomy needs of each custom post type with categories or tags depending on the functionality.

Managing custom fields for custom post types

In normal posts, we rarely use custom fields as the primary feature is displaying content in the WordPress editor along with featured images, tags, and categories. However, custom post type implementations require a considerable amount of data beyond the content in the WordPress editor. So, we need a way to handle the custom data for each custom post type. We can use the default post custom fields feature to store the data in the wp_postmeta table. Let's consider the custom field requirements of a property listing site:

The property listing sites require a large amount of custom data, along with the property title and the main property content through the WordPress editor. We can match some of the property data such as property listing type as categories. However, the majority of the data needs to be handled using custom fields. Such data includes fields such as city, property type, area, price, year, property plans, and so on.

In this section, we are going to add some custom property fields to understand the process of adding and using custom fields in custom post types. Let's start by adding a metabox to define custom fields similar to the technique we used in the *post attachments* plugin. We need to update the constructor of WQCPT_Model_Property with the following action:

```
add_action( 'add_meta_boxes', array( $this, 'add_property_meta_boxes' ) );
```

Now, we have to define the metabox and implement the function for displaying the content of the metabox using the following code inside the WQCPT_Model_Property class:

```
public function add_property_meta_boxes() {
  add_meta_box( 'wqcpt-property-meta', __('Property Details','wqcpt' ),
array( $this, 'display_property_meta_boxes' ), $this->post_type );
}

public function display_property_meta_boxes( $property ) {
  global $wqcpt,$template_data;

  $template_data['property_post_type'] = $this->post_type;
  $template_data['property_nonce'] = wp_create_nonce('wqcpt-property-
meta');
  $template_data['wqcpt_pr_type'] = get_post_meta( $property->ID,
'_wqcpt_pr_type', true );
  $template_data['wqcpt_pr_city'] = get_post_meta( $property->ID,
```

```
'_wqcpt_pr_city', true );

  ob_start();
  $wqcpt->template_loader->get_template_part( 'property','meta');
  $display = ob_get_clean();
  echo $display;
}
```

We already discussed the use of the `add_meta_box` function in the post attachments plugin and how to use a callback function to generate the content. In the post attachments plugin, we used HTML within PHP variables to generate the output. This is not ideal in large projects as it's hard to manage the output within quotes as well as provide extendable capabilities for templates. In the MVC pattern, we use a separate layer for the template called **Views**.

> *Model–view–controller* also known as **MVC** is an architectural pattern commonly used for developing user interfaces that divides an application into three interconnected parts. The MVC design pattern decouples these major components, allowing for efficient code reuse and parallel development.
>
> — *Source :* `https://en.wikipedia.org/wiki/Model-view-controller`

Similarly, we have to separate the template code as much as possible to allow the possibility of future enhancements.

So, we define a global variable called `$template_data` to keep the necessary data for the template used in this function. Then, we assign the post type, nonce value, and the property data to the `$template_data` array. We use the `wp_postmeta` table to store the custom field details for properties. Therefore, we can use the `get_user_meta` function to get the existing property values to be passed to the template. Initially, these functions will return empty strings until we save the data for the first time. Then, we have to use a template loader to load the template for property custom fields.

In this section, we have used our own template loader. You can refer to the `classes/class-wqcpt-template-loader.php` file inside the source code directory of our plugin for the implementation. This class is included in the main file of our plugin and the object is created within the `instance` function. The basic functionality of this class is to include PHP files from the templates directory of our plugin. Those developers who are familiar with using Template Engines such **Twig, Smarty, Mustache** in pure PHP projects may think of this as a similar technique. However, this is just basic PHP file inclusion with template code, and hence doesn't provide any advantages provided by Template Engines.

We can use PHP Template Engines in WordPress plugins with bit of additional development work. However, most plugins including the popular plugins don't use Template Engines and are restricted to template loading as PHP files.

In this function, we have called the `ob_start` function to start the template loading process. This function is used to switch on output buffering, allowing us only to send the necessary content to the browser. Next, we access the object of the template loader class by using the global `$wqcpt` instance of our plugin, and call the `get_template_part` function. We have passed two strings called `property` and `meta` to this function. So, we need to have a template file called `property-meta.php` inside the templates directory of our plugin. Then, we use the `ob_get_clean` function to get the template and clean the output buffer. Finally, we use the `echo` statement to send the content to the browser. The next step in the process is to build the template and use the data specified for the template.

Building the property fields template

We need to begin the process by creating a new directory called `templates` inside the plugin and a new file called `property-meta.php` inside the directory. This file should produce the custom fields to capture property data while keeping the amount of PHP code and logic to a minimum. Let's take a look at the implementation of the template for property custom fields:

```php
<?php
  global $template_data;
  extract($template_data);
?>

<input type="hidden" name="property_nonce" value="<?php echo
$property_nonce; ?>" />
<table class="form-table">
  <tr>
    <th style=''><label><?php _e('Status','wqcpt'); ?>*</label></th>
    <td><select class='widefat' name="wqcpt_pr_type" id="wqcpt_pr_type">
      <option <?php selected( $wqcpt_pr_type, '0' ); ?> value='0' ><?php
_e('Please Select','wqcpt'); ?></option>
      <option <?php selected( $wqcpt_pr_type, 'house' ); ?> value='house'
><?php _e('House','wqcpt'); ?></option>
      <option <?php selected( $wqcpt_pr_type, 'office' ); ?> value='office'
><?php _e('Office','wqcpt'); ?></option>
        </select></td>
  </tr>
  <tr>
```

```
<th style=''><label><?php _e('City','wqcpt'); ?></label></th>
    <td><input class='widefat' name='wqcpt_pr_city' id='wqcpt_pr_city'
type='text' value='<?php echo $wqcpt_pr_city; ?>' /></td>
  </tr>
</table>
```

Let's understand the implementation of the property fields template using the following steps:

1. We begin the template by using the global $template_data array and extracting the values passed as template data.
2. Then, we have to add the HTML fields for keeping the nonce value and property data. In the preceding code, we have limited the fields to city and property type for explanation purposes.
3. Next, we have to use the data passed from WQCPT_Model_Property to load the existing values for these fields.

Now, our template is ready. You can create or edit a property to see the property custom fields, as shown in the following screenshot:

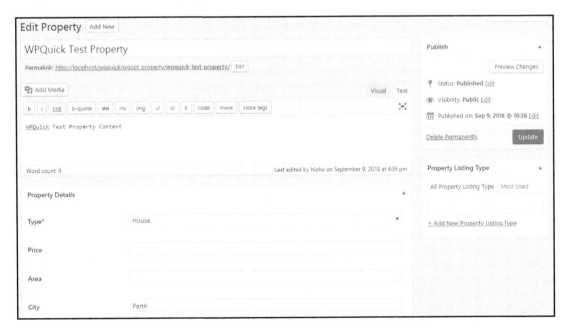

We can use this technique to group all the property fields in a single metabox or use multiple metaboxes to hold related fields. Also, we can change the location and priority of the metabox in the property screen.

Saving property custom fields

We set up a property as a custom post type and hence the main property details will be saved automatically on property publication or update events. However, custom field data will not be saved in this process, and hence we need a custom implementation to store these data. We have chosen to store the custom field data in the `wp_postmeta` table. Let's look at the process of saving custom fields using the WordPress `save_post` action. First, we need to add the following line of code to the constructor of the `WQCPT_Model_Property` class:

```
add_action( 'save_post', array( $this, 'save_property_meta_data' ) );
```

This action is triggered whenever we create or update a post or custom post type. Now, we have to implement the callback function with the following implementation:

```
public function save_property_meta_data( $post_id ) {
  global $post,$wqcpt;
  if (   isset($_POST['property_nonce']) &&  !
wp_verify_nonce($_POST['property_nonce'], 'wqcpt-property-meta')){
    return $post_id;
  }
  if ( defined('DOING_AUTOSAVE') && DOING_AUTOSAVE ) {
    return $post_id;
  }

  if (  isset($_POST['post_type']) &&  $this->post_type ==
$_POST['post_type'] && current_user_can( 'edit_post', $post->ID ) ) {

    $wqcpt_pr_type = isset( $_POST['wqcpt_pr_type'] ) ?
sanitize_text_field( trim($_POST['wqcpt_pr_type']) ) : '';
    $wqcpt_pr_city = isset( $_POST['wqcpt_pr_city'] ) ?
sanitize_text_field( trim($_POST['wqcpt_pr_city']) ) : '';
    update_post_meta( $post_id, '_wqcpt_pr_type', $wqcpt_pr_type );
    update_post_meta( $post_id, '_wqcpt_pr_city', $wqcpt_pr_city );
  } else {
    return $post_id;
  }
}
```

We begin the function by verifying the nonce value assigned to the template. We can just return the post ID on verification failures. Next, we have to apply another validation for checking the autosave. WordPress autosave features periodically save the post content automatically. We don't need to update the custom field values on each autosave. So, the validation only allows the function to process when the user is manually saving the post. The next validation is the most important one since this action is executed on all post types in WordPress.

We have to make sure we use the action only in necessary post types to avoid unnecessary conflicts. So, we check if a property is being saved and the current user has the permission to save properties by using the `current_user_can` function. We didn't assign property-specific capabilities in custom post type registration. Therefore, we have to check for the default post edit permission. Once all the validations are completed, we can retrieve and sanitize the values from the POST request. Finally, we use the `update_post_meta` function to save each property field to the `wp_postmeta` table.

We have the completed the functionality of managing properties from the backend. Now, you should be able to create properties with custom field data and display that data in edit property screens. Once created, you can view the properties from the frontend by using the property link.

 The theme will use the default `single.php` template to display the property. Since we need to display additional property-related fields, we can create a template inside the theme or use our plugin to load a template for handling a single property page.

In this scenario, we used two property fields with basic field types. In real applications, you will have to use more complex fields such as dates, maps, searchable dropdowns, color pickers, and so on. So, manually building custom fields may become an issue for most startup sites with lower development time frames. In such scenarios, we can use custom post type plugins that act as a framework for managing custom fields without the need for manual coding. Let's take a look at some of the custom post type plugins that offer wide range of custom field types:

- **Toolset Types**: This plugin lets you manage custom post types, custom taxonomies, and custom fields without needing any coding. This plugin offers over 20 built-in custom field types. Built-in interfaces allow you to manage custom fields by providing the necessary settings. More details about the features can be viewed from the plugin page at `https://wordpress.org/plugins/types/`.

- **Pods**: This plugin also offers the same set of features, along with the ability to connect multiple custom post types. This plugin offers around 10 custom field types to manage the fields of each custom post type using existing screens. More details about the features can be viewed from the plugin page at `https://wordpress.org/plugins/pods/`.

- **Metabox**: Compared to the other two plugins, this one mainly focuses on managing custom fields by allowing you to add them to metaboxes in the post creation screen. This plugin provides over 40 built-in field types covering a wide range of areas. More details about the features can be viewed from the plugin page at `https://wordpress.org/plugins/types/`.

These plugins are useful for sites that require rapid development process and gives less priority for flexibility and the extendability of the features.

Limitations of storing data as meta values

We use the post meta table in most occasions to store custom data related to different custom post types. However, as the meta tables gets larger, it will be difficult to manage all the meta values. The site will get slower, creating major performance issues. So, we have to consider this limitation when planning the site in the initial stages. Once the posts meta table is used, it's difficult to migrate to a custom solution in later stages, especially when we decide to use custom post type plugins to manage the custom fields.

So, using the post meta table to store custom field data is ideal for small- to medium-scale sites where the posts and post meta tables won't get overloaded with data. In advanced applications, we should consider using a custom table for the custom fields, while using the posts table for the main details of a custom post type item.

Introduction to form management

The majority of WordPress sites consist a of few pages about the site, services, or products while having a blog. Among the rest, a high percentage of sites focus on capturing, processing, and displaying user data. So, form management becomes an important aspect in WordPress development. The forms are mostly used as a data capturing method on the frontend, as we use custom post types to capture data in the backend. We can develop our own custom forms in the frontend, or we can automate the process of managing forms by using an existing form management plugin. The choice between custom forms and form plugins depends on the requirements of the site. Let's take a look at the advantages and disadvantages of using these two methods.

- **Development time**: Form plugins provide a rapid development process with drag-and-drop form creation, while handling all the form field features through configurations. On the other hand, custom forms require considerable development effort and the changes to existing fields require modifications in code.
- **Database usage**: Each existing forms plugin is restricted to using the wp_postmeta table or a single custom table, whereas custom forms can be developed to use either technique according to our preference, while keeping different form data in different tables.

- **Extendability**: Building custom forms enables the possibility of keeping the features open for future enhancements. On the other hand, we will have to work with the limitations of forms plugins when considering the future enhancements of advanced sites.
- **Consistency in design**: We can create our own custom form designs to match the styles of the theme. However, existing plugins may not provide 100% flexibility in modifying the design to match the theme styles.

Due to these reasons, we should carefully choose the development method for custom forms depending on the requirements of each site. Once we complete the upcoming sections on form management, you will have a better idea about the process for making correct decisions.

Building custom forms in the frontend

We have several ways of adding forms to the frontend of a WordPress website. In this section, we are going to discuss two methods used by popular plugins to add forms:

- Adding forms using shortcodes
- Loading forms using custom URLs

We will be implementing both techniques, starting with the shortcode method.

Adding forms using a shortcode

This is one of the most popular methods used by many popular plugins to add data capturing forms to a site. In this method, we use a shortcode to generate the HTML for the form. Then, we add the shortcode to a WordPress post or page and let users access it through the post or page. This is the ideal technique for basic to intermediate level features, where the use of the form doesn't play a critical part in the functionality of the site.

Using shortcode is one of the simplest methods to add a form. However, shortcodes are added to post or page and hence administrators can accidentally delete the page or break the shortcode by mistake. Therefore, it should not be used for advanced sites where the functionality of shortcode is critical. For example, consider a registration form in a basic social network site. The unavailability of the registration page for a limited time is not a major issue since the people register for free to share their activities. However, consider a registration form in a support forum of a site that provides a time-critical service. In such sites, unavailability of registration for even few hours is not acceptable and affects the user. So, we shouldn't use shortcode-based forms in such sites, or prevent modification access to the pages with shortcodes .

In the previous section, we used custom post types to manage the property details in the backend. Now, we need to add the property creation capabilities to the frontend. Let's use the following line of code inside the constructor of the WQCPT_Model_Property class to define a shortcode for the property form:

```
add_shortcode( 'wqcpt_property_form', array( $this, 'display_property_form'
) );
```

Next, we need to implement the callback function to display a property creation form in the frontend. Let's consider the implementation of the display_property_form function:

```
public function display_property_form( $atts, $content ){
    global $wqcpt,$template_data;
    $template_data['property_nonce'] = wp_create_nonce('wqcpt-property-
meta');

    ob_start();
    $wqcpt->template_loader->get_template_part( 'property','form');
    $display = ob_get_clean();
    return $display;
}
```

The implementation of this function is similar to the display_property_meta_boxes function we used in the backend custom post types. In this scenario, this form is only used for property creation and hence we don't have to pass the existing data as template variables. We use a different template called property-form.php for the frontend custom form. Now, we can have a look at the implementation of the property-form.php template:

```
<?php
    global $template_data;
    extract($template_data); ?>
```

```
<form action="" method="POST" >
  <input type="hidden" name="property_nonce" value="<?php echo
$property_nonce; ?>" />
  <table class="form-table">
    <tr>
      <th><label><?php _e('Property Title','wqcpt'); ?>*</label></th>
      <td><input type="text" name="wqcpt_prfr_title" id="wqcpt_prfr_title"
value="" /></td>
    </tr>
    <tr>
      <th><label><?php _e('Property Content','wqcpt'); ?>*</label></th>
      <td><textarea name="wqcpt_prfr_content" id="wqcpt_prfr_content"
></textarea></td>
    </tr>
    <!--HTML for other custom fields -->
    <tr>
      <th>&</th>
      <td><input name="wqcpt_prfr_submit" id="wqcpt_prfr_submit"
type="submit" value="<?php _e('Add Property','wqcpt'); ?>" /></td>
    </tr>
  </table>
</form>
```

The structure of the template is exactly same as the previous scenario on backend. However, we have two additional fields for property title and content, along with a form and a submit button. In custom post types, we had the title and content as built-in fields. We also used the built-in post form and the **Publish** or **Update** buttons. On the frontend, we don't have any built-in features, and hence we have to add them manually. Once the shortcode is added to a page, the property creation form will look similar to the following screen:

Now, we come to the final part where we create the property on the submission of the form.

Creating properties using custom forms

In backend custom post types, we were only coding the custom field saving part, and hence we were able to use the `save_post` action to handle the process. In the frontend, we have to build the process from scratch and hence the `init` action is the ideal hook for the implementation. Let's add the following line of code to the constructor of our `WQCPT_Model_Property` class:

```
add_action( 'init', array( $this, 'save_property_form' ) );
```

Next, we can take a look at the implementation of the `save_property_form` function, as shown in the following code:

```
public function save_property_form() {
  global $post,$wqcpt;
  if( ! isset ( $_POST['wqcpt_prfr_submit'] ) ){
    return;
  }

  if ( !wp_verify_nonce($_POST['property_nonce'], 'wqcpt-property-meta' )
|| ! current_user_can( 'edit_post' ) ) {
    // Handle error
  }

   $wqcpt_prfr_title = isset ( $_POST['wqcpt_prfr_title'] ) ?
sanitize_text_field( trim($_POST['wqcpt_prfr_title']) ) : '';
   $wqcpt_prfr_content = isset ( $_POST['wqcpt_prfr_content'] ) ?
wp_kses_post( trim($_POST['wqcpt_prfr_content']) ) : '';
   $wqcpt_pr_type = isset ( $_POST['wqcpt_prfr_type'] ) ?
sanitize_text_field( trim($_POST['wqcpt_prfr_type']) ) : '';
   $wqcpt_pr_city = isset ( $_POST['wqcpt_prfr_city'] ) ?
sanitize_text_field( trim($_POST['wqcpt_prfr_city']) ) : '';

  // Validations and generate errors
  // post fields and existence of a post
  // Rest of the code for saving data
  }
```

We begin the function by using an `if` condition to check the availability of the **Submit** button in the frontend post creation request, to make sure our code is executed only for the frontend property creation form. Next, we use another conditional check for the nonce value and property creation permissions. In the custom post types section, we executed the permission check by passing the post ID, as we were only saving the custom fields for an already-created property. In this scenario, we are creating a property from scratch, and hence we don't have a post ID yet. So, we can only check for general post editing permissions.

 Once permission errors are generated, we can assign the error messages to a class variable and use it inside the shortcode function to display them.

Once validations are completed, we can retrieve the property data from the POST request and sanitize it before assigning to necessary variables. Here, we have used a function called `wp_kses_post` on the property content. This function sanitizes the content to only keep the allowed tags in WordPress post content by default. Next, we have to validate the data retrieved from the POST request and generate the errors to be displayed inside the shortcode. Now, we can take a look at the rest of the code for this function:

```
$post_id = wp_insert_post(
            array(
                'post_author' => get_current_user_id() ,
                'post_name' => sanitize_title( $wqcpt_prfr_titley ),
                'post_title' => $wqcpt_prfr_title,
                'post_status' => 'publish',
                'post_content' => $wqcpt_prfr_content,
                'post_type' => $this->post_type
            )
        );

if ( !is_wp_error( $post_id ) ) {
    update_post_meta( $post_id, '_wqcpt_pr_type', $wqcpt_pr_type );
    update_post_meta( $post_id, '_wqcpt_pr_city', $wqcpt_pr_city );
} else {
    // Handle errors
}
```

After validating all the property data, we use the `wp_insert_post` function to create the property on the `wp_posts` table. We can pass all the necessary settings as an array to this function. Here, we have used author as the current logged-in user. Then, we assign the property title and content to the respective settings while generating the URL for the post using the `sanitize_title` function. Finally, we set the correct post type and status as publish. This is a built-in function that creates posts while executing all the necessary filters and actions inside WordPress core. In case we use our own query to save the properties, we have to check and execute all the necessary filters and actions to make our feature compatible with other plugins. This function will return `true` or WordPress error based on the status of the execution. Next, we can check the errors and use the `update_post_meta` function to save the property custom fields to the `wp_postmeta` table.

> We can easily use frontend forms to store custom field data on custom database tables for additional flexibility. In such cases, we just have to replace the `wp_insert_post` function with a custom query and necessary data.

Now, we have completed the process of adding data using frontend forms, and you should be able to test the process by assiging the shortcode to a post or page and submitting the form with necessary data.

Loading forms using custom URLs

We already discussed the concept behind this technique in Chapter 6, *Practical Usage of WordPress APIs, Rewrite API* section. The shortcode method is not highly reliable for advanced web sites. So, we create our own URL structures and handle the forms using those custom URLs instead of using post, page, or custom post type. Since we already discussed this technique, we are going to go through the code without major explanations. Let's start by adding a new rewrite rule and a query parameter to handle frontend property creation:

```
add_action( 'init', 'wqcpt _manage_property_routes' );
function wqcpt_manage_property_routes() {
  add_rewrite_rule( '^property-listing/([^/]+)/?',
'index.php?wpquick_property_actions=$matches[1]', 'top' );
  add_rewrite_tag('%wpquick_property_actions%', '([^&]+)');
}
```

This code adds new rewrite rule accessible through `http://www.example.com/property-listing/add` for creating properties from frontend custom forms. We also use a tag called `wpquick_property_actions` to identify the functionality for properties. Ideally, we need to include this code within the main class of our plugin to keep the object oriented nature of our plugin. However, we discussed the need to flush rewrite rules on activation. So, there is a conflict since our plugin is initialized on the `plugins_loaded` action, and the activation handler is executed before that action. Therefore, we have to use the preceding code outside the main class of the plugin, along with the activation handler. The following code contains the activation handler for this plugin:

```
register_activation_hook( __FILE__, 'wqcpt_activate' );
function wqcpt_activate(){
  wqcpt_manage_property_routes();
  flush_rewrite_rules();
}
```

As we did in Chapter 6, *Practical Usage of WordPress APIs*, we register the rewrite rules on the activation handler, just before calling the `flush_rewrite_rules` function. Next, we need to filter the URL and load the custom form for creating properties. We use the built-in `template_redirect` action for this functionality, and we can include the action inside the `WQCPT_Model_Property` class, as shown in the following code:

```
public function property_controller() {
  global $wp_query, $wqcpt, $template_data;
  $wpquick_actions = isset (
$wp_query->query_vars['wpquick_property_actions'] ) ?
$wp_query->query_vars['wpquick_property_actions'] : '';

  switch ( $wpquick_actions ) {
    case 'add':
      $template_data['property_nonce'] = wp_create_nonce('wqcpt-property-
meta');

      ob_start();
      $wqcpt->template_loader->get_template_part( 'property','form' );
      $display = ob_get_clean();
      echo get_header();
      echo $display;
      echo get_footer();
      exit;
      break;
  }
}
```

First, we receive the value of `wpquick_property_actions` using WordPress query variables. Then, we use a `switch` statement to filter different actions for properties. In this scenario, we have only used `add` as a filter. In complete implementation, we will have to include `edit`, `delete`, and `list` actions at a minimum. Inside the `add` case, we load the same template we used for the shortcode process. Then, we include it between the header and footer of the site to display the frontend form. Now, you should be able to access and create properties by visiting `www.example.com/property-listing/add` in the browser URL.

Choosing between custom post types and custom forms

We looked at the features and process of both custom post types and custom forms in the previous sections. We started this chapter by discussing the custom post type features that have changed the way we develop with WordPress. Now, we can compare them with custom forms, and identify the advantages and disadvantages. Let's start by looking at the advantages of custom post types.

You may have already noticed the amount of coding we needed to get to display a custom form and use it for capturing data. We didn't spent even half of the time doing the same thing with custom post types. Let's summarize the additional things we had to do in custom form development, compared to custom post types:

- **Creating fields for title and content**: We had a built-in title field and content field with Rich Text Editor in custom post types, whereas we had to create two new fields to handle them in custom forms.
- **Adding a form and submit button**: We didn't need to add a form or submit button in custom post types as we were using the built-in post functions of WordPress.
- **Saving the property**: We didn't have to create the property and save the main details in custom post types as it was done automatically by the WordPress core process.
- **Handing property validations**: In custom post types, all the necessary validation on main property data is handled by core features. However, we need to check the existence of the property, URL, and make sure to sanitize the property content manually.

- **Post editing and listing**: We have the ability to edit, list, or delete a post as soon as we create one using backend custom post types. However, we only built the create form using the custom form, and hence we have to develop edit, list, and delete features from scratch using more custom forms.

So, in this perspective, built-in custom post types offer a lot more advantages over custom forms. Here are the advantages of using custom forms over custom post types:

- **Frontend interfaces**: Custom post types doesn't offer the data capturing features on the frontend and hence users need to be redirected to the backend. So, we can't match the forms with the styles of themes, whereas custom forms allow us to create any type of design. This also means we will have to manage the permission to other menu items in the backend.
- **Mix of frontend and backend**: When using custom forms, we can let users use the other site features as well as data submissions within the frontend, allowing users to have a consistent set of screens. However, using custom post types means that the user will have to switch between the frontend and backend of the site, creating unnecessary complexity.
- **Flexibility in validations**: WordPress automatically saves custom post types using the autosave feature and hence we can't wait for the custom post creation, until custom validations are completed. So, we have to use some workarounds to validate custom fields and display the error messages, while keeping the post type record inaccessible. In custom forms, we can have the complete freedom for data validation before we actually create the record on the `wp_posts` table.
- **Flexibility in using database tables**: In backend custom post types, the newly created post always saves to the `wp_posts` table. However, in custom forms we can decide whether to use existing tables or use our own custom tables for managing data.

By considering the advantages and disadvantages of each technique, we can come to a conclusion that backend custom post types are mostly suitable for sites with low budget and require a rapid development process. Also, we can consider custom post types when basic functionality is more important than flexibility. On the other hand, custom forms can be used for advanced sites, where performance is crucial and requires flexibility for future enhancements.

Using a form management plugin

We looked at the use of custom post types and custom forms for capturing and displaying the data needed for WordPress sites. However, many startup sites don't have the budget or time to develop a custom solution specific for their sites. So, developers will have to use existing solutions and build the features on top of them. In such cases, WordPress form plugins become the ideal solution. There are some popular form plugins developed to cater a specific area, such as contact forms. We can also find forms plugins such as Gravity Forms, Ninja Forms developed to cater any purpose. Let's understand the features expected from a quality forms plugin:

- **Drag and drop builder**: This is the feature that accelerates the development of custom forms with existing plugins. Instead of writing own HTML for each field, we should be able to drag and drop existing custom fields and build fully working custom forms in minutes.
- **Ajax-based form submission**: This is a very important feature in modern websites as developers don't use the normal post submissions for many features. So, the forms plugin should have the ability use normal form submission as well as AJAX-based submissions.
- **Different field types**: In this plugin, we only used basic text and dropdown fields. However, we need many field types such as dates, google maps, and searchable dropdowns in advanced websites. So, the ability to handle such advanced requirements with the built-in fields in forms plugins is definitely a huge advantage.
- **Form field validations**: Usually, we had to validate each field by applying the necessary validation rules. In a quality forms plugin, we should have the ability to select from an existing set of rules and validate the fields without writing a single line of code.
- **Conditional logic**: In custom forms, we develop each form for specific requirements and hence we can manually apply conditions before loading certain fields. In forms plugins, we add the fields dynamically to a form, and hence we should have the ability to define the conditions before making each field visible on the site.
- **Displaying and exporting data**: We should have the ability to display submitted data in the frontend and export it to common file types when necessary.
- **Saving form data to a custom database table**: Usually, many forms plugins save the data to the `wp_postmeta` table or use the same custom table to save the data of all forms to a single custom table. We should at least have the ability to choose between existing tables or a custom table.

These are some of the features we expect from quality form plugins. Let's take a look at the following screen for the form-creating interface of one of the most popular forms plugins:

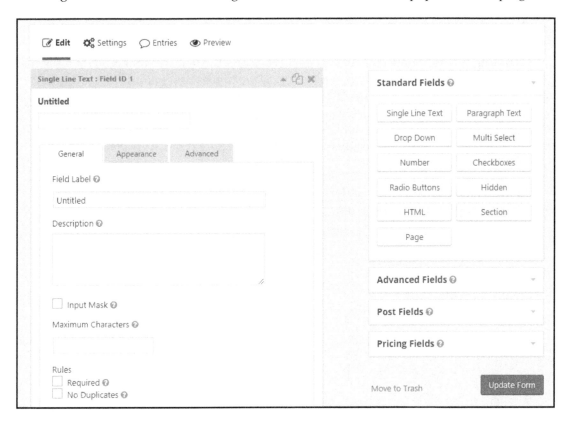

The preceding screenshot previews some of the features we discussed in the previous section. However, it will be difficult to find a forms plugins that provides all these features in a way that we expect to use them. Also, almost all the forms plugin don't provide a frontend interface to let the user edit the submitted data or list them. So, forms plugins are best-suited for scenarios where we want to use one-time forms to capture the user data. Popular examples include registration forms, contact forms, payment forms, and surveys. We should always use custom forms or custom post types to manage forms that requires the user to submit data, update it, and list all the submitted data.

Summary

The process of managing the data is one of the most important aspect of a website or application. WordPress custom post types allow us to model different content types in a standard way, and use built-in features for rapid development. We began the chapter by understanding the importance of custom post types and the features that made it a popular choice in plugin development. Then, we looked at the process of creating custom post types, while understanding the use of taxonomies and custom fields with custom post types. Next, we moved to the process and techniques of developing custom forms for the frontend of a website. Finally, we looked at the need for using forms plugins, and compared the advantages and disadvantages of custom post types and custom forms.

In Chapter 8, *Discovering Key Modules in Development*, we will be exploring the development of key modules in modern web sites, such as UI component integration, improving usability, and customizing core admin features.

Discovering Key Modules in Development

8

Modern website interfaces are mostly built on the concept of blocks, where the site owners can drag and drop reusable components to build the interfaces. UI components and page builders play a major role in developing these interfaces. Therefore, it's important for developers to have the knowledge of integrating any third-party UI component to build amazing interfaces with interactivity. On the other hand, WordPress is chosen by many developers due to the existing CMS features that accelerate the development process. So, developers need thorough knowledge of using backend features as well as customizing the existing features for custom requirements.

In this chapter, we are going to focus on UI component integration as well as customization of common backend features. We begin the chapter by integrating a jQuery slider to WordPress while using menu pages to capture the data. Then, we will integrate another popular component called accordion by using custom post types to capture the data. After this, we will look at the basic steps of integrating any UI component using the two integrations for Image Slider and accordion. Also, we will look at the importance of modern page builders in site development and discuss the basics of creating a custom component with any page builder. Finally, we will look at the process of customizing backend features by creating a basic dashboard widget and modifying list tables to provide custom features.

In this chapter, we will cover the following topics:

- Integrating UI components
- Integrating jQuery image slider
- Integrating jQuery accordion
- Identifying the steps for integrating UI components
- Understanding the use of page builders
- Creating custom dashboard widgets
- Customizing backend list tables

By the end of this chapter, you will have the ability to customize backend admin features as well as integrate UI components into sites with the latest trending methods.

Technical requirements

You will be required to have WordPress 4.9.8 installed to follow this procedure. Even if you have a later version of WordPress, the described examples should work with no significant problems.

The code files of this chapter can be found on GitHub:
```
https://github.com/PacktPublishing/WordPress-Development-Quick-Start-Guide/
tree/master/Chapter08
```

Check out the following video to see the code in action:
```
http://bit.ly/2yGYX03
```

UI components

Modern websites are built on top of interactive UI elements. Many premium WordPress themes include a wide range of UI components with the support of open source JavaScript and CSS libraries. These UI components attract users to a site by simplifying the interfaces as well as providing large content in a limited space. Among hundreds of UI elements, we find image sliders and galleries, tabs being the most popular ones. As a developer, you need to use or build these components to keep up to date with rising UI requirements in modern development. So, it's important to understand the basic process of integrating any UI component into WordPress using plugins or themes. In this section, we are going to look at the integration of two UI components. Let's get started.

Integrating the jQuery image slider

The image sliders and galleries are the most popular UI elements in WordPress sites. You can visit the `wordpress.org` plugin directory or a premium marketplace such as Codecanyon to understand the amount of downloads and purchases of such plugins. We can use these sliders for displaying a set of basic images, as well as to display advanced content and images to promote your products, services, and features.

In this section, we are going to use Basic jQuery Slider (`http://basicslider.com/`) to explain the process of integrating an Image Slider. We will be creating a single Image Slider to display product images in the home page of the site or any other preferred location.

 Image Slider plugins give you the ability to create multiple reusable sliders using custom post types or custom forms. In this scenario, we are only focusing on a single predefined slider.

Before starting the implementation, we have to create another plugin for this chapter. We are going to name it `WPQuick Key Modules` in a directory called `wpquick-key-modules`. We will be using this plugin for the implementation of most of the features discussed in this chapter. The plugin will have the same structure as the previous plugins, with a main class initializing all the other features and classes.

Building a product image slider

We can use sliders to display any type of content, with the common type of content being images. The first step of integrating any UI component is the process of capturing the data. In this scenario, the required data will be a set of images. So, we need to build an interface to let the administrator upload a set of images for the slider. We have two options for creating an interface for such requirements:

- **Menu pages**: We can use the `add_menu_page` function to create a new menu page for the features of our plugin. This will be a top-level menu item in the WordPress admin menu with the ability to support sub menu pages. This is suitable when you need to highlight the menu of your plugin as well as create different menu pages for various features of the plugin. More details about the `add_menu_page` function are available at `https://developer.wordpress.org/reference/functions/add_menu_page/`.
- **Options pages**: We can use the `add_options_page` function to create a new options page for custom settings. This function will create a sub-level menu item on the **Settings** menu item. However, it doesn't support further levels, and hence it will be difficult to use for plugins that require multiple menu pages. This is useful for adding general site specific settings rather than plugin settings. More details about the `add_options_page` function is available at `https://developer.wordpress.org/reference/functions/add_options_page/`.

In this scenario, we are going to choose menu pages for the image uploading interface, as this is a plugin-specific custom requirement. Let's build a menu page to upload the images.

Creating a plugin menu page

WordPress provides built-in functions to add menu pages through plugins. We can add the interfaces as main- menu items or as sub-menu items. Create a class called `WQKM_UI_Components` inside the classes directory of our plugin. Then, we can do the usual file inclusion and object creation within the `includes` and `instance` functions of the main class of our plugin. Next, we can add the following line of code within `admin_menu` action to register a new menu page:

```
add_menu_page( __('UI Component Settings', 'wqkm' ), __('UI Component
Settings', 'wqkm' ),  'manage_options','wqkm-settings', array(
&$this,'ui_settings' ) );
```

The first two parameters of this function define titles for the menu page and the menu item. The third parameter defines the capability to load this page. Here, we have used `manage_options` as the capability to restrict it to the administrator. You can change this capability based on the person responsible for using this interface. The fourth parameter defines a unique slug to access the menu item from the URL. The final parameter defines the callback function to generate the content for this interface. These are the main parameters used for this function.

Now we need to implement the callback function to display the necessary fields to upload the images to the slider. Let's take a look at the structure of the `ui_settings` function:

```
public function ui_settings(){
    // Define global variables
    // Load template and return to browser
}
```

We have already discussed a callback function for template loading in the previous chapters, and hence we will not be discussing the code in detail. First, we define the global variables for holding the main instance of our plugin and passing the data to templates. Then, we load the custom template using the technique we used in the previous chapters, with the support of the custom template loader. You can refer to the source code for the complete implementation. Next, we have to build the custom template to upload files, as shown in the following code:

```
<?php
 global $wqkm_template_data;
 extract($wqkm_template_data);
?>
<form id="wqkm_slider_frm" action="" method="POST" >
 <div id="wqkm-slider-msg"></div>
 <table class="form-table">
   <tr>
```

```
    <th><label><?php _e('Product Slider Images','wqkm'); ?>*</label></th>
    <td> <div id="wqkm-slider-images-panel"></div>
      <input type="file" name="wqkm_slider_image" id="wqkm_slider_image"
value="" />
      </td>
  </tr>
  <tr>
    <th>&</th>
    <td><input name="wqkm_ui_submit" id="wqkm_ui_submit" type="button"
value="<?php _e('Add Image','wqkm'); ?>" /></td>
  </tr>
 </table>
</form>
```

Let's understand the structure of this template for handling image uploads:

1. First, we define the global variable to accept the template data passed from the
   WQKM_UI_Components class. Initially, this variable will be empty, as we don't
   have any template data or settings.

2. Then, we have to define a form to enable data submissions. Inside the form, we
   have an empty container called wqkm-slider-msg to handle the form error and
   success messages.

3. Next, we add a file input field to select and upload the images for the slider. We
   also added a DIV element called wqkm-slider-images-panel, inline with the
   file field to display the current images uploaded to the slider.

4. Finally, we add a button instead of a submit button, as we will be using AJAX to
   handle the form submission.

Now the interface is prepared to upload images to the slider. You can access this interface
by using the UI Component Settings menu item from the main menu.

Saving slider images using AJAX

We can use normal post submissions as well as AJAX submissions, as this is a backend
screen without any other dependencies. However, AJAX gives better user experience, and
hence we will be submitting the form data through AJAX. First, we have to add a new
script using the load_admin_scripts function to handle the AJAX request for saving
slider images. We will be using the exact same code used for the WooCommerce Product
Files plugin, and hence you can refer to the main file inside the source code directory for
the implementation of the load_admin_scripts function.

Next, we have to handle the form submission process using AJAX. The code for the file form submission is available inside the `wqkm-admin.js` file of the source codes directory. The implementation will be the same as the one we used in the `wqwpf-admin.js` file of the `WQWPF Product Files` plugin, except for the following differences:

- In this case, we have get the custom form using the form ID, instead of using a built-in post-submission form
- We use the `wqkm_save_slider_images` action instead of the `wqwpf_save_product_files`
- We remove the post-ID parameter, as we are not submitting a form related to a post

Now we come to the final part of the image-saving process by uploading and capturing the file data. We have to begin by adding the following action to the constructor of the `WQKM_UI_Components` class:

```
add_action( 'wp_ajax_wqkm_save_slider_images', array( $this,
'save_slider_images') );
```

This process is only executed by the logged users, and hence we have omitted the `wp_ajax_nopriv` action. Let's take a look at the implementation of the `save_slider_images` function:

```
public function save_slider_images(){
  global $wpdb;
  $file_nonce = isset( $_POST['file_nonce'] ) ? ($_POST['file_nonce']) :'';
  $user_id = get_current_user_id();

  if(check_ajax_referer( 'wqkm-private-admin', 'file_nonce',false )){
    $result_upload = $this->process_file_upload();
    if(isset($result_upload['status']) && $result_upload['status'] ==
'success' ){
      $file_date = date("Y-m-d H:i:s");
      $uploaded_file_name = $result_upload['base_name'];
      $slider_images = (array) get_option('wqkm_slider_images');
      $slider_images[] = $result_upload['relative_file_path'];
      update_option( 'wqkm_slider_images', $slider_images );
      $upload_dir = wp_upload_dir();
      $display_images = '';
      foreach ($slider_images as $slider_image) {
        if( $slider_image != '' )
          $display_images .= '<img src="' . $upload_dir['baseurl'] .
$slider_image . '" style="width:100px;height:100px" />';
      }
```

```
        $result = array( 'status' => 'success', 'msg' => $result_upload['msg']
, 'images' => $display_images );
    }else{
        $result = array( 'status' => 'error','msg'=> $result_upload['msg']);
    }
  }else{
    $result = array( 'status' => 'error', 'msg' => __('Invalid file upload
request.','wqkm') );
  }
  echo json_encode($result);exit;
}
```

Here's what the previous code does:

1. We begin the function by retrieving the nonce value from the POST request and assigning the ID of the logged-in user.
2. Then, we upload the images in the request using the `process_file_upload` function, after completing the nonce verification. We have made a copy of the `process_file_upload` function from the **Post Attachments** plugin developed earlier. The only difference is the use of image-specific file types instead of the document file types we used earlier.
3. Once the images are uploaded, we use the `get_option` function to retrieve the existing images. Then, we add the uploaded image and save the new image set using `update_option`. In this scenario, we have stored slider images in the `wp_options` table, as it was a predefined slider. In scenarios where we need multiple dynamic sliders, we have to use the `wp_posts` table or a custom table to store this data.
4. Finally, we traverse through the images list and generate the HTML for images to be sent as part of the response for an AJAX request. In the AJAX request, we have to use the necessary keys and display the existing images list inline with the image upload field.

Now we have captured the necessary data required for our image slider component. The next step is to use this data along with the necessary scripts to generate the UI component.

Preparing slider images

We need to prepare the HTML code to include the slider images with the necessary containers. The element structure for each slider varies based on the library. Therefore, we need to refer to the documentation of the slider JavaScript library and find out the expected structure. So, we have to visit http://basicslider.com/ and go to the **Markup** section. This section explains the required elements to implement the slider:

```html
<div id="banner-fade">
 <ul class="bjqs">
 <li><!-- Any content you like --></li>
 </ul>
</div>
```

Now we have to use this structure and add the slider images inside `<li>` elements. We can directly add the HTML to a WordPress post or a page, to display a slider. However, we may need to reuse the slider, and hence it is always a good option to implement it as a shortcode or a widget. The shortcode is the perfect solution, as it can be also included within widgets. Let's start the implementation by adding a shortcode to the constructor of the `WQKM_UI_Components` class:

```php
add_shortcode( 'wqkm_product_slider', array( $this, 'product_slider') );
```

Now we can implement the shortcode callback function to use the uploaded images and generate the HTML structure required for the slider. Consider the following code:

```php
public function product_slider( $atts, $content ){
  $sh_attr = shortcode_atts( array(
    'width' => '520',
    'height' => '320',
  ), $atts );

  $slider_images = (array) get_option('wqkm_slider_images');
  $upload_dir = wp_upload_dir();

  $display = '<div id="banner-fade"><ul class="bjqs">';
  foreach ($slider_images as $slider_image) {
    if( $slider_image != '' )
      $display .= '<li><img src="' . $upload_dir['baseurl'] . $slider_image
. '" /></li>';
  }
  $display .= ' </ul><div>';
  return $display;
}
```

We begin the function by defining the available shortcode attributes and their default values. Here, we have only used the `width` and the `height` of the slider as settings. You may need to define more settings depending on the image slider library of your choice. Then, we retrieve the list of slider images using the `get_option` function with the `wqkm_slider_images` key. Finally, we traverse through the images and add the image HTML within the `<li>` elements while using the main `<ul>` and `<div>` containers to initialize the slider.

Once the shortcode is added to a post or page, you will see a list of images as bullet points, without any sliding functionality.

Integrating jQuery slider

This is the final part of the integration, where we apply the functionality of JavaScript or CSS libraries to initialize the features of the UI component. So, we need to understand the required library files and the order of inclusion. The required files are shown in the **Usage** section of `http://basicslider.com/`. So, we have to download the necessary libraries and add them within our plugin. Once the files are added, we can use the following script and style registering code inside the `load_scripts` function of the main class:

```
wp_register_style( 'wqkm-slider', WQKM_PLUGIN_URL . 'css/bjqs.css' );
wp_register_style( 'wqkm-slider-demo', WQKM_PLUGIN_URL . 'css/demo.css' );
wp_register_script( 'wqkm-slider', WQKM_PLUGIN_URL . 'js/bjqs-1.3.js',
array('jquery') );
wp_register_script('wqkm-front',WQKM_PLUGIN_URL .'js/wqkm-front.js',
array('jquery','wqkm-slider') );
```

We have included the `bjqs.css` and `demo.css` files for styles and the `bjqs-1.3.js` file for scripts with jQuery as a dependency. The third line registers a plugin-specific custom script to initialize the slider. So, we have to use both the jQuery and the slider library as dependencies.

Now we need to include these libraries to WordPress requests. We can use the `wp_enqueue_style` and the `wp_enqueue_script` functions along with registration code to include the files. However, it means these files will be included on every request, even when there are no image sliders in pages. As a solution, we can include them inside the shortcode function, just after the default values for the shortcode attributes. You can refer to the source code for the inclusion of these files.

Then, we come to the final step, where we initialize the component using the necessary scripts. You can refer to the **Activation** section of http://basicslider.com/ to understand the initialization process, as shown in the following code. This code should be added to the wqkm-front.js custom script file:

```
jQuery(document).ready(function($) {
  $('#banner-fade').bjqs({
    animtype : 'slide',
    height : WQKMFront.height,
    width : WQKMFront.width,
    responsive : true,
    randomstart : true,
    showmarkers   : false,
  });
});
```

In this library, bjqs acts as the initialization function. We use it on the container with the ID #banner-fade. We have also assigned the shortcode attribute values for width and height using the data we added with the wp_localize_script function. Now you can refresh the browser and see an image slider, instead of the bullet list.

This is a very basic slider with basic functionality. You can find more advanced sliders with images, content, videos, and some amazing effects. You can try different sliders, as the process of integration is the same, regardless of the slider.

Reusing the slider as a widget

We had a brief introduction to widgets and their role in WordPress. Widgets was intended to add blocks of features to the sidebar of the site. However, with modern themes and widget areas, widgets can be considered as a reusable block of features similar to shortcodes. So, we are going to look at the process of building a frontend widget in WordPress. Let's start by adding a new file to the classes directory of our plugin with a class called WQKM_Product_Slider_Widget.

In this scenario, we will be building a widget to display the product slider created in the previous section. So, we can reuse the shortcode functionality for this widget. Let's take a look at the implementation of the widget, using the following code:

```
class WQKM_Product_Slider_Widget extends WP_Widget {
  public function __construct() {
    parent::__construct( 'wqkm_product_slider', esc_html__( 'Product
Slider', 'wqkm' ), array( 'description' => esc_html__( 'Main product
slider', 'wqkm' ) ) );
  }
```

```php
    public function widget( $args, $instance ) {
        echo $args['before_widget'];
        echo do_shortcode('[wqkm_product_slider width="'.$instance['width'].'"
height="'.$instance['height'].'" /]');
        echo $args['after_widget'];
    }

    public function form( $instance ) {
        $width = ! empty($instance['width']) ? (int) $instance['width']: 640;
        $height= ! empty($instance['height']) ? (int)
$instance['height']:320;?>
        <p>
          <label><?php esc_attr_e( 'Width:', 'wqkm' ); ?></label>
          <input class="widefat" id="<?php echo esc_attr( $this->get_field_id(
'width' ) ); ?>" name="<?php echo esc_attr( $this->get_field_name( 'width'
) ); ?>" type="text" value="<?php echo esc_attr( $width ); ?>">
        </p>
        <p>
          <label><?php esc_attr_e( 'Height:', 'wqkm' ); ?></label>
          <input class="widefat" id="<?php echo esc_attr( $this->get_field_id(
'height' ) ); ?>" name="<?php echo esc_attr( $this->get_field_name(
'height' ) ); ?>" type="text" value="<?php echo esc_attr( $height ); ?>">
        </p>
    <?php  }

    public function update( $new_instance, $old_instance ) {
        $instance = array();
        $instance['width'] = ( ! empty( $new_instance['width'] ) ) ? (int)
$new_instance['width'] : '';
        $instance['height'] = ( ! empty( $new_instance['height'] ) ) ? (int)
$new_instance['height'] : '';
        return $instance;
    }
}
```

WordPress uses the `WP_Widget` class as the base for handling the widget functionality. All the widgets, including the core widgets, should extend this class to use the widget functionality. Therefore, we have extended this class in our custom `WQKM_Product_Slider_Widget` class declaration. Now we can go though the main functions of a widget using the following steps:

1. `constructor`: We have to use this function to call the constructor of the parent `WP_Widget` class, with the necessary parameters. In this case, we have used a unique ID, title, and a description.

2. `widget`: This function is used to generate the output of the widget in the frontend. Here, we have used `wqkm_product_slider` shortcode to generate the output for the widget. You can use a shortcode or call a function to generate the output. The `$instance` variable contains all the settings for the widget, added to the backend. So, we are using the width and height settings as attributes to the shortcode. You may also notice the use of the `$args['before_widget']` and the `$args['before_widget']` statements. These are a predefined set of arguments passed to the widget and the values of these arguments are specified when registering the widgets. These arguments are useful for adding common content before or after each widget.

3. `form`: This function is used to display the form to capture the settings for the widget. We used width and height in the widget function, and hence we need settings to define those values. First, we get the existing values for the settings using the `$instance` variable passed automatically to this function. Then, we generate the input fields for the width and height settings. You may notice the use of the `get_field_id` and the `get_field_name` functions. These are functions defined in the core `WP_Widget` class to provide access to the widget details in a standard way. You should always use these functions without hard-coding names and IDs.

4. `Update`: This function is used to save or update the settings data to the database. Once the **Save** button of a widget is clicked, this function will be called with the old values, as well as the submitted new values. We have to make the necessary validations and assign the new values to the `$instance` variable with the respective keys. Then, the WordPress core widget class will automatically save the values in the `$instance` variable.

This is the standard process for building any custom widget. Once the widget class is created, you have to use these four functions to generate the necessary settings and output for the widget. Even though we have completed creating the widget, it will not be visible in the **Appearance | Widgets** section. We have to register new widgets, before they appear in the widgets section. Let's consider the following code for registering our widget:

```
add_action( 'widgets_init', array( $this, 'register_product_slider_widget'
) );
public function register_product_slider_widget() {
  register_widget( 'WQKM_Product_Slider_Widget' );
}
```

First, we need to include the file inside the `includes` function of the main class. Then, we can add the `widgets_init` action to the constructor of the `WQKM_Admin_Features` class. Finally, we use `register_widget` with the class name of the widget inside the callback function to register the new widget. Now you should be able to use the new widget to add the product image slider to your sidebar.

Integrating jQuery accordion

In this section, we are going to look at the integration of another popular UI component called **Accordion**. The accordion is a component that allows you to display a large amount of content within a limited space using collapsible sections. We have chosen the accordion component of the **jQuery UI** library (`https://jqueryui.com/accordion/`) as a basic solution. You can find many advanced accordion component libraries.

In the image sliders section, we used a menu page to capture data, and limited it to a single fixed-image slider. However, it's also important to have the ability to use same component with different content in various places on the site. So, we are going to build accordions with the ability to create unlimited components with dynamic content. We can either use custom post types and store the data in a `wp_posts` table, or we can use a custom table. Since we are developing a UI element, we are going to use custom post types to simplify the process. Let's get started.

Creating an accordion model and capturing data

We have chosen to use custom post types for accordions. Therefore, we need to register a new custom post type by using the `register_post_type` function with necessary settings. We already created a custom post type and discussed the process in previous chapters, while working with the property post type. Therefore, you can refer to the `WQKM_UI_Components` class inside the source code directory to understand the registration.

 Unlike properties, accordions are not intended to be displayed as individual posts or to achieve page items. Instead, we use them to capture the data to be reused in UI elements within posts or pages. Therefore, we have to set the `public` attribute to `false` while creating the custom post type. This setting makes sure that the accordions are not publicly visible as an individual post type.

Once the post type is registered, we need to use metaboxes to include the necessary fields and capture the data for accordions. The accordion has many sections with dynamic content. So, we need text area fields to capture the content for each section. Let's start by adding a metabox to accordions:

```
public function add_accordion_meta_boxes() {
   add_meta_box( 'wqkm-accordion-meta', __('Accordion Details','wqkm'),
   array( $this, 'display_accordion_meta_boxes' ), $this->post_type );
   }
```

Here, we have registered a new meta box for the accordion post type. The add_meta_boxes action and the post type initialization can be found inside the constructor of the WQKM_UI_Components class. Now we need to implement the callback function using the following code:

```
public function display_accordion_meta_boxes( $accordion ) {
   global $wqkm,$template_data;
   $template_data['accordion_post_type'] = $this->post_type;
   $template_data['accordion_nonce'] = wp_create_nonce('wqkm-accordion-
meta');
   $template_data['wqkm_tab_1'] = get_post_meta( $accordion->ID,
'_wqkm_tab_1', true );

   ob_start();
   $wqkm->template_loader->get_template_part( 'accordion','meta');
   $display = ob_get_clean();
   echo $display;
   }
```

We begin the function by defining the global variables and adding the post type and nonce to the global template data variable. Then, we get the existing data for the accordion sections using the get_post_meta function. Here, we have only included one section. You can find three sections in the source code.

 We have fixed the accordion sections to three, to simplify the development. Ideally, we should allow administrators to dynamically add an unlimited number of sections for accordions.

Finally, we load a custom template for the input fields of the accordion sections. The template for the accordion meta boxes can be found inside the accordion-meta.php file in the templates directory.

This template is similar to the one used for the `Properties` post type, and hence it's self-explanatory. However, you may notice the use of the following line of code instead of the code for text areas:

```
<td><?php wp_editor( $wqkm_tab_1, 'wqkm_tab_1' ); ?></td>
```

We could have used text area fields for the accordion section. However, these sections may contain a considerable amount of HTML, and hence using a text area can be difficult. As a solution, we used the `wp_editor` function that generates the WordPress content editor field with all the formatting. We have to pass the default content and the ID of the content editor. Now we can use the WordPress rich content editor to add content to the accordion sections.

We need to save the section data to complete the data capturing process for accordions. The saving process is implemented using the `save_post` action and the implementation is similar to the property details saving process. The only difference is the use of `wp_kses_post` function to filter the section content generated by the `wp_editor` function. You can refer to the source code for the implementation of the section saving process inside the `WQKM_UI_Components` class.

Preparing accordion content

We already identified the importance of shortcodes for adding UI elements to posts or pages. Therefore, we will be using another shortcode to prepare the content for the accordion. Let's add the following code to the implementation of the accordion shortcode:

```
add_shortcode( 'wqkm_accordian', array( $this, 'display_accordian') );
public function display_accordian( $atts, $content ){
  $sh_attr = shortcode_atts( array( 'id' => '0' ), $atts );
  extract($sh_attr);

  $display = '<div id="accordion">';
  if( trim( get_post_meta( $id, '_wqkm_tab_1' , true ) ) != '' ){
    $display .= '<h3>'.get_the_title( $id ).'</h3>';
    $display .= '<div><p>'.get_post_meta( $id, '_wqkm_tab_1' , true ).' </p></div>';
  }

  // other fields
  $display .= '</div>';
  return $display;
}
```

Here's what the previous code does:

1. We have added a new shortcode called `wqkm_accordian` to the constructor of the `WQKM_UI_Components` class. We used custom post types to allow the creation of unlimited accordions, and hence we need a way to identify each accordion. So, we use the post ID as a shortcode attribute to identify the accordion.

2. Next, we generate the content sections of accordion by loading the data using the ID attribute.

3. Here, we have used the section title and the section content for each section inside a main container. This is the required structure for the chosen accordion library. You will have to find the element structure in case you choose different library for the implementation.

4. Finally, we return the output from the shortcode with accordion sections.

Now you can create and add an accordion to a post or page using the necessary ID. However, like the image slider, you will just see a bunch of HTML sections displayed on browser. To enable the accordion functionality, we need to register the necessary scripts and styles inside the `load_scripts` function of the main class, as shown in the following code:

```
wp_register_style('wqkm-jquery-ui-style', WQKM_PLUGIN_URL . 'css/jquery-
ui.css', false, null);
wp_register_script( 'wqkm-accordion', WQKM_PLUGIN_URL . 'js/wqkm-
accordion.js', array('jquery','jquery-ui-accordion') );
```

First, we have downloaded and added the `jQuery UI CSS` file to our plugin, as it's not provided within the WordPress core. Then, we have added a custom script called `wqkm-accordion.js`, with jQuery and jQuery UI accordion scripts as dependencies. The jQuery UI component libraries are available within the WordPress core, and hence we can directly call the script handle instead of registering the script separately. Then, we can add the following code to the shortcode function to enqueue the files:

```
wp_enqueue_style('wqkm-jquery-ui-style');
wp_enqueue_script('wqkm-accordion');
```

We have the accordion script and style included within the shortcode. Finally, we have to initialize the accordion by adding the following initialization code to the `wqkm-accordion.js` file:

```
jQuery(document).ready(function($) {
  $( "#accordion" ).accordion({ collapsible: true, active: false,
heightStyle: "content"   });
});
```

The accordion is initialized using the ID of the main container we created for the shortcode output. This may vary based on the accordion library of your choice. Now we have completed the accordion integration process, and your accordion should look similar to the following screenshot:

As you can see, we can use these UI components in a limited space to display a large amount of contents.

Steps for integrating UI components

Up to this point, we looked at two implementations for integrating the jQuery slider and accordion UI components using different data-capturing techniques. The implementation may vary based on the type of UI component and its functionality. However, the basic process is similar for most of the common UI components. So, let's summarize the keys for integrating any UI component with WordPress:

1. **Identify component data**: Each UI component works on existing data or elements. So, we need to identify the data needed to use each UI component and the method for storing this data.
2. **Generate component output**: In this step, we have to use the captured data, process it, and generate the HTML output needed to enable the features of a UI component. Usually, we use a reusable component such as a shortcode or widget to add and generate the output for UI components.

3. **Include component libraries**: Most UI components generate their features by applying JavaScript or CSS to the generated output. These features of the component generally come as an open source library. So, in this step, we need to all the necessary scripts and styles for the component, along with the necessary settings. In this process, we use `wp_register_style` and `wp_register_script` functions to include these resources by adding them inside plugins or themes. Then, you can enqueue them conditionally within the main class or inside the UI component generation function.

4. **Passing script data**: Some of the UI element libraries directly apples CSS or JavaScript features on the generated output. However, some element scripts require certain data or settings to initialize the element. In such cases, we have to pass the necessary data to necessary scripts using the `wp_localize_script` function.

5. **Initialize the element**: Once necessary libraries and HTML output is ready, we can initialize the element by using the initialization function of these libraries. These initializations generally takes one to a few lines of code. Usually, we use a CSS class or HTML element ID on the generated output for this initialization.

Once these steps are completed, you will see the interactive features or styles in your UI element. This is the general process for the most common UI elements. However, there may be exceptions that require a different process to initialize the UI element.

Simplifying development with page builders

Page builder is a set of components that simplifies the process of content creation or building the features of the site. These components allow developers to build complex interfaces in super-quick time by choosing and configuring built-in components. Page builders were initially used for simplifying content creation with pre-built design elements. However, page builders have now evolved into a state where we can use the existing components to add advanced site features such as form management, searchable google maps, parallax images, and videos.

Until recently, developers used the page builders included in themes, as well as free and premium page builder plugins. WordPress has introduced a block-based content builder called **Gutenberg**. At this stage, Gutenberg editor supports content editing with a basic set of elements. Currently, it's nowhere near the features offered by popular page builders such as Elementor, Beaver Builder, and Visual Composer. However, the future seems bright, as the WordPress team is backing the Gutenberg editor by making it a default core feature. So, we will soon see more powerful features of the Gutenberg editor, along with the features offered by other page builders.

Understanding the features of page builders

As we discussed, page builders offer a wide range of components that can be dragged or assigned to any post, page, or custom post type. However, many of these page builders provide advanced features beyond using basic built-in components. So, it's important to understand these features to use the existing components, as well as making your solutions integrate with page builders. Let's take a look at the main features offered by modern page builders:

- **Backend and frontend editing**: Usually, we edit or build the site interfaces using the backend content editor, and hence we have to switch to frontend to view the changes. Most page builders provide frontend editing, allowing previews in real time and adjusting them instantly. Also, there is a backend editor, if you want to work with other backend features.
- **Built-in templates**: Many page builders provide built-in template designs by using the existing components. So, the developers can use these templates designed for common requirements and adjust them as needed without writing a single line of code.
- **Advanced styling**: Each component allows various styling options such as margins, paddings, colors and so on. So, you can fine tune the design without going into the code.
- **Responsive design**: This is a must in modern development to cater for different devices, such as personal computers, mobiles, tabs, and so on. Usually, we have to spend lot of time making our designs fully responsive. Page builder structure and components are responsive by default. So, you don't have to do anything to make the content responsive as long as you follow the proper coding standards for your own elements.

As you can see, page builder provides a lot of power for building the content and design of your site. However, these powerful features also come with some limitations. Some of these page builders are completely dependent on shortcodes, and hence you will be locked into the plugin. Also, you might experience performance issues when using some complex features of page builders. Therefore, you need to be responsible with choosing the proper page builder and the features.

Developing components for page builders

Most popular page builders come with a wide range of built-in components as well as additional components using addons. So, we can use the existing components to build general purpose WordPress sites. However, when developing advanced applications or sites with custom requirements, the default functionality of these components may not be sufficient. In such cases, we have to build our own page builder components to provide the necessary functionality. We can always create shortcodes and ask the clients to use them inside the page builder components. But building our components simplifies the process considerably for the client, and hence we have to build components whenever necessary.

Major page builders provides an API or guide for developing components for their plugin. The technique varies for each page builder. So, you need to use the documentation to understand and develop a component for each page builder. Developing a component from scratch with the necessary explanations is beyond the scope of this chapter. However, we will explore the basic steps of component creation using the Elementor page builder as the example. Let's take a look at the main steps for building a page builder component:

- Each page builder identifies its components as modules, widgets, blocks, and so on. So, there should be a way to register new components for the page builder. Elementor uses the `Widget_Base` class and `register_widget_type` function to register new components. The other page builders offer similar techniques.
- After registering the component, you need to specify the input fields for capturing component data. Most page builders provide different types of input fields to capture and save the data for the component. Elementor provides a function called `add_control` on the `Widget_Base` class, supporting over 30 different control types. The other page builders will have similar functions to add input fields to different field types, as well as different data-storing mechanisms.
- Finally, we need to provide the output of the component by building the HTML code or executing an existing shortcode. Elementor provides a function called `render` for retrieving the saved component data and displaying the output. The other page builders should have a similar method, with a similar name.

We have used these steps and built a slider component for the Elementor page builder. You can find the code for this addon inside the `wpquick-elementor-components` directory of the source code for this chapter. The following screenshot previews the component generated by the addon with settings:

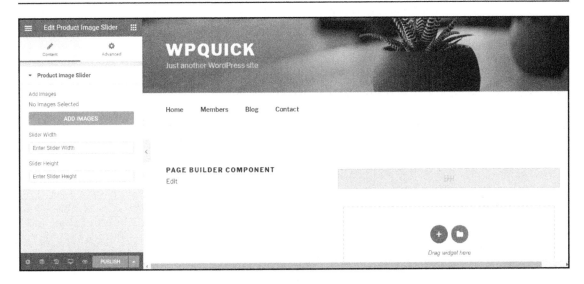

Elementor is one of the most popular and rising page builders at this stage. You can access the documentation at `https://developers.elementor.com/creating-an-extension-for-elementor/` and use the addon code for understanding the step. The process for other page builders will be similar, with the support of plugin-specific component creation functions.

Simplifying and customizing admin features

We have to use the core features as much as possible to get the maximum benefits of using WordPress for site development. This includes the use of frontend theme features, as well as the existing backend features, that mainly focuses on post-related functionality. So, it's obvious that developers need to customize these features to suit the requirements of each website. In this section, we are going to look at several customizations of commonly used backend features.

Creating custom dashboard widgets

We had a brief introduction to the **Dashboard Widget API** in Chapter 6, *Practical Usage of WordPress APIs*. Basically, a *dashboard* is a collection of widgets built for administration purposes. Unlike frontend theme widgets, we don't have an interface for adding or removing admin dashboard widgets. So, we have to build custom solutions to build new dashboard widgets as well as remove the existing ones. In this section, we are going to look at the process of creating a basic dashboard widget.

Registering and building dashboard widgets

First, we have to register the dashboard widget by using the `wp_dashboard_setup` action, instead of the `widgets_init` we used on the frontend widgets. Consider the following code for the widget registration process:

```
add_action( 'wp_dashboard_setup', array( $this, 'dashboard_widgets' ) );
public function dashboard_widgets() {
  wp_add_dashboard_widget( 'wqkm_post_attachments', __('Post
Attachments','wqkm'), array( $this, 'post_attachments_widget' ) );
}
```

Inside the callback function, we use the `wp_add_dashboard_widget` function to register a new widget. The parameters for this function contain a unique widget ID, widget title, and the callback function. Then, we have to implement the function to display the content for the widget, as shown in the following code:

```
public function post_attachments_widget() {
  echo do_shortcode('[wpquick_attachment_posts]');
}
```

Here, we have simplified the process by using a shortcode we developed in earlier chapters. Basically, we have a dashboard widget in fewer than 10 lines of code. This process is simpler compared to the frontend dashboard widget creation process.

The default dashboard widgets are mostly suitable for blogs. In many circumstances, we have to remove the existing widgets and add custom widgets to cater for advanced site-specific business requirements. In custom sites, dashboard widgets are frequently used for displaying the site statistics, reports, or features that need to be executed on a regular basis, without visiting individual screens. You can try the existing plugins with dashboard widgets to understand the usage. WooCommerce, bbPress, and Easy Digital Downloads are some of the popular plugins with built-in custom dashboard widgets.

Customizing backend list tables

WordPress provides backend list tables for the main content types. We discussed the features of list tables in Chapter 7, *Managing Custom Post Types and Processing Forms*, on custom post types. The default features provide data list tables for posts, pages, users, and comments, as well as all the registered custom post types. Also, we can extend the core class used for list tables and create our own custom data list tables. So, it's important to know the existing features as well as customizable features of backend list tables. In this section, we are going to look at the some of the common customizations on the backend user list. Let's get started.

Creating and executing custom bulk actions

The WordPress list tables contains a dropdown called **Bulk Actions** in the top left-hand section of the list. This feature is used to modify multiple records in the table with a single predefined event. We have to choose one or more records, select an action from the **Bulk Actions** dropdown, and click the **Apply** button to complete the process. This is a very useful feature when you want to modify bulk records for custom features.

The WordPress core actions can be used to modify the **Bulk Actions** dropdown and to include custom actions for our projects. Let's add the following action to the constructor of the `WQKM_Admin_Features` class for understanding the process of using custom actions:

```
add_filter( 'bulk_actions-users', array( $this, 'user_actions' ) );
```

This action is used to filter the actions for the users list table. The filter consists of the `bulk_action`-prefix followed by the screen name. So, you can use the same action for other core list tables by replacing users with the screen name for the list. Let's take a look at the implementation of the custom action:

```
public function user_actions($bulk_actions) {
    $bulk_actions['wpquick_featured_user'] = __('Mark Featured
Profile','wqkm');
    return $bulk_actions;
}
```

In this code, we are adding a custom action to the default backend user list by modifying the existing bulk actions list. We have to use a unique slug as the array key for this action and define the label as the array value. In this scenario, we are building an action that allows us to mark certain users as **Featured Users**. Now you will see a new option in the **Bulk Actions** dropdown for handling user-featured status.

Once the records and action is selected, we can click the **Apply** button to make the modifications to the selected records. So, we need to implement the action by adding the following action to the constructor of the class:

```
add_filter( 'handle_bulk_actions-users', array(
$this,'users_page_loaded'),10,3);
```

In this code, we have used `handle_bulk_actions-` filter followed by the screen name for user list table. So, let's take a look at the implementation of the custom action:

```
public function users_page_loaded($redirect_to,$doaction,$featured_users ){
    if ( $doaction !== 'wpquick_featured_user' ) {
      return $redirect_to;
    }
```

```
foreach ($featured_users as $featured_user) {
    update_user_meta($featured_user, 'wqkm_featured_status', 'ACTIVE');
}

$redirect_to = add_query_arg( 'bulk_featured_users', count(
$featured_users ), $redirect_to );
    return $redirect_to;
}
```

Here's what the previous code does:

1. This function automatically receives three parameters for the redirect URL, the action name, and the list of IDs of the records to be modified.
2. First, we check the action and make sure our code executes only for the `wpquick_featured_user` action.
3. Next, we loop through the list of selected user IDs and modify the value to mark the user as a featured user. We can use a different action or toggle the same action to remove the featured status as well.
4. Finally, we redirect the user to the list by adding a custom argument to the URL called `bulk_featured_users`. This value will be used to filter the request and display a custom message using the `bulk_admin_notices` function in the source code.

Now we have a working custom action for the user list. You can test the feature by adding featured status to some of the users and confirming it by checking the database values. This is a simple way of modifying or applying custom data to multiple records for custom requirements. We can't use input fields for these actions, and hence the action should have a fixed feature with predefined values.

Adding custom list columns

The data list tables contains default set of columns, and these columns vary based on the type of the list. In the previous section, we changed the featured status of the user. However, we had to use the database to check the value. Instead, we can display such important information on the data list table by using custom columns. So, in this section, we are going to look at the process of adding custom columns to the default users list as well as identifying the necessary hooks for other lists. Let's start by adding the following filter and action to the constructor of `WQKM_Admin_Features` class:

```
add_filter( 'manage_users_columns', array(
$this,'manage_user_custom_columns') );
add_action( 'manage_users_custom_column', array( $this,
'manage_user_custom_column_values' ), 10, 3 );
```

The `manage_users_columns` filter is used to modify or remove existing columns as well as to add new columns to the user list. The following code previews the implementation to include the featured status as a column:

```
public function manage_user_custom_columns ( $column ) {
  $column['featured_user_status'] = __('Featured Status','wqkm');
  return $column;
}
```

Now you should see an additional column in the user list without any data. The next step is to display the column data for each user. We have to use the `manage_users_custom_column` action to provide the data for our custom column. Let's take a look at the implementation of the callback function:

```
public function manage_user_custom_column_values ( $val, $column_name,
$user_id) {
  $featured_user_status = get_user_meta ( $user_id ,'wqkm_featured_status',
TRUE);
  $featured_user_status = ( $featured_user_status == 'ACTIVE') ?
__('ACTIVE','wqkm') : __('INACTIVE','wqkm');

  switch ($column_name) {
    case 'featured_user_status' :
      return $featured_user_status;
      break;
    default:
      return $val;
      break;
  }
}
```

This function accepts three parameters for the column value, column name, and the user ID. We can use these parameters to get the custom column value for the selected users. Here, we use `get_user_meta` function as we stored the data on `wp_usermeta` table. We can also store these values and display them using custom tables. Next, we use a `switch` statement to return the value based on the column. It's important to use the `default` case and return the default value, to be compatible with other plugins. Now you should see the custom column in the user list with the custom values for each user.

Sorting custom column values

The default list tables provides sorting capabilities for the first column and one or more from the remaining columns. However, these are built-in columns provided by the WordPress core features. So, we need the ability to sort custom column values to effectively use and filter the custom data. WordPress provides a built-in filter for specifying sortable columns. Let's consider the following filter and its implementation:

```
add_filter('manage_users_sortable_columns',
array($this,'users_sortable_columns'));
public function users_sortable_columns( $columns ) {
  $columns['featured_user_status'] = 'featured_user_status';
  return $columns;
}
```

The filter needs to be added inside the constructor of the class. This filter accepts the list of existing sortable columns as a parameter. Here, we have added the key of our custom column to the sortable columns array and return the list. Now you should be able to see a link in custom column to change the sorting value. The final step of the process is to change the default query and enable sorting on the custom column. Let's consider the following action and its implementation:

```
add_action( 'pre_user_query', array( $this, 'users_orderby_filters' ) );
public function users_orderby_filters( $userquery ){
  global $wpdb;
  if( 'featured_user_status' == $userquery->query_vars['orderby'] ) {
    $userquery->query_from .= " LEFT OUTER JOIN $wpdb->usermeta AS
wpusermeta ON ($wpdb->users.ID = wpusermeta.user_id) ";
    $userquery->query_where.= " AND
wpusermeta.meta_key='featured_user_status' ";
    $userquery->query_orderby = " ORDER BY wpusermeta.meta_value ".(
$userquery->query_vars["order"] == "ASC" ? "asc " : "desc " );
  }
}
```

Let's understand the implementation of this function using the following steps:

1. We can use `pre_user_query` action to modify the default query, just before the execution. The `WP_User_Query` object is passed as a parameter to this function.
2. Next, we check the `orderby` clause of the query using the `query_vars` array to make sure our custom code only executes on `featured_user_status` column.
3. Then, we have to modify the query, staring with the `join` statement on the `from` clause to include the `usermeta` table. The modified `where` clause makes sure that sorting is only applied to the values of the `featured_user_status` column.

4. Finally, we change the `orderby` clause to order the list using meta values of the `featured_user_status` column.

Now the process is complete, and you should be able to click the column title to sort the users in both ways using the featured status. The following screenshot previews the features we added to the user list:

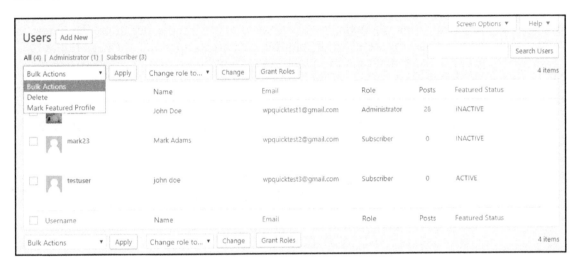

You can follow this technique with the necessary filtering to manage more columns on the user list.

We looked at the list table customization for the backend user list. Similarly, we can apply the same technique to customize the columns of other WordPress list tables using necessary actions and filters.

In most scenarios, we need to customize posts and custom post types lists to include custom columns. We have to use `manage_edit-{post_type}_columns` filter to define the custom columns and the `manage_{post_type}_posts_custom_column` filter to add the values for the custom columns. Then, we can use `manage_edit-{post_type}_sortable_columns` filter to define sortable columns and use `pre_get_posts` action to modify the query for sorting.

So, we need to use these actions and filters whenever necessary to display additional data in list tables and avoid the time-consuming visits to the edit section to check the values.

Summary

The main purpose of using WordPress is to simplify the development process. So, we need to understand the process of customizing important backend features. Also it's important to use modern user interface components to provide all the important in limited space using attractive techniques. We began the chapter by understanding the importance of the integration of UI components. So, we integrated jQuery Slider and Accordion while using two different data-capturing methods. We also looked at the importance of page builders in modern development and the steps for developing custom components for page builders. Next, we moved on to customizing admin features by building a simple dashboard widget. Finally, we looked at the process of adding custom features to built-in WordPress list tables.

In Chapter 9, *Enhancing Security, Performance, and Maintenance*, we will be completing the content for this book by looking at the non-functional aspects of development, such as security, performance, testing, and maintenance.

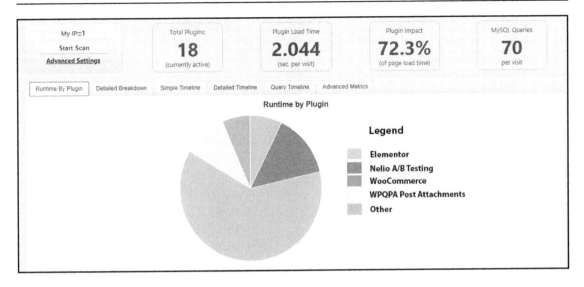

We can see the **Plugin Load Time**, **Plugin Impact**, and the **MySQL Queries** per visit along with various charts in the available tabs. This allows us to directly see the plugins with the most performance impact. In this scenario, the WooCommerce plugin has the highest impact. Earlier, we used the PluginTest service and identified the resource usage of WooCommerce as insignificant. So, we can consider both results and come to the conclusion that this site is not using plugins that affect the performance, as WooCommerce is the plugin with highest impact. If some other plugin is having a higher impact, we can look at the code and use other tools to identify if there is an issue in the plugin that creates a major impact on performance. After such verification, we can keep the plugins or replace them with alternative plugins to reduce the plugin impact on our web site.

Securing WordPress sites

The security of the site is one of the main concerns when developing sites or applications with WordPress. Open source code and the old coding techniques to keep the backward compatibility are two reasons for these security concerns. However, the major threat comes with the use of third-party plugins and themes, as there is no guarantee about the quality of them in many cases. So, it's essential to secure WordPress sites as much as possible to prevent attacks through plugins, themes, or known security concerns.

The WordPress codex provides a separate section called **Hardening WordPress** for defining the necessary security constraints. You can read this security guide at `http://codex.wordpress.org/Hardening_WordPress`. Let's find out the common reasons for WordPress exploits and basic precautions:

- **Username of the admin**: This is one of the most basic and primary reasons for exploits in WordPress sites. Many novice clients and developers keep **admin** as the username of the site administrator. So, the process of hacking becomes simpler as the attacker only has to find the password. So, it's a must to change it to an advanced username including letters, numbers, and maybe some characters.

- **WordPress core updates**: Since it's open source and the community is very large, there is a high-percentage chance of someone finding a bug in each WordPress release or using it to exploit the existing WordPress sites. However, these issues are identified very quickly and an updated version is released immediately to prevent the issue. Many WordPress sites are maintained by non-technical administrators without the support of a developer. So, these administrators don't have the knowledge of updating WordPress or they are afraid of breaking the site by updates. The attackers can easily use the issues in old WordPress versions and exploit them.

- **Plugin and theme updates**: This is even more problematic than WordPress updates. Many of the WordPress sites are done by third-party one-time developers. So, the quality of the plugins or themes is questionable as they only focus on completing the features within the estimated cost. So, there are lot of plugins and themes with exploitable code and many of these are not even actively maintained. So, we can't expect a new version every time for fixing the bugs. Also, these sites are developed using dozens of WordPress plugins and hence manually updating versions of each plugin is not preferred by many administrators. So, the outdated versions of these plugins and themes can cause a major security threat. As a solution, you can enable automatic updates for WordPress.org-based plugins and themes by using `auto_update_plugin` and `auto_update_theme` filters, while returning `__return_true` as the value. However, there is a chance that updates of certain plugins or theme can cause conflicts in other plugins. Therefore, you need to keep a close eye on site functionality when using auto-updates.

- **Configuration file location**: By default, the configuration file is located in the root folder of your WordPress installation and contains the most important database login details. So, it's easier for the attacker as they know the file location. So, we need to protect this file by changing its location to a private directory in your WordPress site.

- **User roles and permissions**: There are five built-in user roles with different capabilities. In most sites, there are two or more people editing the content and managing the site. So, it's important to only give these users necessary features by using user roles and capabilities, while preventing access to important parts of the WordPress site.
- **Login form security**: The default WordPress login functionality is secure. However, attackers may use tools to guess the passwords and gain access to the site. Therefore, we need to implement additional security measures on WordPress login. We can protect the login by implementing features such as limit failed login attempts, using two-factor authentication, restricting to certain IPs, and so on. We can easily find existing plugins to implement these features.
- **Backend file editing**: In case an attacker somehow gets access to a site, he can use the theme or plugin editor to modify the files and add malicious code or completely destroy the site by deleting the data as well as files. So, we need to use `define( 'DISALLOW_FILE_EDIT', true )` in the config file to remove the file-editing capabilities for all users, or conditionally use it for certain users with custom code.
- **Password complexity**: This is one of the basic concerns in any site, not only in WordPress. Most administrators tend to use easy-to-remember simple passwords allowing attackers to guess them. So, the password needs to be long enough for the site to prevent attacks.

These are only some of the basic precautions for securing WordPress sites. We need to use advanced security features, along with these features for sites with sensitive data and functionality. It's impossible to develop these advanced security features for use in development, unless your intention is building a security plugin. So, we have to use one or more top security plugins or services to secure the site. The following is a list of the most popular security plugins provided in the WordPress plugin directory:

- **iThemes Security**: `http://wordpress.org/plugins/better-wp-security/`
- **BulletProof Security**: `http://wordpress.org/plugins/bulletproof-security/`
- **All In One WP Security & Firewall** : `https://wordpress.org/plugins/all-in-one-wp-security-and-firewall/`

We can choose one of these plugins based on the security features needed for a given site. It's possible to use more than one security plugin for providing different security features. However, there is a chance of them conflicting with each other and hence it's ideal to choose one quality plugin.

Migrating WordPress sites

Generally, we develop sites on a staging server before migrating to the live server. The process of manually migrating sites is not practical in most scenarios as we have to manually back up the database, files, uploaded media, and upload to another server via FTP. So, we need to use a tool that allows us to automate the tasks of this process with a smooth migration. There are plugins that allow you to back up the database, files, and media separately, and then import them manually to the live server.

We are going to look at a plugin that offers all these features within the same plugin, making migration a super simple task. You can find a plugin called **All-in-One WP Migration**. This plugin is available at `https://wordpress.org/plugins/all-in-one-wp-migration/`. Once activated, you can click on the **Export** item from the **All-In-One WP Migration** menu item on the left menu. You will get a screen similar to the following:

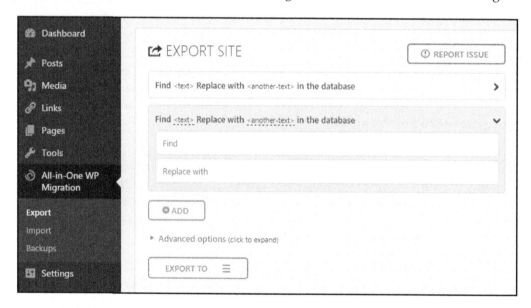

The exporting feature starts with the database replace feature. We can use this feature to find and replace anything in the database. This is quite useful for changing the URLs of custom data to match the live site URL. Next, we can select the File option from the **EXPORT TO** setting, and the plugin will generate the backup of your site to be downloaded as a single file with `wpress` as the extension. We can download the backup to our local machine.

Now, we have to go to the live site and install the same plugin. This time, we have to use the **Import** section, as shown in the following screenshot:

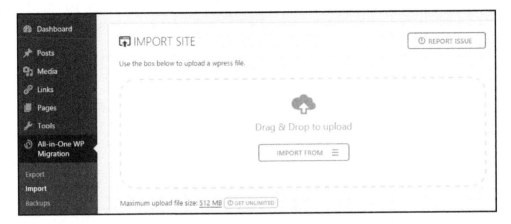

We can click on the **IMPORT FROM** button and add the exported `wpress` file generated in the previous section. Then, the plugin will migrate the entire site within minutes, making it a super-simple solution. Unlike other frameworks, we can completely migrate a WordPress site within a few minutes.

The exported `wpress` files are stored in the `/wpcontent/ai1wm-backups` folder of your server. These files can be very large even for a basic websites. So, you have to make sure to remove the unnecessary backups to prevent the use of a large server space.

We can find all the exported and available backup files in the **Backups** menu of the plugin. So, we can easily restore a site to its previous point using a single click. This is one of the best plugin available for site migration. You can also consider the following plugins as alternatives for site migration:

- **Duplicator**: `https://wordpress.org/plugins/duplicator/`
- **WP Staging—DB & File Duplicator & Migration**: `https://wordpress.org/plugins/wp-staging/`
- **XCloner**: Backup and Restore—`https://wordpress.org/plugins/xcloner-backup-and-restore/`

Each of these plugins offers different migration features including exports to Google Drive and other third-party services. So, you will have to try these plugins and choose the simplest plugin that migrates the sites, while being compatible with your hosting provider.

Maintaining WordPress sites

The process of maintaining sites is another problematic area in WordPress development. Many sites are built by non-technical clients without a developer, and hence they are not aware of the regular tasks in order to maintain the site. Once an issue is occurred, these clients looks for developers to fix them without having the necessary processes and resources. So, as a developer, it's important to keep the site maintainable and transfer the knowledge on the maintenance process to the client, in case you are no longer working on that site. In this section, we are going to look at the primary tasks for properly maintaining a WordPress site and how to implement these tasks:

Backup files and databases

This is one of the must-do tasks in maintenance, ruled out by many non-technical site owners. WordPress powers over 25 percent of the web and hence the number of attacks on WordPress sites are equally high. So, we need regular backups of files and databases to be used in such occasions. Unfortunately, many site owners don't have a proper backup process and some of them assume that it's done automatically by the hosting server.

There are hosting providers and features for automating the backup process from the server side. However, it's better to have our own backups using a manual process or using an existing plugin. There are many plugins that allow us to schedule backups of the sites, such as the following:

- `UpdraftPlus`: This is one of the most popular backup plugins with a wide range of features for file and database backup as well as restoring. You can find all the features at `https://wordpress.org/plugins/updraftplus/`.
- `BackUpWordPress`: Allows you to schedule backups for both files and database. You can find all the features at `https://wordpress.org/plugins/backupwordpress/`.

We already discussed the use of the **All-In-One WP Migration** plugin for migrating WordPress sites. We can also use such plugins as the backup and restore mechanism for the same site as well. So, it's a must to use one of these backup plugins and schedule the backups of your site.

Updating WordPress plugins and themes

We already discussed the need for updating WordPress core, plugins and themes to improve the security of the site in the previous sections. Also, it's an essential part of maintenance, as some of the plugins and themes may not be compatible with older or newer versions of WordPress. So, you need to keep track of the updates in plugins and themes, along with the possible bug fixes in each version. Otherwise, you will have to automate the update process using custom code, or use a plugin like **Automatic Plugin Updates** (`https://wordpress.org/plugins/automatic-plugin-updates/`) for automating updates only for certain plugins.

Optimizing database tables

This is another aspect in maintenance that is not considered by many site owners. We use many plugins in WordPress sites with different data needs. Many of these plugins work on existing database tables, and hence it's difficult to track which plugin is responsible for certain data in core tables. Some of these plugins provide a quality deactivation or delete process, removing all the plugin-related data from the database. However, many plugins don't have such a process and we can find many unused data in the database even after deleting the plugins. Also, WordPress core features such as revisions, transients, caching overloads core tables with unnecessary amount of data.

So, we need to optimize the database time to time by removing these unnecessary data. The first step is only choosing plugins that remove their data on uninstallation. Then, we can choose a database optimization plugin, such as the following:

- **WP-Optimize**: `https://wordpress.org/plugins/wp-optimize/`
- **WP-Sweep**: `https://wordpress.org/plugins/wp-sweep/`
- **Advanced Database Cleaner**: `https://wordpress.org/plugins/advanced-database-cleaner/`

The common features of these plugins include the ability to delete revisions, auto-drafts, comments with certain statuses, and duplicated and orphaned metadata. We have to use one of such plugins to keep the database clean by removing unused data.

Checking request errors and broken links

We use many third-party libraries and resources from external sites when developing sites. So, these resources are loaded through external URLs. Sometimes, we may notice the unavailability of these files due to server unavailability or other errors. So, unavailability of some files may create conflicts in our site features. Also, we might link to no-longer-available content, leading to 404 errors. So, we need to track these issues and resolve them in order to keep the consistency of our site features.

We can use a plugin such as **Broken Link Checker** (`https://wordpress.org/plugins/broken-link-checker/`) to identify the broken posts, pages, or screens on our sites. Also, if you are using an analytics tool such as **Google Analytics**, we can check the requests to the 404 page and them track backward to find the links causing the issue.

We discussed performance-measuring plugins in previous sections. These plugins will show you a list of loaded files with the loading time, along with a list of files with loading errors from external sources. The most common issue is unavailability of CSS or JavaScript files from external sources. So, we can use such plugins to identify these files and update the URLs, or download and include these files locally within plugins.

Checking error logs

Once debug mode is switched off in a live environment, we won't see any errors generated in the site. Many third-party low-quality plugins generate minor and major errors. So, we need to have a error log to regularly check the site for errors as well as identify the cause, when something breaks on your site. The hosting providers also provide error logging features in servers. However, we should use our own error logs by using the core WordPress error log features, or using a plugin such as **Error Log Monitor** (`https://wordpress.org/plugins/error-log-monitor/`) to keep track of the existing errors and fix them as soon as possible.

These are some of the primary tasks for maintaining a site. You can find more minor tasks and plugins for maintaining sites. As a developer, you should have a proper maintenance routine based on the functionality of each site.

Summary

In site development, we mainly focus on the functional aspects, as the client or end users will be involved directly in functionality. However, we will have to give equal importance to non-functional aspects. These non-functional aspects may decide the success or failure of a site as these factors are the keys for using or leaving the site.

We began the chapter by understanding the importance of testing. We looked at several types of functional and non-functional testing with the help of tools such as **P3 Plugin Profiler**, and services such as **PluginTest**. Then, we discussed the need for implementing key security precautions while identifying the plugins for handling advanced security measures. Next, we looked at the importance of automating the site migration process using the **All-in-One WP Migration** plugin. Finally, we looked at the important tasks for properly maintaining a WordPress site, while exploring the existing plugin-based solutions for maintenance.

We began this book by introducing you to the core WordPress features, concepts, and data usage. Then, we developed various features by using core functionality, extending core functionality, and building custom solutions. Finally, we completed the book by looking at the important non-functional requirements for web sites. It's up to you now!

Other Books You May Enjoy

If you enjoyed this book, you may be interested in these other books by Packt:

WordPress Complete - Sixth Edition
Karol Krol

ISBN: 978-1-78728-570-5

- What WordPress is, where to get it, and how to launch your website quickly using it
- How to publish your first content (a blog post or article)
- What the most important sub-pages of a quality website are, and how to create them in WordPress
- How to upload multimedia content such as images, audio, and video
- How to install and work with plugins and widgets
- Where to find quality themes and how to install them
- How to develop your own WordPress plugins and themes

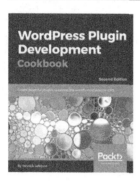

WordPress Plugin Development Cookbook - Second Edition
Yannick Lefebvre

ISBN: 978-1-78829-118-7

- Discover how to register user callbacks with WordPress, forming the basis of plugin creation
- Explore the creation of administration pages and adding new content management sections through custom post types and custom database tables
- Improve your plugins by customizing the post and page editors, categories and user profiles, and creating visitor-facing forms
- Make your pages dynamic using Javascript, AJAX and adding new widgets to the platform
- Learn how to add support for plugin translation and distribute your work to the WordPress community

Leave a review - let other readers know what you think

Please share your thoughts on this book with others by leaving a review on the site that you bought it from. If you purchased the book from Amazon, please leave us an honest review on this book's Amazon page. This is vital so that other potential readers can see and use your unbiased opinion to make purchasing decisions, we can understand what our customers think about our products, and our authors can see your feedback on the title that they have worked with Packt to create. It will only take a few minutes of your time, but is valuable to other potential customers, our authors, and Packt. Thank you!

Index

Printed by Amazon Italia Logistica S.r.l.
Torrazza Piemonte (TO), Italy

The Roman Empire

LOUISE SPILSBURY

raintree
a Capstone company — publishers for children

Raintree is an imprint of Capstone Global Library Limited, a company incorporated in England and Wales having its registered office at 264 Banbury Road, Oxford, OX2 7DY – Registered company number: 6695582

www.raintree.co.uk
myorders@raintree.co.uk

ISBN 978 1 4747 7777 3 (hardback)
ISBN 978 1 4747 7785 8 (paperback)

British Library Cataloguing in Publication Data
A full catalogue record for this book is available from the British Library.

Acknowledgements
We would like to thank the following for permission to reproduce photographs: Cover: Shutterstock: Photolikkk: top; Wikimedia Commons: Diliff: bottom; Inside: Shutterstock: 79mtk: p. 21r; 7th Son Studio: p. 13b; Abxyz: p. 31; Antb: pp. 32–33; Bambambu: p. 29br; BeanRibbon: p. 43b; Benedictus: pp. 40–41; S.Borisov: p. 4–5; Valery Evlakhov: p. 27b; Vitaly Fedotov: pp. 24–25; Gerald Robert Fischer: p. 39t; FlareZT: pp. 18–19; Eric Isselee: pp. 13r, 41br; Kentaylordesign: p. 14–15; Olga Meffista: p. 16t; Mountainpix: pp. 5b, 37r; Marco Ossino: p. 12; Regien Paassen: pp. 26–27; Pattang: p. 11br; Richard Yoshida: p. 7b; Wikimedia Commons: pp. 1, 8, 10–11, 44–45; 1803: purchased from Musée des monuments français, 2011: pp. 6–7; Roberto Bompiani/Digital image courtesy of the Getty's Open Content Program: pp. 36–37; Bristol City Council, Kurt Adams: p. 33br; Helen Cook: p. 9; Jusepe de Ribera: p. 19; Jean-Léon Gérôme: pp. 16–17, 20–21; Jun: pp. 28–29; Rolf Krahl: p. 25b; Poniol60: p. 15b; Hartmann Schedel: p. 45r; Ursus: p. 23b; WolfgangRieger: pp. 30, 38–39; Yeowatzup: pp. 22–23; Zde: pp. 35, 42–43.

Every effort has been made to contact copyright holders of material reproduced in this book. Any omissions will be rectified in subsequent printings if notice is given to the publisher.

All the internet addresses (URLs) given in this book were valid at the time of going to press. However, due to the dynamic nature of the internet, some addresses may have changed, or sites may have changed or ceased to exist since publication. While the author and publisher regret any inconvenience this may cause readers, no responsibility for any such changes can be accepted by either the author or the publisher.

Printed and bound by CPI Group (UK) Ltd, Croydon, CR0 4YY.

Contents

CHAPTER 1

Rome: city of death

Around two thousand years ago, the city of Rome was at the centre of a huge **empire** that ruled more than one-quarter of the people on the planet. The Roman Empire was very creative and smart, but it was also cruel, bloodthirsty and murderous.

The city of Rome was founded, or built, on death. **Legend** says that Romulus and Remus, twin sons of the god Mars, were left to drown in a river by an evil uncle. They were rescued and raised by a wolf. As adults, the boys killed their uncle and then, Romulus killed Remus so that he could build a new city and call it Rome, after himself.

The Romans ruled their large empire with violence, too. Those who broke laws were often killed. There were vicious fights and other blood sports that not only entertained people, but also made them fearful. There are plenty of other horrors in Rome's long history.

Many of the Roman emperors loved blood sports. They made men called gladiators fight one another in vicious, bloody fights to entertain crowds. Gladiators were often prisoners of war, **slaves** or criminals.

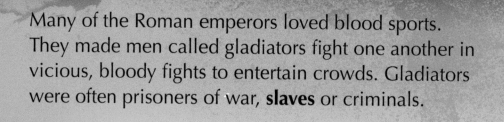

DEADLY DID YOU KNOW?

Emperor Nero blamed a terrible fire in Rome on the Christians living there. As punishment, he set fire to many of them, and used the burning bodies as evening lights.

Emperor Nero took money from ordinary people to build a marble and gold house with a 30-metre- (98-foot-) high statue of himself at the door.

CHAPTER 2

Bloody sports

When the Romans went to see a show at an **amphitheatre**, they wanted to see blood and violence. One sport that proved very popular was men fighting fierce wild animals such as lions and crocodiles.

Trained hunters wearing light body **armour** carried long spears to attack and fight the animals. As well as lions and crocodiles, they also fought leopards, tigers, rhinoceroses, elephants and giraffes.

The wild animals were kept in cages beneath the floor of the amphitheatre. They were lifted up and released suddenly into the arena through trap doors. When leopards, lions and tigers were in the amphitheatre, barriers were put in place to stop these dangerous animals leaping into the audience.

Animal fights were brutal, and up to ten thousand animals may have been killed in just one day.

The Romans were fascinated with and terrified by fearsome crocodiles.

KILLER FACT!

The wild animals were treated very badly before a fight. They were beaten and starved so they would be more vicious but also weak. This meant that the human hunters usually won.

Violent chariot races

The most popular Roman sport was the violent and bloody **chariot** racing. Bloodthirsty crowds loved these races because they were dangerous for the drivers and the horses that pulled the speeding chariots.

The chariot drivers and the horses were often badly injured or killed in their races.

The chariot races were not just about speed. Drivers tried to force other chariots to crash. The chariots were light, delicate and easily destroyed. Drivers were often thrown from their chariot. If they then became entangled in the long reins, they were dragged across the ground and under the chariots' wheels.

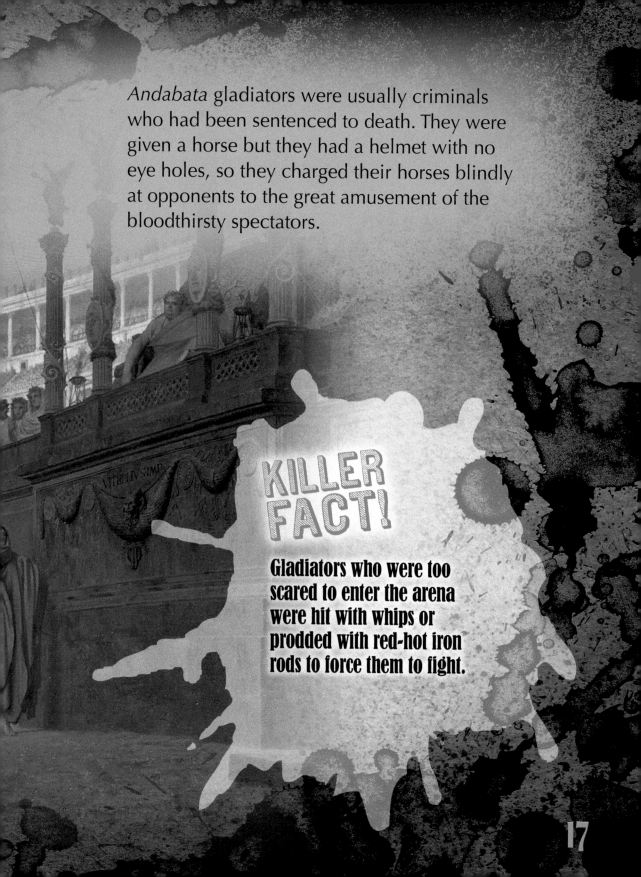

Andabata gladiators were usually criminals who had been sentenced to death. They were given a horse but they had a helmet with no eye holes, so they charged their horses blindly at opponents to the great amusement of the bloodthirsty spectators.

KILLER FACT!

Gladiators who were too scared to enter the arena were hit with whips or prodded with red-hot iron rods to force them to fight.

Terrible training

Gladiators were trained under the eye of their owner in gladiatorial schools. These schools were surrounded by a **fortress** and were more like prisons. Gladiators lived in cells and their training was tough.

Gladiators came out to exercise, to train and to learn how to use their weapons. At one school, trainees were shown how to fight wild animals. Gladiators were also taught how to die because Roman crowds expected them to die gracefully and with honour.

These are the remains of a Roman gladiator school. The buildings would have contained kitchens, sleeping areas and weapons stores.

Life must have been made even more unpleasant because of the food they were given. Gladiators were fed a lot of beans to build up layers of fat. It was thought this would protect them when they were hit, but they must have been very gassy. They washed down dinner with a drink made from plant ashes and vinegar, which was supposed to build up their bones.

Though female gladiator contests were rare, the women probably fought to the death, just like the men.

Doomed to die?

At the Colosseum, a typical day at the races included many deaths, all watched over by the emperor who paid for the games. He watched from a special seat where all the spectators could see him and he could enjoy watching the victims who were doomed to die.

Before gladiator fights in the afternoon, criminals and prisoners of war were pushed into the arena to be executed. Dangerous animals killed some of them. Others were forced to fight one another to the death. Some executions were set up to look like scenes from **mythology**.

Gladiators fought to the death – it was a case of kill or be killed!

A siege tower was a clever fighting tool. It had a drawbridge that was lowered from the top, allowing the soldiers inside the tower to climb onto the enemy's wall or shoot at them with bows and arrows.

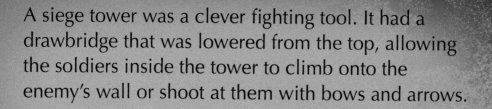

KILLER FACT!

The Romans used a kind of large and powerful wind-up crossbow called a ballista. This could fling heavy bolts or stones more than 480 metres (0.3 miles) to hit and kill enemies instantly.

The Romans also used small ballistas, like this one, on battlefields.

A soldier's sorrows

Roman soldiers faced great risks on the battlefield, but they almost always followed orders. If they disobeyed, they faced a harsh punishment.

Roman soldiers were divided into groups called legions. The legions were then divided into groups of one hundred soldiers. The centurion who led them carried a short rod. He would use this to beat any soldiers who disobeyed him. Soldiers who fell asleep on duty or behaved in a cowardly way were often executed.

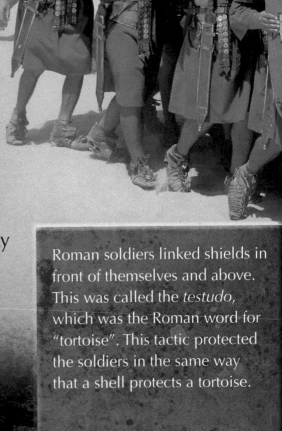

Roman soldiers linked shields in front of themselves and above. This was called the *testudo*, which was the Roman word for "tortoise". This tactic protected the soldiers in the same way that a shell protects a tortoise.

Strict discipline meant the soldiers learned clever battle tactics that made them deadly. If attacked by arrows from above, soldiers linked shields to surround and protect themselves. They moved forward like this, only lifting their shields when they were close enough to attack and defeat the enemy.

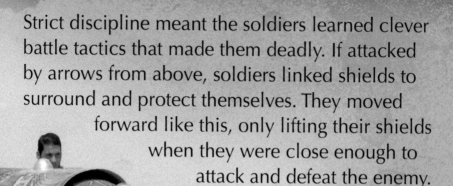

DEADLY DID YOU KNOW?

Roman soldiers were brutal killing machines. For their bloodthirsty work, they were paid in salt! The Latin word for salt was "sal". This is where the English word "salary" comes from.

A bag of salt does not seem a great reward for risking life and limb in battle!

CHAPTER 5

Long-suffering slaves

Roman armies sent thousands of captured soldiers back to Rome to be sold as slaves. Slaves became the property of their new owner and had to work for free. Some slaves were treated fairly, but others were worked to death.

Slaves were often badly treated and whipped. Those who tried to run away were branded – marked with a hot iron. Slave owners were allowed to kill slaves for any reason they chose.

Rich Romans might own as many as five hundred slaves.

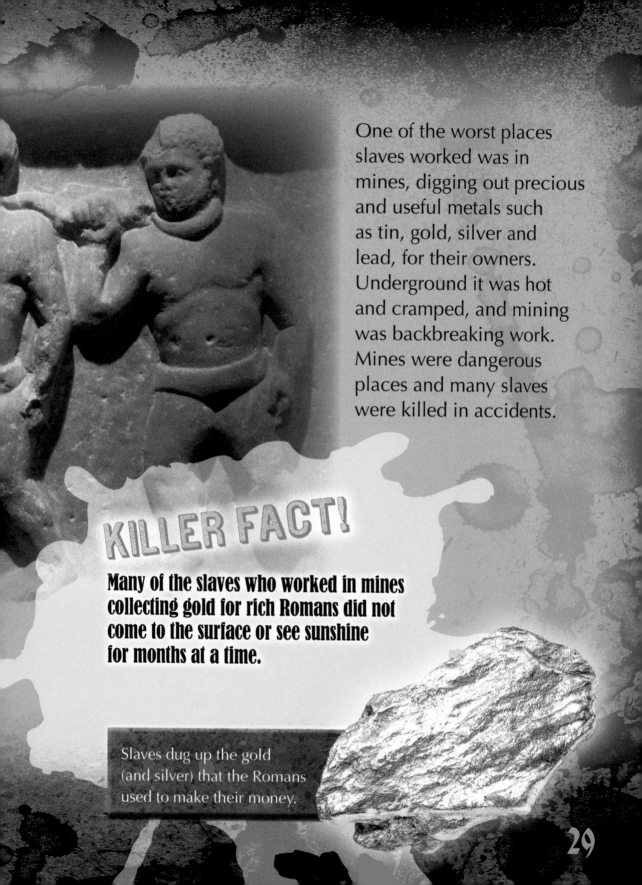

One of the worst places slaves worked was in mines, digging out precious and useful metals such as tin, gold, silver and lead, for their owners. Underground it was hot and cramped, and mining was backbreaking work. Mines were dangerous places and many slaves were killed in accidents.

KILLER FACT!

Many of the slaves who worked in mines collecting gold for rich Romans did not come to the surface or see sunshine for months at a time.

Slaves dug up the gold (and silver) that the Romans used to make their money.

Horrible jobs

Slaves did a lot of the work in Rome. While some worked as teachers, farmers, builders and even doctors, many were forced to do some really horrible jobs.

Some slaves were hairdressers. This was a less-appealing job than it sounds. Hairdressers had to use hair dyes made from ingredients such as pigeon **faeces**, rotting **leeches**, squid ink and urine.

Roman women spent a lot of time having their hair styled. Well-cared-for and styled hair was a sign of wealth.

Sacrifices were part of a ceremony that had different stages. First, there was a **procession** to the altar. Then there was a prayer. Wine and a **sacred** cake were sprinkled over the animal's head before the creature was killed with a special knife. The dead animal was cut up and parts of it were roasted over a fire.

KILLER FACT!

After a sacrificed animal was cut up, its internal organs were examined to see if they showed messages from the gods.

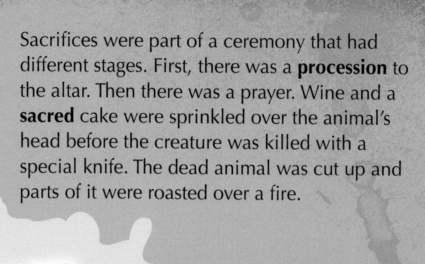

The Romans often used a special bowl for catching animal blood at a sacrifice. The blood was poured over the altar.

Disgusting dinners

At banquets, emperors and very rich Romans wanted to show off their wealth by serving foods that were rare and expensive. These banquets could last for up to eight hours.

Some of the most unusual meals that rich Romans ate included peacocks' brains, flamingos' tongues and the heads of parrots and pheasants. One emperor liked to serve camels' feet and another had a taste for elephant trunks. One emperor even sprinkled pearls over his food instead of pepper.

Wealthy Romans were waited upon by slaves at mealtimes. The slaves poured drinks and carried food to and from the table.

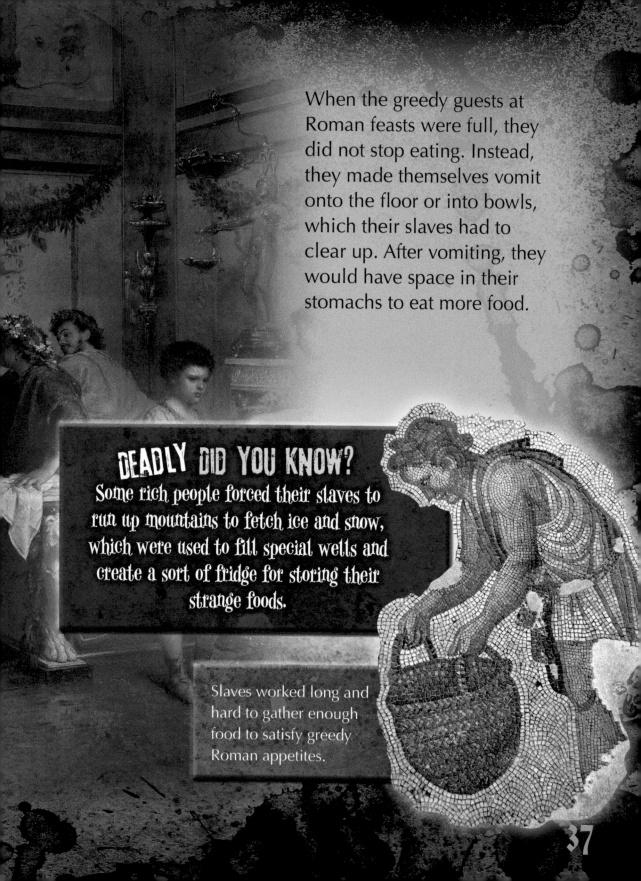

When the greedy guests at Roman feasts were full, they did not stop eating. Instead, they made themselves vomit onto the floor or into bowls, which their slaves had to clear up. After vomiting, they would have space in their stomachs to eat more food.

DEADLY DID YOU KNOW?

Some rich people forced their slaves to run up mountains to fetch ice and snow, which were used to fill special wells and create a sort of fridge for storing their strange foods.

Slaves worked long and hard to gather enough food to satisfy greedy Roman appetites.

Festering fashions

Roman emperors wore purple to show how important they were. Purple dye was so expensive to produce that it was more valuable than gold. The colour may have looked beautiful, but the way Romans created it was quite horrible.

Purple dye was made by crushing thousands of small, rotting sea snails and leaving them to bake in the sun. Then they were boiled in giant lead pans for several days. The slaves who had the unpleasant job of making the dye had to suffer the terrible stench it created. The smell was so bad that dye-making workshops were built far away from the cities.

The slaves that made dye, coloured fabric and washed an emperor's clothes had a smelly and unpleasant job.

Malaria spread easily because people travelled around the empire and because foreign **invaders** attacked Rome. The disease killed so many people in Rome that it became known as "Roman fever".

The Romans tried various medicines to cure their diseases. There are reports of people collecting the blood of dead gladiators and selling it as a medicine. Some Romans seemed to believe that drinking gladiator blood would cure certain conditions. Some people went one step further – they pulled out a dead gladiator's liver and ate it raw!

KILLER FACT!

Mosquitoes thrived in the marshy damp land around Rome, and malaria was spread when infected mosquitoes sucked on human blood.

A female mosquito sticks a straw-like part of her mouth through skin to suck blood.

A violent end

The Roman Empire began to fall apart in the fifth century. Some say that the Roman Empire ended much as it began – with blood and violence.

Rome's power was weakened by a series of useless emperors and bloody wars between different parts of the empire. Tribes such as Goths, Huns and Vandals from northern Europe took advantage of this weakness and started energetic and brutal attacks.

These invaders destroyed many of Rome's great buildings, stole its valuables and made many of its inhabitants slaves or murdered them. In AD 476, the last Roman emperor was forced to step down from power and a German prince made himself king of Italy.

The Vandals were a tribe that attacked and destroyed parts of Rome.

DEADLY DID YOU KNOW?

Rome named the invaders who attacked them barbarians. Roman soldiers greatly feared the heavy battleaxe weapons used by barbarians from Germany because these could smash through their shield, armour and helmet in a single blow!

Attila the Hun was one of the fiercest barbarian rulers who attacked the Roman Empire.

Glossary

altars tables or platforms on which religious rituals were carried out

amphitheatre oval or circular building with stepped seats around an open central space for spectators to watch contests and races

aqueducts artificial channels and bridges that carry water long distances for people to use

armour clothing worn by soldiers for protection

battering ram weapon that consists of a large wooden beam with a head of iron, which is used to beat down walls

chariot two-wheeled vehicle pulled by horses

conquer use force to take over a city or country

defeated beaten

emperors male leaders or rulers of an empire

empire large area of land or group of countries ruled over by one leader

execution killing of someone when given the order to do so

faeces digestive waste

fortress large, strong building that can be defended from attack

invaders people, armies or countries that use force to enter and take control of another country

leeches bloodsucking creatures

legend story from ancient times that is not always true

luxuries things that add to pleasure or comfort but that are not absolutely necessary

malaria disease spread by mosquitoes

mythology traditional stories about gods and heroes

offerings things that people give as part of a religious ceremony or ritual

procession group of people moving along in an orderly way, especially as part of a ceremony

sacred important to a religion

sacrifices animal or human that is killed to honour a god or gods

slaves people who are owned by other people and have to obey them

surrendered gave up or admitted defeat in battle

taxes money paid to a ruler or government

temple building where people go to worship their god or gods

toga loose outer garment worn by people in ancient Rome

trident three-pronged spear

Find out more

Books

Ancient Rome (History Hunters), Nancy Dickmann (Raintree, 2016)

Daily Life in Ancient Rome (Daily Life in Ancient Civilizations), Don Nardo (Raintree, 2016)

DKfindout! Ancient Rome, DK (DK Children, 2016)

Geography Matters in Ancient Rome, Melanie Waldron (Raintree, 2015)

Life in Roman Britain (A Child's History of Britain), Anita Ganeri (Raintree, 2015)

The Roman Empire and its Impact on Britain (Early British History), Claire Throp (Raintree, 2016)

Websites

www.bbc.com/bitesize/articles/z2sm6sg
Learn more about life in ancient Rome.

www.dkfindout.com/uk/history/ancient-rome
Find out more about ancient Rome.

Index